NATIONAL ACADEMIES
Sciences
Engineering
Medicine

NATIONAL ACADEMIES PRESS
Washington, DC

Impact of Burnout on the STEMM Workforce

Convened October 1–2, 2024

Katie Wullert and Paula Whitacre,
Rapporteurs

Committee on Women in Science, Engineering, and Medicine

Policy and Global Affairs

Proceedings of a Workshop

NATIONAL ACADEMIES PRESS 500 Fifth Street, NW Washington, DC 20001

This activity was supported by a contract between the National Academy of Sciences and the National Institutes of Health (HHSN263201800029I/ 75N98023F00017). Any opinions, findings, conclusions, or recommendations expressed in this publication do not necessarily reflect the views of any organization or agency that provided support for the project.

International Standard Book Number-13: 978-0-309-73567-4
International Standard Book Number-10: 0-309-73567-X
Digital Object Identifier: https://doi.org/10.17226/29078

This publication is available from the National Academies Press, 500 Fifth Street, NW, Keck 360, Washington, DC 20001; (800) 624-6242; http://www.nap.edu.

Copyright 2025 by the National Academy of Sciences. National Academies of Sciences, Engineering, and Medicine and National Academies Press and the graphical logos for each are all trademarks of the National Academy of Sciences. All rights reserved.

Printed in the United States of America.

Suggested citation: National Academies of Sciences, Engineering, and Medicine. 2025. *Impact of Burnout on the STEMM Workforce: Proceedings of a Workshop*. Washington, DC: National Academies Press. https://doi.org/10.17226/29078.

The **National Academy of Sciences** was established in 1863 by an Act of Congress, signed by President Lincoln, as a private, nongovernmental institution to advise the nation on issues related to science and technology. Members are elected by their peers for outstanding contributions to research. Dr. Marcia McNutt is president.

The **National Academy of Engineering** was established in 1964 under the charter of the National Academy of Sciences to bring the practices of engineering to advising the nation. Members are elected by their peers for extraordinary contributions to engineering. Dr. John L. Anderson is president.

The **National Academy of Medicine** (formerly the Institute of Medicine) was established in 1970 under the charter of the National Academy of Sciences to advise the nation on medical and health issues. Members are elected by their peers for distinguished contributions to medicine and health. Dr. Victor J. Dzau is president.

The three Academies work together as the **National Academies of Sciences, Engineering, and Medicine** to provide independent, objective analysis and advice to the nation and conduct other activities to solve complex problems and inform public policy decisions. The National Academies also encourage education and research, recognize outstanding contributions to knowledge, and increase public understanding in matters of science, engineering, and medicine.

Learn more about the National Academies of Sciences, Engineering, and Medicine at **www.nationalacademies.org**.

Consensus Study Reports published by the National Academies of Sciences, Engineering, and Medicine document the evidence-based consensus on the study's statement of task by an authoring committee of experts. Reports typically include findings, conclusions, and recommendations based on information gathered by the committee and the committee's deliberations. Each report has been subjected to a rigorous and independent peer-review process and it represents the position of the National Academies on the statement of task.

Proceedings published by the National Academies of Sciences, Engineering, and Medicine chronicle the presentations and discussions at a workshop, symposium, or other event convened by the National Academies. The statements and opinions contained in proceedings are those of the participants and are not endorsed by other participants, the planning committee, or the National Academies.

Rapid Expert Consultations published by the National Academies of Sciences, Engineering, and Medicine are authored by subject-matter experts on narrowly focused topics that can be supported by a body of evidence. The discussions contained in rapid expert consultations are considered those of the authors and do not contain policy recommendations. Rapid expert consultations are reviewed by the institution before release.

For information about other products and activities of the National Academies, please visit www.nationalacademies.org/about/whatwedo.

BURNOUT IN STEMM AND IMPLICATIONS FOR EQUITY WORKSHOP PLANNING COMMITTEE

RESHMA JAGSI, M.D., D.Phil. (*Chair*) (NAM),[1] Chair, Department of Radiation Oncology, Emory University and Winship Cancer Institute
KELLEY BONNER, M.S.W., Founder and CEO, Burn Bright Consulting
ELENA FUENTES-AFFLICK, M.D., M.P.H. (NAM), Chief Medical Officer, Association of American Medical Colleges
LONNIE GOLDEN, Ph.D., Professor of Economics and Labor-Human Resources, Pennsylvania State University, Abington
ALICIA KOWALSKI, M.D., Professor of Anesthesiology, The University of Texas MD Anderson Cancer Center
JOSÉ A. PAGÁN, Ph.D. (NAM), Chair and Professor of Public Health Policy and Management, New York University

Staff

KATIE WULLERT, Ph.D., Study Director and Program Officer, Committee on Women in Science, Engineering, and Medicine
ASHLEY BEAR, Ph.D., Director, Committee on Women in Science, Engineering, and Medicine
PAMELA LAVA, Senior Program Assistant, Committee on Women in Science, Engineering, and Medicine

Consultant

PAULA WHITACRE, Consultant Writer

---

[1] Designates membership in the National Academy of Sciences (NAS), National Academy of Engineering (NAE), or National Academy of Medicine (NAM).

Reviewers

This Proceedings of a Workshop was reviewed in draft form by individuals chosen for their diverse perspectives and technical expertise. The purpose of this independent review is to provide candid and critical comments that will assist the National Academies of Sciences, Engineering, and Medicine in making each published proceedings as sound as possible and to ensure that it meets the institutional standards for quality, objectivity, evidence, and responsiveness to the charge. The review comments and draft manuscript remain confidential to protect the integrity of the process.

We thank the following individuals for their review of this proceedings:

BRIGID SCHULTE, New America
J. MARGO BROOKS CARTHON, University of Pennsylvania
PASCALE CARAYON, University of Wisconsin-Madison (retired)

Although the reviewers listed above provided many constructive comments and suggestions, they were not asked to endorse the content of the proceedings nor did they see the final draft before its release. The review of this proceedings was overseen by **J. NICHOLAS ODOM**, University of Alabama at Birmingham. He was responsible for making certain that an independent examination of this proceedings was carried out in accordance with standards of the National Academies and that all review comments were carefully considered. Responsibility for the final content rests entirely with the rapporteurs and the National Academies.

Preface and Acknowledgments

Science, technology, engineering, mathematics, and medicine (STEMM) occupations have long been understood to be greedy institutions—demanding an immense amount of time, dedication, attention, and resources from individual workers. It is perhaps no surprise then that rates of burnout are high for those working in these domains, especially in medicine. In March of 2024, our committee began to meet to plan a workshop to unpack burnout—what it is, how it has been conceived and misconceived, what causes it, what its impacts are, and what we can do about it. All of this was discussed within a context in which STEMM disciplines remain highly unequal for women, people of color, and other marginalized or undersupported groups, such as individuals with disabilities and individuals with caregiving responsibilities. Our focus was also to understand what burnout means for fostering a STEMM environment that best engages all people because, while anyone can experience burnout, the implications are uneven across the population given the ways in which experiences of discrimination, microaggressions, and other significant stressors unevenly affect different groups.

This document details the key takeaways from a 2-day workshop held October 1–2, 2024, at the National Academy of Sciences building in Washington, D.C. Day 1 of the workshop focused on background knowledge to ensure a shared understanding of what burnout is, how it comes to be, and what this means for individuals and organizations within STEMM.

Day 2 shifted to focus on interventions to provide insights into current knowledge on efforts to mitigate and address burnout.

We are immensely grateful to the sponsor of this workshop, the Office of Research on Women's Health within the National Institutes of Health. Their guidance and support made this possible. We are also grateful to our many outstanding speakers and commissioned paper authors. We had a unique opportunity to turn to experts in the field not only to share their insights at the workshop but also to craft papers providing an essential summary of our current scientific knowledge on the causes and consequences of burnout and interventions to address it. You will find these papers in Appendixes B, C, and D of this proceedings.

Personally, there is much I took away from this workshop. First and foremost, burnout must be recognized as the consequence of chronic, unmanaged workplace stress. Burnout often results from the accumulation of many small insults, so-called pebbles in the shoe that, in isolation, might be brushed aside but when taken together can conspire to cause tremendous harm. The causes of burnout are complex, multifactorial, and multilevel, and the consequences, which include detriment to talented individuals' physical, mental, social, and professional outcomes, are not borne equally by all individuals. As the workshop highlighted, burnout has clear implications for gender and racial equity within STEMM. Additional research to understand the ways burnout affects the vitality of STEMM professionals, including those who may be most vulnerable due to multiple marginalized identities, such as the unique experiences of women of color, for example, is critical to target interventions to support the essential segment of the workforce that STEMM constitutes.

Nevertheless, models already exist to guide interventions that seek to prevent burnout and to mitigate its effects. We have a great opportunity to build on a strong foundation of evidence already collected—much of which has been synthesized herein—to transform our organizations. We must implement locally appropriate initiatives, evaluate them, and disseminate what we learn. We must honor the voices of all those within organizations so that decisions include their invaluable perspectives, and we must maintain the focus on the worthy and inspiring purpose that motivates us. I look forward to partnering with all those reading these proceedings in the all-important work of continuous improvement of our work environments.

Reshma Jagsi, Chair
Planning Committee for the Burnout in STEMM
and Implications for Equity Workshop

Contents

1	INTRODUCTION	1
2	UNDERSTANDING BURNOUT AND CHALLENGING MISCONCEPTIONS	7
3	CAUSES OF BURNOUT AND ASSOCIATED RISK FACTORS	15
4	CONSEQUENCES OF BURNOUT AND MEASUREMENT CHALLENGES	23
5	DEEP DIVE ON BURNOUT, IDENTITY, AND INTERSECTIONALITY	31
6	CURRENT AND INNOVATIVE APPROACHES TO MANAGING BURNOUT	41
7	INTERVENTIONS TO MANAGE BURNOUT: DEEP DIVE ON MEDICINE	51
8	IMAGINING A FUTURE OF GREATER SUPPORT: AN INTERACTIVE DISCUSSION	59
	REFERENCES	63

APPENDIXES

A	Public Meeting Agendas	69
B	Understanding the Causes of Burnout and Gender and Race Disparities in STEMM: A Multilevel Approach	73
C	Job Burnout: Consequences for Individuals, Organizations, and Equity	107
D	Breaking the Burnout Cycle: Building Organizational Strategies to Address Burnout Sources and Symptoms	149
E	Biographical Sketches of Planning Committee Members and Speakers	207

Boxes, Figures, and Tables

BOXES

1-1 Workshop Statement of Task, 3

5-1 Sample Participant Takeaways from Workshop Day 1, 38

C-1 Summary of Individual, Occupational, Organizational, and Societal Consequences of Burnout Highlighted in This Paper, 111

C-2 Summary of the Equity-Based Consequences of Burnout Highlighted in This Report, 124

FIGURES

1-1 Word cloud resulting from participants poll responses, 4

4-1 Burnout and stress levels by racial and ethnic groups, 27

6-1 Individual, Group, Leader, Overall Organization (IGLOO) interventions for healthy workplaces, 44
6-2 Burnout intervention chart, 45
6-3 BUILD model, 46

D-1 Burnout antecedents and outcomes and corresponding levels of interventions, 153
D-2 Template for a holistic perspective in addressing burnout, with example initiatives, 196

TABLES

4-1 Individual-Level Consequences of Burnout, 25
4-2 Occupational-Level Consequences of Burnout, 25

D-1 Meta-Analysis-Based Studies of Burnout Interventions, 160
D-2 Examples of Individual and Organizational Interventions to Address Burnout, 174

1

Introduction

The term *burnout* was coined in the 1970s to describe the intense stress faced by individuals in professions focused on helping others, such as doctors and nurses (Maslach and Leiter, 1976). Today, however, people recognize and study burnout across many different occupations. The World Health Organization (WHO) defines burnout as "a syndrome conceptualized as resulting from chronic workplace stress that has not been successfully managed." WHO characterizes burnout by three dimensions: (1) decreased energy or exhaustion; (2) negativity and/or cynicism toward, or feelings of distance from one's job; and (3) feelings of reduced efficacy at work (WHO, 2019).

Though burnout has long created challenges for many workers in science, technology, mathematics, and medicine (STEMM) fields, the COVID-19 pandemic had sweeping effects on the STEMM workforce and led to increased burnout for many that has drawn greater attention to issues of burnout in recent years. Faced with health and economic uncertainty, along with workplace challenges from an ever-changing and overtaxed system, many workers in STEMM fields experienced and continue to experience heightened symptoms of burnout (Gewin, 2021; Lievens, 2021; Linzer et al., 2022). Pandemic-related strains and increased demands at home and work exacerbated long-standing gender differences in burnout (Dillon et al., 2021; NASEM, 2021). Indeed, prior to COVID-19, women experienced greater rates of burnout, as well as associated symptoms such as exhaustion, cynicism, and low feelings of efficacy (Gold et al., 2016; Jensen and Deemer, 2019; Rabatin et al., 2016). A 2021 National Academies of

Sciences, Engineering, and Medicine report on the impact of COVID-19 on the careers of women in STEMM found that the combined uneven effects of the pandemic, coupled with existing inequities in burnout, could worsen the gender gap in these fields (NASEM, 2021). Taken together, burnout is a long-standing, but recently significantly exacerbated issue with important gender implications for the STEMM workforce.

Addressing burnout is important for healthy workplaces and healthy individuals. As detailed in the workshop and this proceedings, burnout comes with many significant consequences for workers who may face physical and mental health challenges as well as organizations that can suffer from absenteeism, attrition, and diminished engagement, all of which can reduce growth and innovation. In healthcare settings, consequences have the potential to be even more dire. It has been shown that burnout can be related to negative patient outcomes as individual providers are struggling to manage overwhelming caseloads and hours. The uneven effect of burnout is also cause for concern for a thriving STEMM ecosystem, as this can diminish the kind of creativity and innovation that thrives in environments when a broad set of voices are represented. Taken together, these challenges make clear the need for continued attention to burnout and interventions in STEMM fields.

To explore these challenges in greater detail, the Committee on Women in Science, Engineering, and Medicine of the National Academies convened a workshop on October 1 and 2, 2024, in Washington, D.C., to examine burnout and its implications for gender equity in STEMM (see Box 1-1 for the Statement of Task and Appendix A for the workshop agenda). Through three commissioned papers, panel and breakout discussions, and participant engagement, the workshop was designed to examine current knowledge, share lessons learned, and consider ways to address burnout in STEMM settings. Though the committee was explicitly tasked only with looking at the implications of burnout for gender equity, in the process of planning the workshop, committee members decided to extend their attention to race as well given the ways in which issues of gender and race are deeply intwined in the workplace and broader society. Additionally, the workshop while looking broadly at STEMM gave particular attention to healthcare settings for two key reasons. First, burnout among healthcare providers is particularly acute given the challenges of exceptionally long hours, high expectations of devotion, and work with potentially challenging consequences. Second, likely as a result of the high rates of burnout in healthcare, the literature on burnout in healthcare settings is the most extensive of that in any other STEMM field.

> **BOX 1-1**
> **Workshop Statement of Task**
>
> The National Academies of Sciences, Engineering, and Medicine will hold a two-part, hybrid workshop that will examine the impact of burnout on gender equity in science, engineering, and medicine. Specifically, the workshop will
>
> 1. examine the current state of knowledge on the prevalence, nature, and impact of burnout on gender equity in science, technology, engineering, mathematics, and medicine (STEMM), including in both clinical and research careers;
> 2. describe policies and practices that provide greater support for those experiencing burnout as well as proactive measures to prevent burnout;
> 3. discuss gaps in the current research, with particular attention to gaps in understanding the experiences of the most marginalized groups of women;
> 4. examine the causes of burnout and potential variation in causes of burnout across settings of care (e.g., community based, private, public, corporate health systems, and academic institutions) and diverse populations of workers; and
> 5. explore the relationship of the degree of burnout to characteristics such as age, sex, gender, and sociocultural demographics.
>
> The planning committee will commission papers on these topics to be discussed/presented at the workshop.
>
> This two-part workshop will engage a diverse array of scholars and practitioners with expertise in burnout. Following the events, the National Academies will publish a proceedings that provides an overview of the key points from the presentations and community discussion.

OPENING REMARKS

Planning committee chair Reshma Jagsi (Emory University) welcomed participants in person and virtually to the workshop and thanked the National Institutes of Health Office for Research on Women's Health for sponsoring the workshop. Representing the planning committee, she said, "We're here to learn from many incredible speakers but also to learn from you, our audience. We spoke at length about the topics most pressing on our

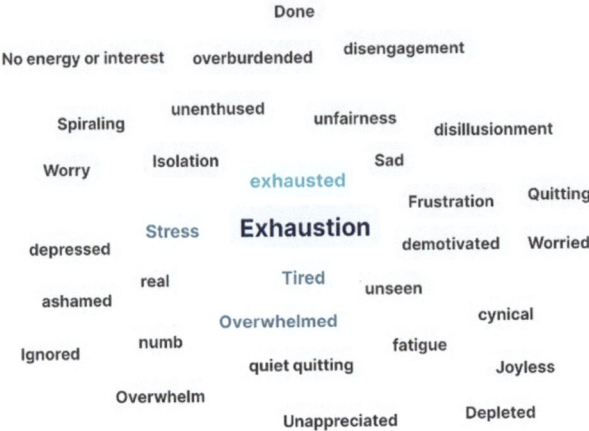

FIGURE 1-1 Word cloud resulting from participants poll responses.
SOURCE: Poll 1, Workshop, October 1, 2024; 44 participants, 73 responses.

minds and likely the minds of many people about what it means to grapple with being burned out at work." The committee designed the workshop to unpack burnout, she continued—what it is, how it has been conceived and misconceived, how it comes to be, what its impacts are, and what can be done about it. "Throughout, we focus on the implications for equity," Jagsi said. "While acknowledging that anyone can experience burnout, the implications are uneven across the population."

As an initial way to engage all attendees and learn from their experiences, Jagsi asked them to participate in a quick online poll to share one word that comes to mind when they think of burnout. Frequent responses were "exhaustion," "overwhelmed," "stress," and "isolation" (see Figure 1-1). "These are concepts that we will rely on our expert speakers to help us unpack and understand the relationships between them," she said.

ORGANIZATION OF THIS PROCEEDINGS

The remainder of this publication summarizes the presentations and discussions from the workshop. The workshop began with a moderated discussion with two leading experts to understand burnout and challenge misconceptions about it, which is summarized in Chapter 2. Highlights from two of the commissioned papers follow, with Chapter 3 on the causes and associated risk factors and Chapter 4 on consequences of burnout, both followed by moderated discussions. Chapter 5 summarizes a panel that took a deep dive on burnout, identity, and intersectionality. Chapter 6 highlights the third commissioned paper on current and innovative approaches to managing burnout, followed in Chapter 7 by another deep dive panel, this one on interventions to manage burnout in medicine given particular challenges of burnout in healthcare professions. The workshop concluded with interactive discussions on three interrelated topics focused on interventions to address burnout. Report-outs from these discussions and concluding comments from the workshop organizers are reported in Chapter 8. Though the workshop was designed to have Day 1 provide important context and background on burnout and Day 2 examine interventions, given the hunger among both presenters and audience members for actionable policies and practices that can mitigate burnout, questions and discussions of interventions occurred throughout the two days. The workshop agenda, biographical sketches of the speakers, and full text of the commissioned papers can be found in the appendixes.

In accordance with the policies of the National Academies, this proceedings does not attempt to establish any conclusions or recommendations about needs and future directions for research, focusing instead on key issues and themes discussed by the speakers and workshop participants. The proceedings was prepared by the workshop rapporteurs as a factual summary of what was presented and discussed at the workshop. The planning committee's role was limited to planning and convening the workshop. The statements made are those of the rapporteurs and do not necessarily represent positions of the workshop participants as a whole, the planning committee, or the National Academies.

2

Understanding Burnout and Challenging Misconceptions

> **Highlights from the Presentations**
> - The World Health Organization defines burnout as "a syndrome characterized as resulting from chronic workplace stress that has not been successfully managed" (WHO, 2019). It is not an individual medical condition or illness (Maslach).
> - The Maslach Inventory is a discovery tool to measure burnout in a given situation and not intended as a diagnostic tool for individuals (Maslach).
> - Six areas in a work environment that can help to predict burnout in the workforce include overload, lack of control, insufficient rewards, breakdown of the work community, absence of fairness, and values conflict (Maslach).
> - Burnout occurs on a continuum and treating it as an individual problem is counterproductive (Shanafelt).
> - Anchoring to a common, research-based definition and showing how burnout affects organizational priorities can help organizations recognize that addressing burnout is necessary to accomplish their missions, and not just a "nice thing to do" (Shanafelt).

- Small steps to address "pebbles in the shoe"[1] can make a huge difference in addressing burnout and do not need to cost a lot of money (Maslach, Shanafelt).

The workshop began with a discussion facilitated by planning committee member Elena Fuentes-Afflick (Association of American Medical Colleges) with two pioneering experts in burnout research: Christina Maslach (University of California, Berkeley) and Tait Shanafelt (Stanford University School of Medicine). The goal of this panel was to establish a shared definition and common understanding of burnout to guide all further workshop conversations. This panel did not take a specific science, technology, engineering, mathematics, and medicine (STEMM) focus, but rather aimed to set the stage by unpacking the phenomenon of burnout more generally.

PANEL DISCUSSION

Definition of Burnout

Maslach began by noting that there is an agreed-upon definition of burnout in the research literature. She referred to the classification by the World Health Organization (WHO) in its 11th Revision of the International Classification of Diseases (ICD) of burnout as an occupational phenomenon, which is based on decades of work. The ICD-11 states that "burnout is a syndrome conceptualized as resulting from chronic workplace stress that has not been successfully managed" (WHO, 2019). She called attention to several salient points. It results from chronic stressors, and recovery from chronic conditions is often more difficult than from other, more intermittent, stressors. It results from conditions that "are not successfully managed," which implies they could be better managed, and people would not necessarily experience burnout. She also called attention to WHO's characterization of three dimensions as the "trifecta of burnout":

---

[1] "Pebbles in the shoe" and related concepts like "daily hassles" refer to seemingly small everyday challenges and inefficiencies at work that can build up over time to create much greater problems. For more on pebbles in the shoe and how this has been conceptualized in the medical field, see https://www.ama-assn.org/practice-management/physician-health/identifying-pebbles-contribute-physician-burnout.

exhaustion, increased negativism or cynicism, and reduced professional efficiency. WHO made clear that burnout is not a medical condition or illness, but rather an occupational phenomenon with health consequences, akin to how stress can lead to heart disease.

Shanafelt opened his remarks by dispelling the idea that a person either experiences burnout or does not. "The symptoms are on a continuum," he clarified. "We look at the effect of changes on a scale." He suggested thinking of the range akin to blood pressure, with thresholds above which undesirable consequences may be the outcome. He also cautioned against conflating depression and burnout, which he said is inconsistent with the literature. "Depression is a mental health condition with a biological basis that is treated at an individual level," Shanafelt clarified. Miscategorizing burnout is also counterproductive in terms of interventions. Another misconception, he continued, is that burnout is the only form of occupational stress. An example of a source of stress that is distinct from burnout but related is moral distress. This was particularly prevalent in healthcare professions in the early days of COVID-19, as many people in these fields were without adequate personal protective equipment. Many employees felt betrayed that they were not sufficiently protected.

Many organizations have responded to burnout with individual solutions to create "more resilient workers." He noted that the business world rejected a similar notion 50 years ago in trying to build "strong workers." Looking for solutions like this "is like a first-aid station on a factory floor to help when people are injured," rather than redesign processes so they do not get injured in the first place, he commented.

Measuring Burnout

Maslach provided context for her development of the Maslach Inventory, which she explained grew out of years of research with colleague Susan Jackson to develop a measurement of burnout (Maslach and Jackson, 1981). While she was setting up a new lab at the University of California, Berkeley, she began interviewing subjects on emotionally challenging work and how people deal with this during the workday. She heard a consistent story across hundreds of people in many occupations, who described the chronic stressors they experienced at work. At the time, the term "burnout" did not exist for the situation she was documenting but the interviews became the basis for creating a measure to capture what respondents were expressing. She stressed that the inventory was not designed as a diagnostic tool and is used incorrectly when it is employed to diagnose individuals. It is a discovery tool for research. It can answer questions about what burnout is, under what conditions it might be aggravated, and interventions that might help.

Shanafelt also noted the need for effective measurement tools to understand whether and when interventions are effective. In many instances, well-constructed interventions do not have the hoped-for effect. Given organizations' finite resources, it is important to quantify effectiveness before scaling or promulgating interventions. "I look at that as a very high risk for resource utilization and diverting resources away from things that are effective," he said. He also urged anchoring around a good, common definition that ties into at least four decades of research on the mechanistic drivers of burnout, such as workload, community, and balance. This allows for understanding what fuels burnout in a particular setting, which may lead to improving upstream drivers.

Systemic Focus

Maslach commented on the tendency to ask "who questions," such as "Who is burned out?" By focusing on individuals, the action becomes what is wrong with them, how to fix them, where to move them, and the like. It leads to interventions that do not address root causes[2] in the environment. Those who experience greater burnout are a signal that something is not working in general across the workplace. She urged changing to "what and why questions," such as "What is causing burnout?" and "Why is it happening?" This encourages us to look at causes and proactive prevention of burnout, not just treating people when they have it.

She said research from herself and her colleagues has identified at least six challenges that can arise in the workplace and that can predict burnout problems in the workforce:

1. Overload (high demand, low resources)
2. Lack of control (no autonomy or choice to do the job right)
3. Insufficient rewards (in terms of praise and opportunities)

---

[2] We use the term "root causes" to highlight the multiple causes that are at the heart of burnout. There is no singular cause that produces burnout; however, there are multiple factors that are central to producing burnout. It is these root causes that are referenced throughout this proceedings.

4. Breakdown of the workforce community (bullying, social toxicity, lack of clarity about who to turn to for help)
5. Absence of fairness (such as discrimination and barriers to advancement)
6. Values conflict (an environment where the worker feels the values are "eating away my soul")

Stigma

Fuentes-Afflick commented that many medical professionals experience or fear stigma if they disclose feelings of burnout. She asked how a clear understanding of burnout could challenge norms and promote conversations that could break down this stigma. Shanafelt harkened back to the WHO definition of burnout that states the root issue is the work environment and workplace systems, not a problem with the individual. Stigma occurs when someone feels marginalized or feels they are not seen as dedicated or tough enough and if they were to acknowledge the challenges they are facing, they would be viewed negatively. He stated that anchoring to the fact that this is a structural rather than an individual issue is helpful to challenge that stigma. It also enables a tie-in to the literature that can provide motivation for organizations to act. For example, there is robust data that burnout in nurses and physicians can affect quality-of-care outcomes, costs of care, and access, all of which are healthcare priorities. When organizations recognize that burnout is linked to these priorities, acting on it is not just a "nice thing to do, but is essential to accomplishing the core mission." Anchoring to burnout also allows interventions to be evidence-informed, albeit not evidence-based, since what works in one situation will not necessarily work elsewhere.

Why It Matters

Before turning to audience questions, Fuentes-Afflick asked both panelists to share one element about burnout that they wish was better understood and why it matters for organizations and individuals. Maslach underlined the need to understand that burnout involves job conditions as much as, if not more than, qualities of individuals. It is critical to reduce or eliminate chronic job stressors that are causing the problem. Solutions might be to redesign jobs, using new processes or technologies, and putting in positives and not just negatives. She offered an acronym for this: GROSS, or Get Rid of Stupid Stuff.

To Shanafelt, the important thing to point out was, "We can address this issue. It has been done." He acknowledged a sense of nihilism that nothing can be done given large systemic issues such as national payment models or economic belt-tightening that might make it seem like certain interventions are not feasible or could not tackle the broader issues. "You do not need a lot of money. It has to be prioritized. The most important asset is not financial capital, but leadership attention and behaviors," he said. Flexibility and control do not have to cost a lot, and aligning values and leaders' behaviors are in scope for many quality improvement efforts. Building a community of support, as well as giving people agency and voice, can have huge effects in all organizations, not just well-financed ones.

OPEN DISCUSSION

Worker Agency

Fuentes-Afflick opened the conversation to audience questions. One questioner noted that workers are often "at the mercy of employers," and asked how workers can have more control, as Maslach and Shanafelt suggested. Shanafelt agreed that individuals may feel they are at the mercy of organizations, and organizations are also at the mercy of regulatory agencies, accrediting bodies, payment structures, and other actors. He paid tribute to work by the National Academies of Sciences, Engineering, and Medicine, such as a 2019 report from the National Academy of Medicine on clinician burnout, that has led to engagement by legislative bodies, payors, and professional societies in different conversations than were happening a decade ago (NASEM, 2019). However, he noted, macro policy changes may not always have the intended benefit. As an example, after years of work, the Centers for Medicare and Medicaid Services redefined some billing codes for physicians with the goal to reduce burnout. He credited the effort, but said penetration was modest and did not affect the day-to-day experience in the clinic. He urged looking at the different levels of individual, work group, and organization to make changes, not just the overall health system. He also urged not being distracted by the large, structural factors that will take decades to change while more limited changes are attainable and can contribute to future structural change.

Maslach reflected on Shanafelt's notion of pebbles in the shoe and suggested thinking about scale. Reducing burnout does not require transforming healthcare. Everyday things that pose obstacles can be improved without costing a lot of money. Ask workers about the main things that bother them, she recommended, then collaborate with them to make changes. When she recently worked with an organization, interviews revealed that workers desired simple interventions such as not holding meetings during lunch hour or at the end of the day. "What I hear from the top and from employees often do not match," she observed. She also suggested that conversations take place regularly to identify problems and solutions to make things better for everyone.

Shanafelt added that each department in an organization has different needs. A classic impact/feasibility grid would show that some changes could have high impact but low feasibility, while others may make less impact but are very feasible now. Start with the latter, he urged. Higher-impact changes may become more feasible over time. He clarified that these less feasible but greater impact changes should not be avoided but recommended not getting distracted in seeking changes that will take years; instead, do the things that can give workers a better experience in the next 3 months. At the work unit level, if people have meaningful work, a well-led team, and agency, what is happening in the broader organization matters less. Maslach added that these steps build optimism and breed a sense of more control.

Quality of Care

The next question came from a participant interested in the relationship between burnout and quality of care in healthcare settings. They noted that research shows strong linkages using subjective measures but mixed evidence using objective measures such as clinical charts and asked about this discrepancy. Shanafelt said the majority of studies are subjective, although some good objective studies have taken place as well. He suggested that the Maslach Inventory can predict measures like patient experience prospectively. Other studies have looked at links between burnout and objective measures such as line infections, quicker discharge of patients, and post-operational pain in ensuing weeks. In the aggregate, they tell a compelling and consistent story. He added that he does not think more studies about the problem are needed. He would rather see rigorous research to test interventions. He also noted that looking at patients' charts to measure the effect of burnout should not be the gold standard in this regard. "Near misses are not documented in the chart," he commented. As an example, Shanafelt highlighted that a doctor writing an incorrect dose of chemotherapy that is intercepted by a chemotherapy pharmacist before affecting the patient does not end up in the chart, but if thousands of those events happen, some will sneak through and result in negative outcomes. As a new measure to look at burnout, he pointed to entries in electronic health records, and specifically when a potential medical error is retracted within 60 seconds.

Continued Confusion

In closing, a virtual participant brought up continued confusion or conflation of burnout with other conditions, despite the WHO definition. Maslach posited that part of the confusion is that the term "burnout" is commonly used for all kinds of things in everyday life, highlighting how the term can become muddled when it is applied to so many different scenarios, some of which look nothing like what the WHO defines as burnout. Understanding and addressing burnout, however, requires a shared definition about the issue.

3

Causes of Burnout and Associated Risk Factors

> **Highlights from the Presentation and Discussion**
>
> - Burnout is a multilevel phenomenon with factors at the macro, meso, and micro levels that have a disproportionate impact on women and minoritized STEMM workers (Cha).
> - Macro factors at the societal level include economic, cultural, and demographic shifts, including the effects of globalization, persistence of the "ideal worker" norm, and persistence of stigmas when people take advantage of flexible policies that do exist (Cha).
> - Meso factors include factors within an organization such as high job demands or expectations of work hours as well as lower job resources or limited utilization of resources that do exist (Cha).
> - Micro factors at the individual level include hampered identification with work, lack of cultural fit, and intersectional inequalities (Cha).
> - When a policy is framed as a gender issue, it may not be used because of stigma. Flexible policies should be designed as a legal entitlement, not an accommodation (Cha).

- The Healthy Work Design and Well-Being Program at the National Institute for Occupational Safety and Health provides resources that can apply to issues of burnout in the workplace (Pana-Cryan).

A panel on the causes of burnout and associated risk factors revolved around a commissioned paper developed by Youngjoo Cha (Indiana University) along with her collaborator Cassie Mead. She presented a high-level summary of the paper (see Appendix B for the full paper), followed by comments by planning committee member Lonnie Golden (Pennsylvania State University, Abington), discussant Rene Pana-Cryan (National Institute for Occupational Safety and Health [NIOSH]), and other attendees.

The purpose of the commissioned paper and this panel were to address the various factors at the root of high rates of burnout in the science, technology, engineering, mathematics, and medicine (STEMM) workforce and to understand how this might vary across diverse populations of workers, particularly along lines of race and gender. It additionally was developed to provide insight into how burnout relates to other demographic characteristics.

BURNOUT CAUSES AND FACTORS IN STEMM

As context about the prevalence of burnout, Cha began by pointing to the American Psychological Association's 2023 Work in America Survey. Fifty-seven percent of workers said they experience emotional exhaustion and mental disengagement from work (APA, 2023). Cha said her review of the literature shows that burnout is a multilevel phenomenon caused by factors at the macro, meso, and micro levels. She elaborated on each of these levels.

At the macro level, Cha noted the impact of economic, cultural, and demographic shifts. Economic factors included globalization and union declines. These broad economic conditions pressure organizations to cut costs and to downsize. These changes lead to increased demands and lower job security for those who survive layoffs. She also noted the research on a "time divide," in which high-skilled workers have seen an increase in hours and low-skilled workers a decrease (Jacobs and Gerson, 2004), as well as the rise of "gig" or contract work in STEMM fields, which can contribute to stress and strain as well as insecurity at work and can affect burnout (Kunda et al., 2002; Wingfield, 2019).

Turning to macro-level cultural factors, Cha highlighted a few key challenges such as pressure to comply with the "ideal worker norm," or the expectation that individuals must show complete dedication to their work, exemplified through long hours and undivided focus at all times, and intensified work-life conflict. Even when flexible policies are available, there is often a stigma to using them, so they go underutilized. Parenting norms have also intensified, which increases overall time demands and has gender implications because women still disproportionately provide care for children as well as other kin. "Both the family and the workplace have gotten greedier," Cha commented. In STEMM fields, the strong ideal worker norm and flexibility stigma have led to higher turnover (Cech and Blair-Loy, 2014).

Finally turning to macro-level demographic changes, Cha pointed out that dual-earner households have increased, with a mean increase in work hours at the family level. Although an older example, heterosexual married couples' joint weekly work hours increased from 52.5 hours in 1970 to 63.1 hours in 2000 (Jacobs and Gerson, 2004). Workers do not have the spousal support of the past, and time pressures can increase the likelihood that workers experience burnout.

At the meso or workplace level, job demands are increasing, Cha continued. These conditions include long and inflexible hours, "work-work conflicts"[1] when people have dual appointments or other multiple occupational roles that can conflict with each other and cause strain, an increase in "hidden work" such as service or mentorship efforts that more often go unnoticed and unrewarded, and the use of new communication technology that can mean workers are constantly logged in and basically "sleeping with their smartphones." She noted that women and minoritized STEMM workers, including faculty, are particularly affected by work-work conflicts and hidden work phenomena. Resources that can mitigate these conditions include more control over schedules, creative and meaningful work, autonomy, and relationships. STEMM workers typically face higher job demands than those in other fields but also have more resources than

---

[1] Work-work conflict refers to potential conflict between multiple organizational roles or activities an individual might hold or be engaged in that can produce stress and strain. For more, see Wynn et al., 2018.

workers in other fields. However, referring to her comments above, strong ideal worker norms often offset the benefit of these resources.

At the micro level, Cha looked at STEMM professionals' identification with their work and perceptions of fit. Failing to attach meaning to their work in the face of job and family demands is a major factor of elite workers leaving their jobs. On the flip side, strong identification with the work shields some people from burnout when they feel they have a calling or passion project or when they receive organizational rewards or cultural appreciation. Perception of cultural fit affects burnout in STEMM jobs and, as with the intensification of parenting, has gendered implications. Cultural ideals of many STEMM fields are based on White male heterosexual values, and others often feel they must hide their lifestyles and bodily experiences. These ideals are communicated in many ways including through socialization in engineering education (Seron et al., 2016) and the language or images used in recruiting efforts (Wynn and Correll, 2018). Research shows that being a numerical minority is also a stressor (Jackson et al., 1995; Kanter, 1977; Taylor, 2016), Cha continued. Status beliefs and stereotypes can lead to a sense of underappreciation and inequality, which, in turn, lead to lower job satisfaction, higher turnover, and increased psychological distress for women and other minoritized STEMM workers (Beck et al., 2022; Hall et al., 2015, 2019; Pascoe and Richman, 2009; Wingfield and Chavez, 2020). Emotional labor and gendered and racialized "feeling rules," or expectations that individuals perform certain emotions, such as expectations of being friendly or open, regardless of their own emotions, additionally create a double burden for women and other minoritized STEMM workers (Hochschild, 1983; Wingfield, 2019).

These macro, meso, and micro conditions affect gender and race disparities in STEMM and potential burnout, Cha concluded. This occurs both through seemingly gender- and race-neutral factors such as workplace resources. When these are combined with gender and race segregation in jobs, they produce gender- and race-specific outcomes in working conditions, job resources, and identification with work. They also have gender- and race-based implications due to implicit biases built into workplace culture, norms, practices, and interactions, Cha concluded.

REFLECTIONS ON COMMISSIONED PAPER

Golden commented on Cha's presentation as a labor economist. Overwork is not new, he pointed out; Adam Smith wrote about it in 1776.

Future research questions may include whether there is a tipping point beyond which burnout risk cannot be reduced, and whether workers choose to leave a particular job, the entire field, or the labor force entirely. Burnout has multiple causes and should be viewed with multiple frameworks: the economics of labor supply and demand economics, time use/allocation between work and nonwork time, individual and organizational psychology, health risk, and salutogenesis,[2] or what supports or creates health and well-being rather than just looking at negative or unhealthy factors.

A salutogenic approach applied to burnout has at its core a sense of coherence with three dimensions: (1) comprehensibility (the degree to which a person perceives work, job, and life as structured and predictable); (2) manageability (the extent to which a person feels they have the resources to cope with multiple demands); and (3) meaningfulness (how much a person feels their workplace challenges are worthy of investing time and emotional energy). Reflecting on Cha's literature review and presentation, Golden said burnout is a culmination of a variety of factors that can build up at the macro, meso, and micro levels. He offered three questions: How do we disentangle the three levels, what is the role of the ideal work norm, and can they be addressed?

Discussant Pana-Cryan briefly introduced NIOSH, which is within the Centers for Disease Control and Prevention. In her remarks, she specifically highlighted the Healthy Work Design and Well-Being (HWD) Program.[3] While acknowledging the importance of macro and micro factors as described by Cha, she explained HWD's focus on the meso, or organizational, level. Proximal outcomes are related to burnout, fatigue, and stress, but the program also recognizes economic and evaluative outcomes to rate quality of life now and in the future.

HWD complements the observations from previous presenters, she noted, such as spillover effects and feedback loops across macro, meso, and micro levels. HWD has delineated "healthy work design elements" that encompass flexibility, workload, and other topics. HWD is also looking at the differential effects between direct employment and contract work, as well as availability and use of paid leave policies.

---

[2] Salutogenesis was developed by sociologist Aaron Antonovsky to argue for a move away from focusing on the "pathogenesis" of disease but instead consider what advances and maintains health. For more on salutogenesis, see https://pmc.ncbi.nlm.nih.gov/articles/PMC7014834/.

[3] For more information, see https://www.cdc.gov/niosh/research-programs/portfolio/hwd.html.

OPEN DISCUSSION

Following the moderated discussion, the floor was opened to general questions. When asked by Golden about how to disentangle the levels and tackle norms and stigmas, Cha recognized the levels are a useful analytical framework, but real life offers a more complex picture. Interventions at the workplace level seem the most fruitful. She agreed that the root causes are important, and changing laws and culture should be considered but it takes a long time. For example, the norm in most workplaces is that a household has a single breadwinner, which contributes to policies that often produce more strain for families with multiple working members as is increasingly more often the reality of today's workforce.

At the micro level, she expressed skepticism about the fix to "give employees a spa day." Other individual interventions are more effective, such as confronting day-to-day discrimination and stereotypes that are chronic stressors. These micro-level dynamics must be recognized, and interventions to address them may originate at the meso level. Regarding combatting the ideal worker norm, she noted that a root cause to address is that currently most people are rewarded when their job demands increase. She is undertaking a study on flexible work policies and has found how they are implemented makes a difference. A differentiator is whether the policies are up to the discretion of managers versus policies for everyone to use in a gender-neutral way. She echoed the value of starting with "small wins," and normative changes might eventually follow. Elaborating on the impact of globalization, Cha said an increase in competition and participation in the global economy brings a faster pace and greater pressure to reduce labor costs.

Golden then gathered a series of questions from attendees, and Cha responded to the series in totality. A participant asked about the balance between expanding accommodations broadly to avoid stigma while faced with finite resources. Another participant asked how the different levels can talk with each other. Questions about identification with work and building the evidence base were also raised.

Framing policies is important, Cha stressed. When a policy is framed as a gender issue, it may be more stigmatized and therefore not be used as frequently. Instead, flexible policies should be seen as a legal entitlement, not an accommodation. She noted that in Germany, workers are entitled to 4 weeks of vacation, and they take it. Cha noted that the mindset toward vacation is very different when seen as an entitlement versus an accommodation. In the United States, vacation is not seen as a legal entitlement. As a result, people may be required to ask co-workers to fill in and feel that taking vacation is an imposition on their team, resulting in taking less vacation time. In dealing with how to distribute work when it is seen as a zero-sum game, Cha said the response must come from the organization. Stigma is enhanced when others must pick up the extra work, she noted. She discussed the importance of considering each level when designing policies. At the macro level, why are we having this problem? At the meso level, how can we mitigate individual factors, such as through different hiring practices, mentoring and networking, or sending out signals related to cultural fit? A participant urged engaging the individuals affected in the design of meso and macro policies. Pana-Cryan underscored the need for workers' voice. She referred participants to NIOSH's Worker Well-Being Questionnaire as a resource.[4] It provides free, de-identified data to use in designing policies, learning from each other, or serving as a benchmark. She also noted that mental health is part of what NIOSH considers as worker health.

When asked about making the business case for childcare, Cha noted that many studies have shown how flexible work improves the bottom line. They have not been effective in convincing most employers. This might be a situation in which political will is needed and not just the business case. Pana-Cryan added that a business case must be tailored for each environment. As a future research question, a participant raised generational shifts in the workplace and tailoring interventions to respond to rapid changes.

---

[4] To access the questionnaire, see https://www.cdc.gov/niosh/twh/php/wellbq/index.html.

4

Consequences of Burnout and Measurement Challenges

Highlights from the Presentations

- Individual-level and occupational-level consequences of burnout have been well and sufficiently documented with enough data to implement and test interventions (Lai).
- Early-career STEMM workers are particularly vulnerable to burnout but there is relatively less on gender differences and especially on racial differences in burnout implications (Lai).
- One study reported particularly high burnout and stress among respondents who chose not to identify by race or ethnic group, which merits further exploration to understand how individuals of various racial identities choose to report or not report burnout (Lai).
- There is a need for more research on gender and racialized consequences of burnout for organizations, such as potential implications of uneven turnover. There is also a need for research on leader burnout and spillover effects of this (Lai).
- Besides looking at what is not working or who is experiencing burnout, it is valuable to look at the places where things are working or those individuals who are not experiencing burnout (Porta).

> - Accountability is important, but care must be taken in determining what to measure to avoid unintended consequences (Lai, Porta).

Planning committee member José Pagán (New York University) moderated the next workshop session on the consequences of burnout in science, technology, engineering, mathematics, and medicine (STEMM). Alden Lai (New York University) shared key observations derived from the commissioned paper he undertook with colleagues. (For the full text of the paper, see Appendix C). Carolyn Porta (University of Minnesota) served as discussant followed by general discussion with in-person and virtual attendees.

The paper at the heart of this panel was commissioned to examine the impact of burnout for individuals and organizations and how this might vary by key demographics such as gender and race. The paper and presentation also provided insight into areas where scientific knowledge of burnout, particularly along lines of gender and race, is still lacking.

REVIEWING CURRENT KNOWLEDGE TO SUGGEST FUTURE DIRECTIONS

Lai began by introducing the methodology of the literature review he conducted along with co-authors Mark Linzer, Amber Stephenson, Erin Sullivan, and Kenneth Wee. He explained that they took a review-of-reviews approach, a search for non-reviewed articles, and a backward and forward reference search to find the set of relevant scientific knowledge on the consequences of burnout in STEMM fields. He concurred with previous speakers that based on this review, "We have enough data to act." Ultimately, he argued that doing more studies to identify consequences would be less helpful than studies to chart new areas of inquiry.

Researchers have captured a sufficient breadth of individual- and occupational-level consequences of burnout, although most are in medicine and other healthcare settings with less in other areas of STEMM. The individual-level consequences can be categorized into somatized symptoms, poorer quality of life, physical and mental health conditions, poorer cognitive function, substance use, and suicide ideation, with a range of manifestations (see Table 4-1).

TABLE 4-1 Individual-Level Consequences of Burnout

Categories	Manifestations
Somatized symptoms	Headaches, neck pain, body pain
Poorer Quality of Life	Loss in appetite, loss in sleep, chronic fatigue
Physical health conditions	Gastrointestinal infections, respiratory infections
Mental health conditions	Anxiety, depression, post-traumatic stress disorder, mood disturbances
Poorer Cognitive function	Poorer prospective memory, delayed memory
Substance use*	Alcohol use, medication use
Suicide ideation	Suicide ideation

* Indicates mixed evidence, in part due to inconsistency in measurement tools.
SOURCE: Alden Lai, Workshop Presentation, October 1, 2024.

Occupational-level consequences include talent loss, poorer work performance, poorer employee well-being, and less talent growth (see Table 4-2).

Lai noted that the studies reviewed show that early-career STEMM workers are particularly vulnerable to burnout (e.g., Laschinger et al., 2015; Rudman and Gustavsson, 2012). For example, one study found that employees with 1 to 3 years of experience were most likely to leave, compared with those with fewer than 6 months or more than 5 years (Trinkenreich et al., 2024). It is important to be sensitive to those workers, Lai said.

TABLE 4-2 Occupational-Level Consequences of Burnout

Categories	Manifestations
Talent loss	Intention to leave training programs, job, or profession
Poorer work performance	Absenteeism, reduced ability to work, less professionalism
Poorer employee wellbeing	Lower job satisfaction, regretting career choice
Less talent growth	Reduced engagement in professional development activities

SOURCE: Alden Lai, Workshop Presentation, October 1, 2024.

Occupations, work responsibilities, and work settings drive some of the differences in the consequences of burnout, Lai continued. For example, nurses had higher burnout and reported more changes in their workload during the pandemic than did physicians (Peck and Porter, 2022). Those with direct involvement in treating patients are at higher risk for burnout (Mukherjee et al., 2022), and work settings such as emergency medicine and intensive care also affect the consequences of burnout (Hodkinson et al., 2022). In this way, the contexts of care in medicine as well as in the general context of work across other STEMM fields matter for how burnout manifests.

"Even without all the data, we can take meaningful action," Lai said, echoing Tait Shanafelt's earlier point that evidence-informed, rather than evidence-based, research can be sufficient. "The time to take action is now." He underscored the lack of attention within the research to pronounced gender differences in burnout and urged implementation and testing of interventions. Drawing for existing evidence, women report higher burnout than men and a higher rate of intention to leave their jobs (Apple et al., 2023). Another study found that female neurologists were more likely to report suicide ideation than male neurologists (LaFaver et al., 2018).

Lai argued it was also very important to understand burnout and race. Specifically, he noted, "We need to better understand how persons of color choose to report burnout, as well as their lived experiences in the context of burnout." To this point, Lai shared data on levels of burnout reported by Black, White, and Latinx healthcare workers as well as healthcare workers who did not share their racial identity (Prasad et al., 2021). Almost 13 percent of the respondents chose not to identify their race or ethnicity. This group ultimately reported the highest rates of burnout and stress: 62 percent reported burnout and 42 percent reported stress (see Figure 4-1). This raises the question of who the people are who prefer not to identify and why and what barriers this might pose to our understanding of racialized implications of burnout.

Another area where Lai argued more research is needed is to link the mechanisms between worker burnout and organizational and societal consequences, such as the domino effect in which leaders' burnout has detrimental effects on their direct reports and the consequences of absenteeism and attrition. Other future work might include measurement issues related to subjective and objective measures to develop a more cohesive call to action; organizational and social contexts in which human capital is being eroded or lost (thus upending careers and losing out on innovation); and translating knowledge into action for workers, employers, and institutions.

Highest burnout and stress levels noted for U.S. health care workers who preferred not to identify race or ethnicity (12.9% of 20,947 respondents) in a national survey

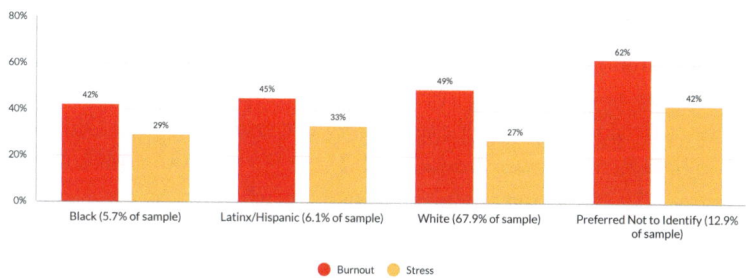

FIGURE 4-1 Burnout and stress levels by racial and ethnic groups.
SOURCE: Alden Lai, based on Prasad et al. (2021), Workshop Presentation, October 1, 2024.

REFLECTIONS

Porta is a nurse-scientist involved in workforce and public health, as well as a forensic nurse, an area with high turnover and experience with trauma. She offered two personal examples in which family members made choices based on the work environment about whether to stay or leave their jobs to ground her remarks. An uncle retired in 2022 but returned to the workplace as a consultant. In contrast, Porta's daughter left a job where she felt objectified, and her manager did nothing to support her.

Most of the time people spend during the day is at work, and she expressed concern that the state of workforce science lags other sciences. The budget of the National Institute for Occupational Safety and Health is small compared with other research agencies. They are the healers charged with keeping society healthy, yet they have limited capacity to understand and improve workplace conditions. Porta commented on the disconnect between burnout and big data and called for more sophisticated tools to understand and predict burnout to prevent it. Sensors are used for all kinds of things, from vehicle tires to animal health, she commented, and real-time data collection, artificial intelligence, and predictive analytics may be useful in workforce well-being.

Porta also suggested looking at protective factors and what works. For example, if a study shows a burnout rate of 60 percent, what is going on with the 40 percent who do not experience burnout, she posed. It is also important to look at thriving workforce members and their workplaces.

The paper developed by Lai and colleagues is a good place to start, she concluded.

Pagán asked about the broader impact of the consequences in the studies identified by Lai. He responded that many of the studies reviewed pointed to the financial effects, such as an estimate that turnover costs $4.6 billion annually (Han et al., 2019). While they should be taken in account, he noted that the individual- and organizational-level consequences that surfaced are not captured by the numbers alone. Only a few studies have looked at the societal level. He noted that one study suggested more opioid prescriptions are given to patients when physicians are experiencing higher burnout.

Porta added that the costs of not retaining workers and of onboarding new workers are well known. Less well known are the costs of other factors. For example, she asked, how do we quantify and demonstrate the effect of inaction versus action in addressing workplace well-being. Pagán agreed that the information is hard to capture and asked why more organizations do not attempt to do so. Porta posited that many react to day-to-day operations and do not take the time to step back despite the importance. She has stayed with her organization because of the team, supervision, and organizational values, but a neighboring health system has a high turnover. It is important to find the space to look at why and seek transformational excellence.

Lai referred to Cha's comments about workplaces in which family-friendly policies are widely used (see Chapter 3). Research by the Oxford Wellbeing Research Centre has shown that employee well-being improves firms' performances, and the top 100 in terms of well-being outperform the Standard and Poor (S&P) index.[1] Another immense challenge is that burnout can result from system failure and inefficiency. He agreed that unit-level action can be undertaken, and perhaps other pockets of opportunity can be identified.

OPEN DISCUSSION

During audience questions, a participant commented that healthcare organizations are accountable for many measures but are generally not accountable for workforce well-being and some upstream factors, such as workload, measured through self-reports or another type of measurement that were being implemented by healthcare organizations to address this. Lai said his review did not find research engaging directly with the ways

---

[1] For more information, see https://wellbeing.hmc.ox.ac.uk/.

in which to use burnout measures as tools of accountability. He reminded the group that the Maslach Inventory (see Chapter 2) is intended as a discovery tool, not a diagnostic tool. He added that the Oxford Centre convinced S&P Global to include questions related to job satisfaction, stress, happiness, and other measures when reporting on corporate sustainability, although he does not see this happening widely in the healthcare space. Now might be the time to consider it, he urged. Porta offered lessons learned from Occupational Safety and Health Administration (OSHA) regulations: regulations incentivize industry to engineer out risk. When an entity is self-driven to protect itself, people are sometimes disincentivized to report a mental or emotional health need. Federal policies are important, but organizations must take the initiative to examine what is happening internally, especially if they are losing workers.

Echoing previous comments, a participant noted that the business case is well established to prevent burnout but does not lead to change. Measurements alone do not work, but retention as a metric may work. Porta said underreporting is a significant issue, which is why other ways of knowing beyond measurements are needed. One participant noted that those who are leaving are the very people who might otherwise advocate for more work-life balance if they stayed. Porta said that when people leave, an organization is losing creativity and the next big idea, and it must decide whether to transform. She pointed to an annual letter that finance leader Ross Stevens sends to stakeholders, in which he says his company is tough on ideas but kind to people.

Tait Shanafelt pointed to an important dimension related to accountability: If the wrong outcome is measured, it can foster gaming and underreporting and worsen the situation. In addition, less-resourced healthcare systems could be disadvantaged if the wrong metrics are focused upon. He suggested looking at a study under way by The Joint Commission[2] as well as a piece by John Ripp and himself (Ripp and Shanafelt, 2024) about how to hold hospitals accountable for clinicians' well-being. It is important to hold each other accountable, Porta agreed. "Team member, ally, accomplice—all have a role to play," she said. Lai also called for internal accountability within a healthcare system to learn why some units are performing differently regarding burnout. Accountability can catch the

---

[2] For more information, see https://www.jointcommission.org/our-priorities/workforce-safety-and-well-being/resource-center/worker-well-being/.

"bad apples" but also identify those with good intentions that need help in achieving the best outcomes.

Commenting on the role of leaders and training to effect change, Porta stressed the importance of an employee's immediate supervisor, which she said is backed up in the literature and her own experience. She noted some health systems base part of leaders' bonuses on their workers' well-being, but leaders must be prepared for this role through support and mentorship.

5

Deep Dive on Burnout, Identity, and Intersectionality

Highlights from the Presentations

- Even with more limited data on burnout among those with multiple marginalized identities, it is clear that a lack of psychological safety and a need to mask are chronic workplace stressors (King, Reede, Rodriguez).
- The concept of "bringing your whole self to work" has implications for professional and personal safety, especially for women and minoritized STEMM workers (King, Reede, Rodriguez).
- Not everyone feels equally safe to report burnout, especially those with intersecting marginalized identities. Current measures of burnout rely on self-report, which creates challenges and may impact findings (Rodriguez).
- Mentoring and support groups are "good news stories" as resources to thrive in the workplace for marginalized groups (King).
- It is necessary to help trainees and younger faculty with multiple marginalized identities not take on the added burden of feeling they are responsible for individually solving the societal problems that institutions must solve (Reede).

> - Takeaways from the first day of the workshop include the complexity of the topic, the energy and ideas to address it, and the need for shared definitions and goals to develop effective interventions (Jagsi, Wullert).

Planning committee member Kelley Bonner (Burn Bright Consulting) facilitated a roundtable discussion on burnout, identity, and intersectionality with Jean King (Worcester Polytechnic Institute), Joan Y. Reede (Harvard Medical School), and José Rodriguez (University of Utah). A short wrap-up by planning committee chair Reshma Jagsi (Emory University) and National Academies of Sciences, Engineering, and Medicine program officer and workshop study director, Katie Wullert, wrapped up the first day of the workshop.

This panel was developed in recognition of the fact that there is still a relative dearth of scientific literature examining experiences, causes, and implications of burnout for those at the intersection of multiple marginalized identities. It was intended not just to highlight gaps, but as Bonner noted in her introduction, as "an opportunity to get at where there's absence of research and where we can lean on experiential data and what we know to be intuitively true about intersectional identities" to better understand experiences that are not currently captured in our scientific literature.

TYING BURNOUT TO IDENTITY AND INTERSECTIONALITY

The panelists began by offering thoughts about how burnout is tied to identity and intersectionality for workers in general and science, technology, engineering, mathematics, and medicine (STEMM) professionals specifically. King said as a neuroscientist, she has studied the effect of stressors on the brain for 30 years. "We bring ourselves to every interaction we have," she pointed out. Each person's construct is unique. When a person has multiple underrepresented identities, these identities overlap, change in different situations, and become a response and an experience. There is not a lot of research that ties intersectionality with burnout, although there is research on the link with stress, which can serve as a proxy. It is important to identify who is suffering, not specific individuals but the experiences of particular groups at work. If you cannot show up at work as yourself, especially in STEMM, and if you have to buck the system on a daily basis, identity cannot be disambiguated from stress and burnout, she said.

Reede raised the multiple identities that everyone must address, such as those related to race, gender, work, and discipline. Time and place are also critical, such as what is happening in one state in the country versus another, or in the field of public health versus another field. Another variable that changes the stressors is working in an academic STEMM environment versus industry, government, or nonprofit, and, within that environment, being at different stages, such as entry level versus leadership.

Rodriguez commented he is a family physician that until July 1, 2024, was the associate vice president for health diversity, equity, and inclusion (DEI) at his institution. The Utah legislature passed a law that made DEI offices illegal in public institutions in the state. He was able to preserve jobs, and a portion of what employees were doing in the new Office for Health Sciences Workforce Excellence. Burnout can be a diagnosis, but it is almost an identity because the individual has to report experiencing it. That brings up issues in academic medical centers where underrepresented minorities experience "minority taxation" and safety—if you do not say you are burned out, people will not know. Yet, there can be safety issues in telling other people you are hurting, he said.

SELF AND WORK

Reede commented on the expression "bring your whole self to work," first noting that no one should feel they have to be their whole selves at their workplace. She called for a clearer understanding of what the term means. She described it in terms of whether she has to filter what she says and does, feels safe saying no or disagreeing, or worries about being misinterpreted or made to feel uncomfortable. Everyone has this, but being a woman and person of color is an additional pressure. She also said that another factor in her mind is that what she says does not just have implications for herself, but for others. "These are dimensions of thinking and worrying that others may not have to take into consideration," she said. Part of survival is not to have to deal with these concerns alone, but through a group and connective process.

Rodriguez agreed about the challenge of bringing one's whole self to work, and the masking and filtering needed for minoritized individuals to survive particularly in academic medical settings, which he knows best. In terms of easing the experience, he recalled that when he was asked to take on the health equity vice president's role in 2018, the first thing he did was go to the university's resiliency center to set up a relationship with a therapist before issues arose. He also continued his work at a Spanish-speaking clinic in Salt Lake City as a way to reduce isolation. When he was told to stop because he is in administration, he refused because he realized its importance to his own well-being. But he also recognized that early-career professionals cannot assert themselves like he was able to. Those who burn out early cannot access many mitigation strategies because they may not have the voice of more senior professionals.

King added that when she thinks of bringing one's whole self to work, she considers the impact of multiple identities. For example, she has been asked why she conducts research on Black women and stress and noted the perception that the topic was not "real science." Being interested in a particular group when one is a member of that group diminishes the work, she observed. Yet, when thinking of the many intersectional studies that are not done, she observed, "Look at most of the principal investigators—they are not at the different intersections, so the questions will not come to them." Research teams should consciously reflect different communities, she urged. The voices of the voiceless can be where innovation resides. When junior scientists want to bring their whole selves to work, she advises them not to do so to protect themselves. To this point, she commented on the people who chose not to identify by race or ethnicity in the study cited by Lai (see Figure 4-1 in Chapter 4) and their level of comfort in expressing their sense of marginalization.

Reede commented on an added burden for many in medicine who often carry a strong weight and responsibility for the health of their communities. "We have to recognize that we do not own it ourselves, but rather it is the institutions that put or do not put resources in communities," she said. She urged conversations to recognize wanting to be part of doing a better job while not taking on the pressure of feeling they have to fix everything as individuals. She also reflected that younger scientists often do not realize the ways they are stressed and are not taking care of themselves. Many do not have an opportunity to talk about and acknowledge these issues.

DISCRIMINATION IN THE WORKPLACE

Rodriguez commented on one implication of anti-DEI laws in many parts of the country. Those who study diversity are not seen as pursuing science, while it is also very personal work. He suggested a job for senior leaders is to provide a place for newer people to process the pressures they face, something they do not learn in medical school or residency. Physicians think or are taught that they are different from their patients. Therefore, he said, "We don't take sick days or vacation, or take care of ourselves. That may have a sense of nobility, but it is not sustainable."

Bonner also asked panelists about the role of microaggressions, or everyday experiences of discrimination, that are more common for those with multiple marginalized identities and how this relates to burnout. As another workplace discrimination issue, Rodriguez noted the no-win situation of how to react to microaggressions and discrimination. If a person files a complaint, there can be repercussions. If a person does nothing, they are hurt because they internalize it. "We have not examined how to deal with this effectively yet," he said, but added that "all the literature that talks about underrepresented faculty is clear on one point: We are the canaries in the mine. [If it is happening to us,] it will happen to others."

Reede called out the term "microaggression," noting it makes the experience sound small when it is anything but to the individual facing it. It denies the impact on the recipient, while presenting the concept from the perspective of the person doing the aggression. King concurred and said that if a person asks for help after a microaggression, they are seen as reacting to something that should not be "a big deal." She also pointed to invisibility faced by women and minoritized scientists, in which one's ideas or comments are ignored or repeated by someone else who gets the credit. "Being invisible in science is not a good thing," she noted. Bonner offered another term instead of microaggression, as explored by researchers Tiffany Jana and Michael Baran: "subtle acts of exclusion." Panelists supported this term and the role this exclusion could have in issues like burnout.

RESEARCH ON RACE AND BURNOUT

A participant asked the panelists their reaction to Lai's research in which people who experienced a high degree of burnout were reluctant to self-identify by race or ethnicity. Lai first offered that a hypothesis is that these respondents did not feel safe disclosing their identity, but more research is needed about this finding and respondents' lived experiences. King offered her concurring hypothesis that those with marginalized racial identities might not feel safe both admitting who they are and what they are experiencing because of potential implications this may have for their community. She commented on the need for data about people with multiple identities to better understand how they are affected by stress and burnout. Identity is not just one more factor among many, she said, but intensified wear and tear on the system, in what is known as allostatic load.

She called for research to generate strong data. Reede called for more rigor in DEI-related research to understand nuance, as needed in all types of research. She said she is excited about new people coming into the field with new questions and methods.

Rodriguez commented that in reporting race and other identities, there is a concept that connects identity with advantage or disadvantage. The concept is not as concrete as one would think, as he noted that a large part of the White population thinks they are disadvantaged. It will take some time before people feel comfortable talking about vulnerabilities, like experiences of burnout especially in demanding STEMM fields, without fear of being hurt by doing so.

MENTORSHIP

When asked how mentorship could help navigate burnout, Rodriguez described a fellowship he runs for early-career faculty who identify as underrepresented in family medicine. Aspects of the training include self-care and expectations about what they should produce in the scientific realm. They are learning how to collect information about things they are already doing to show their achievements and how to find help for their scientific work within the academy. The group meets in person and virtually, and they often have questions that Rodriguez and the other fellowship organizers had not thought of. The most important part is to teach them how they can help change the system.

Reede underscored the value of creating safe spaces to ask questions, feel comfortable, and not feel isolated. In the past week, she met with 10 residents of color for valuable conversations about what they hear and how they cope. She also noted that the flip side to mentorship is an added stressor for the mentor and sponsor, especially if they are the only mentor who is a person of color and feel a huge sense of responsibility. Institutions need to recognize and value mentoring in considering promotion and in growing the scientists of tomorrow. She also warned about situations when mentoring is not good, what she referred to as "de-mentoring" and "tormenting."[1] It is important to protect trainees and younger faculty from

---

[1] These terms are used to refer to toxic or unhelpful mentorship relationships. Tormenting in particular has been used colloquially to distinguish from a positive, supportive mentor and a mentor who causes challenges and works against the individual being mentored. For an example of how this distinction has been used, see https://www.forbes.com/councils/forbescoachescouncil/2021/07/22/how-to-know-if-you-have-a-mentor-or-tormentor/.

these situations and types of mentors because they can serve as substantial stressors that promote burnout. King said overall mentoring is "the good news story." She also suggested support groups and peer-to-peer mentoring as effective and with less burden on specific individuals.

A participant commented on the importance of looking for and disseminating best practices related to mentorship and role-modeling. The literature base on authentic leadership could also be digested and shared. Institutions often offer coaching for people at higher levels, but it is also needed at early levels of leadership. As an example of how to make an intervention more widespread, trauma debriefs used to be opt-in for nurses at the participant's institution and most did not participate, but now they are required.

FINAL TAKEAWAYS

Bonner asked each panelist for a final takeaway. King said she wants organizations to truly see people of multiple identities, try to understand them, and look for ways to help so that they receive support if they are facing burnout, as well as other stresses at work. "If we could change the invisible to visible, we have a start," she said. "If no one is looking or talking about it, it cannot get solved."

Rodriguez acknowledged negative mentors are out there, but there is also the good news of excellent mentors that can help to reduce stress and strain that contribute to burnout. It is a trying time in the United States. Identities are being put on trial with the end of affirmative action and anti-DEI laws and this can generate stress and challenges, but "we have the opportunity to look beyond identity on the surface and address problems more deeply."

Reede commented on the fact that the conversation is even happening. It would not have occurred in this way 10 years ago. There is backlash, but she urged people to keep in mind that this is not the first time that DEI has been under attack or there has been pushback, but it is important to march forward. Through good scholarship, working together, and understanding the value and work of all, science and health will improve.

WRAPPING UP DAY 1 OF THE WORKSHOP

Planning committee chair Jagsi commented on the complex nature, multilevel causes, and the profound consequences of burnout as seen through an intersectional lens and from a diverse array of disciplinary backgrounds. She acknowledged that while this is not a happy topic, she was excited and motivated to see the intellectual firepower and energy that was brought to addressing this issue and was anticipating an engaging conversation on interventions for the second day.

National Academies program officer Katie Wullert reflected on some of the points raised for her from the presentations and discussions. She called attention to who reports burnout and how safety is important for people to acknowledge and report it. In looking ahead to the next day's discussion about interventions, she noted the importance of understanding the environments where burnout occurs to move forward. Shared definitions and goals are needed to know the crux of the issue to solve it. There are gaps in the literature, as was pointed out, but also a lot is known that can be acted upon.

Wullert also conducted a quick online survey to ask attendees what they saw as their main takeaways from the workshop sessions to date. She reported several of the responses: Burnout can be defined and addressed, the importance of making the invisible visible, the complexity of burnout and how to intervene, and burnout is a failure of the system and not the individual. Selected additional responses from participants can be found in Box 5-1.

BOX 5-1
Sample Participant Takeaways from Workshop Day 1

"Burnout is a systemic issue that requires attention at every level—micro, meso, macro. Preventing burnout requires a focus on root causes, a collaborative, equitable process, and human/leadership capital. Small wins can matter, measures at the micro level build toward transformational change."

"We need more research on this topic, a deeper understanding of how diversity, equity, inclusion, and intersectionality impact burnout and the well-being of individuals. Then, we need more tools to implement at the organization level, and more accessible resources for those impacted, since we know that reporting isn't often accessible because of fear of repercussions that are real and can be devastating."

"Burnout interventions need to take into account which workers' experiences are reflected."

"Leaders and systems are critical to influencing workplace and burnout contributors."

"Building on past successes, failures, and other lived experiences to develop novel research methods and techniques."

"Need a holistic approach including research, individual, and system."

"Burnout is a shorthand for organizational failures that should be fixed through interaction of public policy and organizational interventions."

"I'd forgotten about intersectionality in thinking about how burnout might affect groups differently. I also was heartened to know that people are looking at multiple levels at which to effect change. I see gaps in the approach, though, so that's something that needs to be addressed."

"The inequities in society lead to workplace experiences that then disproportionately impact some groups, and we need to figure out how to break the vicious cycle."

"Burnout is a failure of the system, not the individual, and needs to be addressed at the system level."

"Hope. Burnout can be addressed."

SOURCE: Poll 2, Workshop, October 1, 2024.

6

Current and Innovative Approaches to Managing Burnout

> **Highlights from the Presentations**
> - Most current interventions as well as current research on interventions focus on supporting individuals rather than changing environments (Day).
> - A holistic approach to addressing burnout considers four areas: Individual, Group, Leader, and Overall Organization, or IGLOO (Day).
> - One potentially fruitful model to introduce an intervention within an organization is the BUILD model, which encompasses Buy-in, Understand, Implement, Learn, and Develop sustainability (Day).
> - As an analogy to burnout as a job hazard, a broken wrist or concussion from a fall can be treated, people can learn to watch for and avoid hazards, but, ideally, the hazard is removed (Day).

- A fallacy in the realm of policy is that easy tips and tricks will solve more complex challenges. Deeper investments are required (Adibe).[1]
- Unless and until the economic basis of burnout is addressed, rather than addressing it for altruistic reasons, interventions will be limited (Adibe).

The second day of the workshop turned from understanding the causes and consequences of burnout in science, technology, mathematics, and medicine (STEMM) to interventions. To launch the day, attendees took a quick online poll to rate the efficacy of current interventions. None saw current interventions as very effective, 62 percent saw them as somewhat effective, and 38 percent saw them as not effective. In sharing the poll results, planning committee chair Reshma Jagsi (Emory University) commented, "Maybe the discussions from yesterday show the reasons why. One size does not fit all."

Alicia Kowalski (University of Texas MD Anderson Cancer Center) then moderated a session on current and innovate approaches to managing burnout that began with a presentation by Arla Day (St. Mary's University) based on a commissioned paper. (See Appendix D for the full paper.) Bryant Adibe (Princeton University) served as discussant, followed by open discussion.

This paper was commissioned to provide current knowledge on effective interventions to address burnout in terms of both policies and practices that support those experiencing burnout and work to proactively mitigate burnout. In discussions with the author while planning this paper, it was determined that limiting to only interventions tested within STEMM would provide an incomplete picture. The decision instead was made to focus generally on a framework for understanding different types of interventions that could be employed in STEMM fields.

---

[1] While speakers on Day 1 noted the value of addressing small "pebbles in the shoe" as meaningful but low-cost ways to address burnout, speakers in this panel were more divided. There was acknowledgment that smaller efforts can make a difference but also concern about focusing too much on the idea that individual nudges could accumulate and change societal problems significantly when deep investments are needed.

ADDRESSING BURNOUT

Day drew on the World Health Organization (WHO) definition of burnout, and noted it is an occupational syndrome that leads not only to exhaustion but also to cynicism and lack of accomplishment. She underscored the six causes elucidated by Christina Maslach and Michael Leiter (see Chapter 2). Workload alone does not create burnout. Although not the simple answer that one might wish for, it is caused by many things and is very context dependent. Research shows it comes from workload combined with (1) a lack of autonomy and control; (2) interpersonal relationships related to lack of work support, community breakdown, bullying and ostracism (e.g., Thompson et al., 2020), and incivility (Leiter et al., 2011, 2012); (3) organizational changes (Day et al., 2017); and (4) lack of transformational leadership (Day and Hartling, 2016). Outside the workplace, burnout can come indirectly from additional demands placed by friends and family and from within oneself (Bakker and de Vries, 2020; Hakanen et al., 2011).

Two general ways to address burnout are to focus on the symptoms or focus on the sources. Addressing symptoms might involve caring for workers who have burnout (e.g., through counseling, leave, and resources for resiliency). Addressing the sources involves reducing the organizational causes and not just "healing the wounded." She likened interventions to primary, secondary, and tertiary levels of medicine. For burnout, she suggested, the tertiary level would be to treat the symptoms, the secondary level would be to change perceptions and strengthen coping skills and resilience, and the primary level would be to change the environment through increased resources and decreased demands.

She offered another framework from the EMPOWER Healthy Workplace Partnership, with interventions at the levels of Individual, Group, Leader, Overall Organization, or IGLOO (see Figure 6-1). Approaches must be holistic, she stressed, so that all four levels are considered.

Elaborating on the framework, most interventions that are implemented and have been studied in the scientific literature are individual based, such as mindfulness and therapy to change perceptions of the workplace and improve coping and resilience. Other individual-focused interventions include family and friend support, healthy eating and sleeping practices, and delegation of responsibility.

Group- or team-focused interventions aim to maintain positive relationships, such as CREW (Civility, Respect, and Engagement in the

FIGURE 6-1 Individual, Group, Leader, Overall Organization (IGLOO) interventions for healthy workplaces.
SOURCE: Arla Day, Workshop Presentation, October 2, 2024.

Workplace), led by Michael Leiter (Osatuke et al., 2013). Day explained the CREW framework was not specifically designed to reduce burnout, but it has been shown to improve workplace relationships and reduce burnout. She stressed CREW must be tailored to a specific work unit and implemented through a participatory process. The members of the unit decide the issues to tackle and what constitutes appropriate behavior.

Moving to leader-focused interventions, Day described a study in a West Coast healthcare system in which management allowed physicians to identify key issues and how to fix them. One thing that emerged was to place physicians' health on par with financial performance as a priority. Leaders can also support mentorship and allyship, bring teams together, and treat all team members with respect. These actions will not change whole systems, but they also do not cost a lot. As she posed, how much does it cost to treat employees with respect? Little steps can lead to larger ways of well-being and lower burnout. Leadership self-care should also be incorporated into training, she continued. Leaders need to care for themselves and learn how to support their team's well-being.

Organizational-focused interventions are varied and can take many approaches. She noted that one topic on which she wanted to see greater work that arose on the first day of the workshop was the issue of person-job fit. From an organizational perspective, she noted that this was important

CURRENT AND INNOVATIVE APPROACHES TO MANAGING BURNOUT 45

		PRIMARY *reduce sources of burnout*	SECONDARY *resilience; reframe issues; improve self-care*	TERTIARY *heal the wounded*
Burnout Invention Chart	INDIVIDUAL	Job skills training (PJ-fit)	Self-care → CBT; ACT; Wellbeing Apps	EAPs Return to Work
		Interpersonal communications/conflict training		
	GROUP	Group/Team-based civility training	Team-based well-being 'skills'	EAPs Team Mediation
	LEADER	Inclusive Leadership Mentorship/Allyship Training (to reduce others' burnout)	Leadership self-care (to reduce own burnout)	EAPs (for self) RTW training (to support DRs' RTW)
	OVERALL ORGANIZATION	Recruit/Select (PJ-fit) IDEA (trust) Reducing BO sources Surveys (actionable items) Policy change, etc.	Wellbeing & Healthcare Initiatives (exercise opportunities; healthy eating; CBT/ACT training	Leave policies RTW policies EAP offerings

FIGURE 6-2 Burnout intervention chart.
SOURCE: Arla Day, Workshop Presentation, October 2, 2024.

in recruiting and training employees and giving them what they need to do their jobs. People are less burned out when they do things effectively.

Pulling together the primary, secondary, and tertiary levels, and IGLOO, Day offered a menu of potential interventions (see Figure 6-2). This menu highlights that burnout can be addressed at three levels. At the primary level, interventions can work to reduce the actual sources of burnout. At the secondary level, interventions can aim to improve resilience to experiencing burnout. At the tertiary level, interventions can respond to those who are already burned out. Interventions at each of these levels can operate across different groups or targets of the intervention. That is, a primary intervention addressing causes of burnout may target individuals by providing job skills training that helps them engage in their work more effectively and efficiently but could also target leadership by having leaders engage in mentorship training that may improve how they are engaging with employees. Overall, the model highlights the multiple levels and potential targets of interventions and what types of interventions sit at each intersection.

Where to start to create healthy workplaces? Day offered the idea of a BUILD model: Buy-in, Understand, Implement, Learn, and Develop Sustainability (see Figure 6-3). The model begins with gaining buy-in from key constituencies and engaging supporters to advance change. Next, the goal is to increase understanding—what are the needs and constraints of the

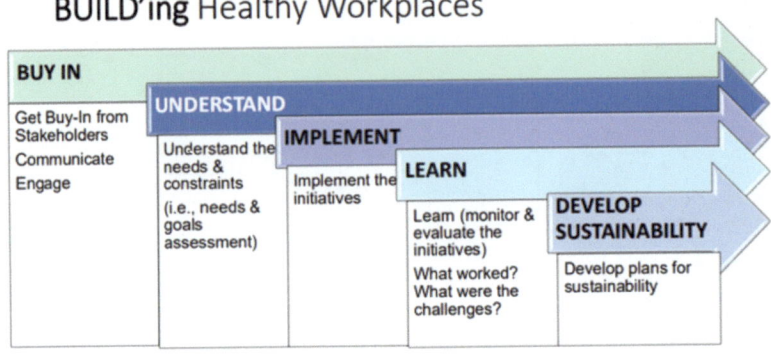

FIGURE 6-3 BUILD model.
SOURCE: Arla Day, Workshop Presentation, October 2, 2024.

workforce that need to be addressed? From there, the next step is to take this knowledge and implement an initiative aimed at addressing the key pebbles in the shoe. After implementation, Day argued, it is important to learn and evaluate what worked and what did not. Finally, the goal is to develop sustainability to ensure that new and successful initiatives remain in place.

As key take-home messages, Day summarized that (1) burnout is not just emotional exhaustion but affects job performance; (2) most current interventions focus on supporting individuals, rather than changing the environment; (3) the best interventions are those that do not focus on the syndrome per se but on the causes; (4) there are no simple cure-alls to burnout, though there are simple actions that can be taken to improve environments; and (5) an ongoing process must be built. As an analogy to burnout as a job hazard, she noted that while a broken wrist or concussion from a fall can be treated and people can learn to avoid hazards, ideally, the hazard is removed so no one is at risk of injury in the first place.

REFLECTIONS

Kowalski highlighted Day's observation about the lack of interventions and best practices at the organizational level and asked how more can be done. Day suggested looking at European organizations that tend to do better in this regard. She called for encouraging organizations to look broadly and to change the culture to realize the benefits and value of reducing burnout.

Adibe agreed that looking at organizational versus individual interventions is critical and noted some evolution in the literature over the past 20 or so years. Abide expressed skepticism that small "nudges" in individual behavior and fixes could have a broader impact. The nudge effect or nudge theory comes from a 2008 book from Richard Thaler and Cass R. Sunstein and posited that environments could be adapted in ways that influence how individuals and groups make decisions and potentially address larger societal problems such as choices in health or retirement (Thaler and Sunstein, 2008). In response to this theory, "nudge units" were set up both in the United States and abroad, with the hope that individual-level interventions could solve larger societal problems at less cost and social capital. Cumulative data show they have had limited impact. A 2022 systemic review by two proponents of the nudge effect showed an effect size of 1 percent or less (Chater and Loewenstein, in press).

In his view, a fallacy in the realm of policy is that easy tips and tricks or quick wins will solve more complex challenges. He argued that deeper investments are required, and burnout serves as an example. Some studies show that another effect of the focus on individual interventions is decreased public support for broader societal solutions. Without addressing core systemic issues, it will be tough to fight burnout, he said. He expressed some optimism that once it is recognized that societal-level problems cannot be solved by individual-level interventions, tools can be developed to investigate what he called the "well-being black box." He and his team, for example, have developed a tool to help organizations understand the economic and other drivers of burnout within their system and provide recommendations for the organization to get at the root of them. "This allows the organization at the system level to provide better solutions and more closely mirrors what frontline providers actually want," he said.

Day reiterated the point that rather than more research on the causes, efforts should be focused on organizations using tools in their specific context. Longitudinal work is also needed. There are no quick wins to the broader challenges producing burnout but instead a need to focus on the long term. She said she has optimistic and pessimistic perspectives. On the optimistic side, people want to and are thinking of how to tackle burnout. Pessimistically, she questions if organizations, and the people within them, really want to change.

Kowalski commented that many interventions are reactive, although more should be proactive. Day said a focus on the reactive might have limited outcomes. From a healthcare lens, Adibe commented that people are in a reactive state because healthcare organizations are in a tough period economically. With declines in revenue, leaders may reduce staffing ratios, by decreasing administrative support or increasing productivity by raising Relative Value Units, or RVUs, thresholds.[2] This gap drives burnout, but unless and until the economic basis is addressed, interventions will be limited. Economic arguments are what gets attention, rather than promoting well-being through the lens of altruism.

The demands on healthcare providers increase every year, Kowalski observed. Given that, she asked what could be studied further to mitigate the increased burden. Adibe responded that on a simple level, he urged leaders to listen to providers. Leaders are now making decisions with insufficient information. They need to know the trade-offs. For example, what does reducing administrative support do for turnover for physicians and nurses? What is important to the providers? He joked that a rallying cry should be "No more yoga!" (signifying a simple fix to a larger problem). Looking at the data from doctors and nurses, a study in *JAMA* ranked operational drivers like improved workflows and more autonomy in the clinic as more critical than wellness efforts (Aiken et al., 2023). Leaders need better metrics like this to make more informed decisions, he said.

Day underscored the problem with cosmetic approaches, such as offering apples in the cafeteria, while toxic bosses and ineffective processes persist. However, the challenge is finding the balance between changing systems and the smaller changes that Christina Maslach and Tait Shanafelt discussed that can snowball (see Chapter 2). If too much is done for individuals, bigger things are ignored until a crisis. She is a proponent of looking at what is possible within an organization but is tired of having to make the argument about cost and return on investment. "I would like to say 'Stop hurting people as an organization.' We have to hold organizations accountable," she stated. Burnout should not be a "cost of doing business." The challenge is to create a more efficient system and work environment where people are not getting sick. Referring to civility and efficiency, Kowalski commented on the physical layout of workplaces as a topic to study, such as the effect of the role of the physicians' cafeteria in increasing communications through "casual collisions." She wondered about other opportunities to think differently and creatively. Adibe expanded on the role of the built environment on well-being. In healthcare settings, for example, it has been

---

[2] For more on RVUs, see https://www.cms.gov/cms-guide-medical-technology-companies-and-other-interested-parties/payment/physician-fee-schedule.

documented that the view from a hospital room affects patient outcomes. It is important to understand the optimal healing environment. Day added that remote work also highlighted that isolation can be detrimental to well-being, problem-solving, and culture.

OPEN DISCUSSION

Referring to Day's comment about the need for a fit between an individual and an organization, a participant queried whether that blames the individual for any problems. Day said it is not a blame situation, but individuals must have the right training to maximize their capabilities. A mismatch of expectations might also occur, for example, when individuals say the workload is too heavy, but the system has set that amount of work as the target, a participant observed. Day suggested this is where participation comes in. A job analysis can show what is required and get people to talk about requirements and expectations.

Organizations in the midst of budget tightening have to deal with people, space, and data components, a participant commented. Adibe noted the overall state of the health system is reactive. Value-based care does not solve everything, but it is a proactive approach to patient care that may help ameliorate many challenges.[3] A compounding factor of burnout for many physicians is when their patients cannot get needed care and resources, which contributes to the physicians' sense of moral injury and defeat. A broader transition toward a more preventive healthcare system and support of social challenges outside the hospital is key.

Day noted that improvement requires more than just collecting data. It must be shared to get organizations and leaders to buy in. Another participant shared her experience implementing interventions. She noted there is often a different language between the people who work in the field of organizational development and related issues and the people who are working in the organizations themselves. She finds it effective to frame the issue through an enterprise risk lens, she said. She reminds leaders of tiers of risk, encompassing not only economic but also human, reputational, and management risks. Once embedded, workplace culture is part of an enterprise's risk dashboard. Leaders need adequate information, Adibe agreed. A big challenge is that well-being and burnout have been considered separately

---

[3] For more information from the Centers for Medicare and Medicaid Services on value-based care, see https://www.cms.gov/priorities/innovation/key-concepts/value-based-care.

from other enterprise factors. An enterprise risk dashboard or other tools such as a well-being dashboard[4] he and his colleagues are developing that considers both economic and human factors may move it to more operational considerations and as part of all that an enterprise is doing. Day suggested that costs and return on investment can be part of the framing of risk, such as related to absenteeism and turnover. For example, a poor reputation affects employee recruitment, insurance, and other costs. She called for both a theoretical moral high ground and pragmatic considerations to get things done. A classic tenet is that attitudes need to change before behavior does, but maybe behavior change can lead to attitude change, she posited.

Kowalski suggested that well-being must be embraced as part of the fiber of the organization at the same level of professionalism, safety, and other aspects of quality. Adibe said one challenge of promoting wellness is the dearth of quality research. While a systematic review of well-being initiatives found that individual-focused interventions had little to no effect, the quality of studies was in general poor, which contributes to a lack of direction on how best to support physician well-being (Haslam et al., 2024). Philosophically, well-being is seen as an add-on or footnote, while other issues are prioritized. COVID-19 helped to change that, when widespread resignations placed enterprises at risk. If leaders do not have the tools to codify the risks, they will not find appropriate solutions. He called for better transparency around costs. Wellness must be at the "big table," Day said. She noted some organizations put the concept in their mission, vision, or policies but do not act on it, which she called "wellness washing." Clients and patients are always placed first, but British entrepreneur Richard Branson has advocated to put employees first and they will treat the customers well.

---

[4] For more information on well-being dashboards, see https://catalyst.nejm.org/doi/full/10.1056/CAT.22.0219.

7

Interventions to Manage Burnout: Deep Dive on Medicine

> **Highlights from the Presentations**
>
> - Healthcare settings have a unique intensity, although ideas discussed to manage burnout in medicine apply to other settings (Jagsi).
> - Many practices, such as match day for trainees and how physicians who recently gave birth are thrown back into the workplace, create trauma and stress (Silver).
> - Healthcare workers, including primary care physicians and those in critical care settings, are expected to be on 24/7. When physicians, particularly women, reduce their hours, they end up working full-time while being paid part-time (Kerr).
> - There is not only a stigma around acknowledging a mental health condition, but doing so in some states can affect licensure and institutional accreditation (Dyrbye, Kerr).
> - Dealing with stigma to prioritize self-care starts at the top of the organization. Leaders who model and talk about self-care can tackle the stigma (Dyrbye).
> - A care delivery model that focuses on peer-to-peer support has improved well-being and mitigated bullying among hospital unit nurses (Cineas).

> - Exit and stay interviews can provide leaders with useful input about what employees need to thrive and what causes them to leave (Cineas).

A second deep dive workshop discussion focused on burnout in medicine and healthcare. In introducing the session, planning committee chair Reshma Jagsi (Emory University) said healthcare settings have a unique intensity, although some of the ideas will fit to other settings. Natalia Cineas (NYC Health and Hospitals), Eve Kerr (University of Michigan Medical School), Julie Silver (Wake Forest University School of Medicine), and Liselotte Dyrbye (University of Colorado School of Medicine) provided perspectives based on their research and workplace experiences.

The purpose of this panel was to give greater attention to medicine and other healthcare professions given especially high rates of burnout in this field. This panel examined the unique case of healthcare as well as variation in burnout across care settings and discussed effective interventions for those in medical fields.

UNIQUE FACTORS AFFECTING BURNOUT IN MEDICINE AND HEALTHCARE PROFESSIONS

The panelists began by discussing unique factors about healthcare that provide context for particularly high rates of burnout in these domains. Cineas said data from 2018 to 2022 from the Centers for Disease Control and Prevention show the critical state of the healthcare workforce. One in four U.S. essential workers had a mental health diagnosis, and burnout increased from 11.6 to 19 percent during this time (Nigam et al., 2023). Suicides among nurses and other providers increased. Three in 10 resigned during the "great resignation." Kerr noted the heavy workload healthcare professionals face and the unique demands of being in a helping-focused role. "Professionals feel it all the time. You don't know when your day ends, yet you are driven by service," she said, both to treat patients and train the next generation. There is not only a stigma around acknowledging a mental health condition, but also doing so in some states can affect licensure. She also noted the differential impact on women, who generally have more home responsibilities in addition to work responsibilities. Silver highlighted the match system for physician trainees as another unique factor in medicine that could heighten burnout. In this lottery-type system, on a certain day, trainees are notified where they will be deployed. The system can create trauma and stress for the trainees and their families as they wait to find out where in the country they may have to move and may need to be far away from their current support systems. Dyrbye related that the substrate of undergraduate students entering medical school is strong, but the situation flips in a few years when depression and burnout are high. In large studies conducted every 3 years since 2014, she and colleagues have seen that physicians are more likely to experience burnout than other U.S. workers, even adjusting for work hours. "It is a good moment for us to reflect on what is happening," she said. Some aspects might be related to moral distress and mistreatment by patients and their families, which contribute to job stress and to burnout.

Jagsi commented on several relevant studies by the National Academies of Sciences, Engineering, and Medicine's Committee on Women in Science, Engineering and Medicine, including on sexual harassment, bias, and family caregiving (NASEM, 2018, 2020, 2024) that highlight challenges and lack of support in the medical system particularly for women that may contribute to burnout.

BURNOUT ACROSS HEALTHCARE

Medicine is not a monolith, Jagsi pointed out, and asked how burnout affects different groups by specialty, level of experience, or other factors. Kerr sees a lot of distress as a primary care physician because primary care is the foundation of the healthcare system. As an example, there is a 50 to 100 percent increase in the number of portal messages that primary care physicians receive. Women physicians receive more and longer messages than their male counterparts and spend more time in patients' electronic health records than their male counterparts. The expectation is to respond 24/7, without being paid for this time. There is a need to acknowledge that individuals are not on duty all the time. When physicians, particularly women, reduce their hours, they often end up working what is still a full-time schedule while being paid less. She referred to Jagsi and colleague's study of successful clinical researchers that showed that gender and climate affect burnout (Paradis et al., 2024).

Silver spoke about the importance of taking an individual lens for each group in medicine given the needs and challenges they have. She then turned to suicide as one example, where nurses are at particular risk and discussed the importance of a sense of belonging in combatting this. She highlighted the Interpersonal Theory of Suicide from Joiner and colleagues (2009), which has two key components: perceived burdensomeness and thwarted belongingness. As an example of how these factors relate, she noted that many women in medicine who may take leave to give birth or care for children return and are expected to immediately get back into work with no ramp up and with expectations that she "owes call, she owes long shifts." The system is not set up to support reentry and can leave individuals feeling as if they are failing and as a result can internalize that they are a burden to their colleagues and do not belong in their role. These systems issues thus can produce circumstances that sit at the heart of the interpersonal theory of suicide.

Dyrbye pointed out that the primary driver of burnout is work hours and workload. Within healthcare, different job categories have specific drivers, and no one size fits all. Some solutions can be found at the systems level, such as those related to electronic health records or policies about mistreatment, but the level of the work unit is what drives stress. Changes can be made at a high level but, most importantly, must be felt by the local work unit or team.

Cineas commented on the effect of specialty selection, in her case, as a nurse. People need more tools to understand what each specialty involves. For example, oncology nurses say they are used to dealing with patients' death, but the impact on their mental health has not been fully explored. Night nurses deal with fatigue, which can lead to more errors, yet new, young nurses are usually placed in night shifts. The workforce is getting younger, and they need more resources. She called attention to the *Impact Wellbeing Guide: Taking Action to Improve Healthcare Worker Wellbeing* recently enrolled by National Institute for Occupational Safety and Health as a useful tool in this regard.[1]

TARGETING STIGMAS

Jagsi reflected that the intensity described by the panelists stems from medical providers' commitment to mission, often to the detriment of their own health. "Regardless of the specialty or level of training, we have internalized that expectation," she commented. The flip side is the tremendous stigma that exists when people feel a need to slow down, take a break, or attend to other commitments outside of work. She asked the panelists how to recognize, call out, and target stigma.

Silver called for normalizing behavior to combat stigma. She also called out structural sexism and racism, which she defined as policies, practices, procedures, and culture that predict a certain outcome along race and

---

[1] See https://www.cdc.gov/niosh/healthcare/impactwellbeingguide/index.html for a link to download the guide.

gender lines. Drawing on the example of anesthesiologists giving birth, Silver suggested developing policies or practices that help them return to a high level of work while considering physical characteristics such as their recent surgery or lactation. Making policies, practices, and procedures standard, not special, could destigmatize them.

Dyrbye said dealing with stigma starts at the top. The reluctance to engage in self-care for fear of looking selfish needs work at the top of healthcare organizations. Modeling and talking about self-care can tackle the stigma. Outside of the healthcare organization, there needs to be work on medical licensure and hospital credentialing questions, such as not asking intrusive questions about mental health. "Stigma in medicine comes in multiples places, from the healthcare industry and also inside our own walls," she said.

Cineas agreed with the need for self-care and noted that many employees do not take the personal leave time they are due. She also called for the integration of well-being into daily operations. Her institution has developed a care delivery model that integrates peer-to-peer well-being. At the beginning of every shift, nurses huddle, articulate a value, then discuss methods and operations. A staff member volunteers to be the well-being buddy for the day to ensure colleagues have taken breaks and check how they are doing. This normalizes the reality that things may not be okay on any given shift. Though they are just starting to examine the impact of this approach, Cineas noted that, based on early results, they are seeing that because some unexpected people have emerged as volunteer buddies, the staff has gotten to know each other better, they are providing better care for patients, and bullying has been mitigated. Wellness becomes integrated into operations.

Kerr highlighted the stigma around vacations and taking time off. She detailed an experience where she emailed colleagues to explain that she was missing an important meeting to celebrate her wedding anniversary. In response, she received emails thanking her for sharing the information and helping to normalize her choice. Systems must be in place for coverage so as not to burden others. As one idea, she pointed to a practice that employs a dedicated individual, such as a nurse or other provider, to serve as an "inbox-ologist" who handles the in-box of a colleague when they are away.

OPEN DISCUSSION

A participant asked about dealing with organizations that believe that burnout during the COVID-19 pandemic was an outlier, rather than a continuing issue. Dyrbye agreed that burnout spiked during the pandemic, but emphasized it is not new. Research from 20 years ago showed burnout was most intense in hospitals and critical care, and that has persisted. Most recent studies show a decline in burnout in the healthcare workforce compared with the peaks of the COVID-19 pandemic but is still high compared with the rest of the U.S. population. When asked whether there are fields without a high rate of burnout, Kerr shared results of a survey that showed relatively high levels throughout her institution but especially for those in clinical care. Researchers and those with limited clinical care had lower levels.

Another participant who researches childbearing physicians reported on a ripple effect: As efforts are made to regulate women in their third trimester or when they give birth, others have to take up their work and they feel more burned out. Given limited resources, more support cannot be brought in, so she asked how to implement policies and procedures without further stigmatizing the accommodated group. Silver commented that this dilemma is "why we are all here." Big system-level issues are not getting the attention and resources to solve them. In a resource-constrained environment, the burden shifts to others. There is no way around the fact that there must be another model with additional resources. Trying to make it work otherwise is a "nonstarter," she said.

A participant queried how the medical industry is learning from those who experience burnout to feed that information back in the system. Cineas said one way is to reengineer exit interviews to understand why employees are leaving. She acknowledged that this comes late in that the person is leaving and each person is different, but they provide information that could help others. She also suggested "stay interviews" to ask employees what will lead them to stay. Another participant commented that the culture for early-career professionals, including lack of sleep and pressure not to speak up, has burnout baked in. Dyrbye acknowledged the extra challenges for early-career workers. They may work less advantageous shifts, have more work-home conflicts, and need to establish their reputations. Another participant pointed to the work of Mark Linzer, who runs the Institute for Professional Worklife at the University of Minnesota. He has conducted a randomized control trial on physician well-being and found workplace champions are helpful, as Cineas described. Dyrbye also pointed to work by Tait Shanafelt on how to galvanize improvements in the work environment at a local level to lead to meaningful change. His model is like one used at her institution, she said, in which funded well-being leaders develop and share a local-level climate assessment and then galvanize action within the department's sphere of concern and control. Developing local leaders to lead systems-level change is part of the path forward.

PRIORITIES FOR CONSIDERATION

Following this panel, the workshop moved into breakout sessions where participants and presenters would discuss interventions. To kick this off, Jagsi asked each panelist for one point that the groups should consider in their discussions. Dyrbye urged thinking about leadership buy-in and the role of leadership development and fostering wellness-centered leadership behaviors within a work environment. Cineas pointed to architectural design, and how spaces where healthcare providers work, sleep, and eat while they are on a shift can affect well-being. Kerr called for creating a climate of inclusion and advancement at the macro, meso, and micro levels. Silver urged attendees to consider ageism and ableism. Older physicians are now a more homogenous group. Behind them are more diverse individuals, but what will happen to this workforce in the decades ahead, she asked.

8

Imagining a Future of Greater Support: An Interactive Discussion

Participants became part of the process through an interactive discussion examining interventions to address burnout. In in-person and virtual breakout groups, they were asked to discuss and bring forward ideas in three overlapping areas: (1) ensuring interventions are fair and equitable and help those most at risk without introducing new inequities along the way; (2) implementation of interventions discussed throughout the workshop and what implementation might look like in their own organization; and (3) brainstorming of ideas to target burnout not previously discussed, along with key issues that would need to be addressed. After an hour of discussion, the small groups returned to the main room to share what each had covered.

REPORTS BY THE BREAKOUT GROUPS

Equity

The Equity breakout group discussed the importance of representation at the design phase to ensure those most affected by burnout are at the table to develop interventions to address it. A potential tool is power mapping, which fosters thinking about such factors as career stage, generational differences, and diversity, equity, and inclusion principles. Considering the different levels of interventions discussed throughout the workshop, the group noted that too much focus on individual-level interventions can reinforce inequity, even unintentionally. When people are pressured to solve the problem themselves, with such examples as yoga and mindfulness training, inequity becomes rife in terms of who has access to and gets rewarded for undertaking these practices. It is critical to acknowledge the power differences between those who do the work and those who have the resources that affect the people doing the work. The language and images behind many of the concepts discussed at the workshop, such as well-being and risk, also have equity implications. For example, looking for images online of who does risk management work results in images of White men, while a search for people who do equity work results in images of Black women. The group also urged using repetition to continually raise the issue of equity and learning lessons from community-based collaboration.

Implementation

The Implementation group divided into two groups—those in person and those online. Each reported back their discussion. The in-person group urged a focus on the organizational level to address burnout. Benefits would include enhanced well-being, a commitment to the organization and its people, demonstrated compliance with regulations and standards, and a reduction in risk. Drawbacks involve potential challenges with creating culture change, which may not be measurable or feasible. It is important to convince an organization that the investment is worthwhile. To deal with unintended consequences for individuals, a safety net or alternative is essential. To build support within an organization, the group said, it is important to make business, moral, and scientific cases. A business case needs clear benchmarks and a return on investments, and a business plan supported by people from all demographics who will be affected. The moral case could show the impact on the health and welfare of individuals but should be supported by data. The scientific case would examine the evidence, both data and practical wisdom. The two main barriers are sustainability and pushback. To overcome these barriers, the group looked to the BUILD process (Buy-in, Understand, Implement, Learn, and Develop Sustainability; see Chapter 6). Vetting and allowing for feedback by the group affected could help address pushback.

The online group called for thinking at multiple levels, collecting data, and holding leaders accountable to act based on the data. They urged interventions that do not add to the burdens of time and money to already busy people and under-resourced institutions. A challenge is not to add more to the burnout of already burned-out people. They harkened to an acronym brought up by Christina Maslach (see Chapter 2): GROSS, or get rid of stupid stuff.

Brainstorming

The Brainstorming group similarly divided into two groups. The in-person group suggested developing structures and process measures linked to downstream performance metrics, such as physician retention, as well as systems to recognize programs and institutions that are doing things well. Asked to prioritize one idea to share with the group, they suggested a way to benchmark well-being practices, somewhat akin to quality metrics for patient safety. A starting point might be the Joy in Medicine Health System Recognition Program of the American Medical Association.[1] Organizations apply for bronze, silver, and gold status, with criteria at each level. A practical way to get more involvement in such a model would be to get payers or accrediting bodies involved. Challenges to overcome may be an overfocus on particular measures and the need to standardize how well-being is measured across an organization.

The online group acknowledged the fundamental challenge of understaffing as a cause of burnout and sought to think about interventions that could address this. The easiest solution, e.g., hire more staff, is not always viable. Thus, they looked at what can be meaningful without fully addressing the root cause. Transparency in work responsibilities can help people understand their own and others' workloads. Training, mentorship, and validation are also important to help people get past the challenging learning curve of starting a new job/working in a new area and acknowledge their efforts. The group also discussed a shift in reward systems so that people feel they can take time off and care for themselves. A complex issue is that when people take on extra work, they receive extra compensation or other rewards, as they should—but that can reinforce a belief that extra work is expected and encouraged.

CLOSING REMARKS

Planning committee chair Reshma Jagsi thanked participants for insights about the critical issue of burnout. She noted that it is important

---

[1] For more information, see https://www.ama-assn.org/practice-management/physician-health/joy-medicine-health-system-recognition-program.

to maintain the joy that exists in science, technology, engineering, mathematics, and medicine (STEMM) fields and structure the work environment at every level to facilitate the thriving of the people who choose these fields. Creating a sustainable system can expand access to the full talent pool and strengthen the mission of STEMM. She expressed hope in that the conversation has begun and will continue.

References

Aiken, L. H., K. B. Lasater, D. M. Sloane, et al. 2023. Physician and nurse well-being and preferred interventions to address burnout in hospital practice: Factors associated with turnover, outcomes, and patient safety. *JAMA Health Forum* 4(7). DOI: 10.1001/jamahealthforum.2023.1809.

APA (American Psychological Association). 2023. *2023 Work in America Survey: Workplaces as Engines of Psychological Health and Well-Being*. https://www.apa.org/pubs/reports/work-in-america/2023-workplace-health-well-being.

Apple, R., E. O'Brien, N. Daraiseh, et al. 2023. Gender and intention to leave healthcare during the COVID-19 pandemic among U.S. healthcare workers: A cross-sectional analysis of the HERO registry. *PLoS One* 18(6): e0287428. DOI: 10.1371/journal.pone.0287428.

Bakker, A. B., and J. D. de Vries. 2020. Job demands–Resources theory and self-regulation: New explanations and remedies for job burnout. *Anxiety, Stress, & Coping* 34(1): 1–21. https://doi.org/10.1080/10615806.2020.1797695.

Beck, M., J. Cadwell, A. Kern, et al. 2022. Critical feminist analysis of STEM mentoring programs: A meta-synthesis of the existing literature. *Gender, Work & Organization* 29(1): 167–187. https://doi.org/10.1111/gwao.12729.

Cech, E. A., and M. Blair-Loy. 2014. Consequences of flexibility stigma among academic scientists and engineers. *Work and Occupations* 41(1): 86–110. https://doi.org/10.1177/0730888413515497.

Chater, N., and G. Loewenstein. In press. The i-frame and the s-frame: How focusing on individual-level solutions has led behavioral public policy astray. *Behavioral and Brain Sciences*.

Day, A., and N. Hartling. 2016, July. Avoiding burnout: The relationship between transformational leadership and leader well-being. *International Journal of Psychology* 51: 732–733.

Day, A., S. N. Crown, and M. Ivany. 2017. Organisational change and employee burnout: The moderating effects of support and job control. *Safety Science* 100: 4–12.

Dillon, E. C., C. D. Stults, S. Deng, et al. 2021. Women, younger clinicians' and caregivers' experiences of burnout and well-being during COVID-19 in a US healthcare system. *Journal of General Internal Medicine* 37(1): 145–153. https://pubmed.ncbi.nlm.nih.gov/34729697/.

Gewin, V. 2021. Pandemic burnout is rampant in academia. *Nature* 591: 489–491. https://www.nature.com/articles/d41586-021-00663-2.

Gold, K. J., L. B. Andrew, E. B. Goldman, et al. 2016. I would never want to have a mental health diagnosis on my record: A survey of female physicians on mental health diagnosis, treatment, and reporting. *General Hospital Psychiatry* 43: 51–57. https://doi.org/10.1016/j.genhosppsych.2016.09.004.

Hakanen, J. J., A. B. Bakker, and M. Jokisaari. 2011. A 35-year follow-up study on burnout among Finnish employees. *Journal of Occupational Health Psychology* 16(3): 345.

Hall, W. M., T. Schmader, and E. Croft. 2015. Engineering exchanges: Daily social identity threat predicts burnout among female engineers. *Social Psychological and Personality Science* 6(5): 528–534. https://doi.org/10.1177/1948550615572637.

Hall, W., T. Schmader, A. Aday, et al. 2019. Decoding the dynamics of social identity threat in the workplace: A within-person analysis of women's and men's interactions in STEM. *Social Psychological and Personality Science* 10(4): 542–552. https://doi.org/10.1177/1948550618772582.

Han, S., T. D. Shanafelt, C. A. Sinsky, et al. 2019. Estimating the attributable cost of physician burnout in the United States. *Annals of Internal Medicine* 170(11): 784–790.

Haslam, A., J. Turia, S. L. Miller, et al. 2024. Systematic review and meta-analysis of randomized trials testing interventions to reduce physician burnout. *The American Journal of Medicine* 137(3): 249–257. https://doi.org/10.1016/j.amjmed.2023.10.003.

Hochschild, A. 1983. *The Managed Heart*. University of California Press. https://www.ucpress.edu/books/the-managed-heart/paper.

Hodkinson A., A. Zhou, J. Johnson, et al. 2022. Associations of physician burnout with career engagement and quality of patient care: Systematic review and meta-analysis. *BMJ* 378: 1–15.

Jackson, P. B., P. A. Thoits, and H. F. Taylor. 1995. Composition of the workplace and psychological well-being: The effects of tokenism on America's Black elite. *Social Forces* 74(2): 543–557. https://doi.org/10.1093/sf/74.2.543.

Jacobs, J. A., and K. Gerson. 2004. Understanding Changes in American Working Time: A Synthesis. Pp. 25–45 in *Fighting for Time: Shifting Boundaries of Work and Social Life*. Russell Sage Foundation. https://www.jstor.org/stable/10.7758/9781610441872.5.

Jensen, L. E., and E. D. Deemer. 2019. Identity, campus climate, and burnout among undergraduate women in STEM fields. *Career Development Quarterly* 67(2): 96–109. https://doi.org/10.1002/cdq.12174.

Joiner, T. E., K. A. Van Orden, T. K. Witte, et al. 2009. *The Interpersonal Theory of Suicide: Guidance for Working with Suicidal Clients*. American Psychological Association.

Kanter, R. M. 1977. Some effects of proportions on group life: Skewed sex ratios and responses to token women. *American Journal of Sociology* 82(5): 965–990. https://doi.org/10.1086/226425.

Kunda, G., S. R. Barley, and J. Evans. 2002. Why do contractors contract? The experience of highly skilled technical professionals in a contingent labor market. *ILR Review* 55(2): 234–261. https://doi.org/10.1177/001979390205500203.

LaFaver, K., J. M. Miyasaki, C. M. Keran, et al. 2018. Age and sex differences in burnout, career satisfaction, and well-being in US neurologists. *Neurology* 91(20): e1928–e1941.

Laschinger, H. K. S., C. A. Wong, and P. Greco. 2006. The impact of staff nurse empowerment on person-job fit and work engagement/burnout. *Nursing Administration Quarterly* 30(4): 358–367.

Laschinger, H. K., L. Borgogni, C. Consiglio, et al. 2015. The effects of authentic leadership, six areas of worklife, and occupational coping self-efficacy on new graduate nurses' burnout and mental health: A cross-sectional study. *International Journal of Nursing Studies* 52(6): 1080–1089. DOI: 10.1016/j.ijnurstu.2015.03.002.

Leiter, M. P., H. K. S. Laschinger, A. Day, et al. 2011. The impact of civility interventions on employee social behavior, distress, and attitudes. *Journal of Applied Psychology* 96(6): 1258.

Lievens, D. 2021. How the pandemic exacerbated burnout: A Q&A with pioneering researchers Michael Leiter and Christina Maslach. *Harvard Business Review*. https://hbr.org/2021/02/how-the-pandemic-exacerbated-burnout.

Linzer, M., J. O. Jin, P. Shah, et al. 2022. Trends in clinician burnout with associated mitigating and aggravating factors during the COVID-19 pandemic. *JAMA Health Forum* 3(11): e224163. https://pubmed.ncbi.nlm.nih.gov/36416816/.

Marquis, C., and A. Tilcsik. 2013. Imprinting: Towards A Multilevel Theory. 7(1): 193–243. The Academy of Management Annals. https://doi.org/10.5465/19416520.2013.766076.

Maslach, C., and S. E. Jackson. 1981. The measurement of experienced burnout. *Journal of Organizational Behavior* 2(2): 99–113.

Maslach, C., and M. P. Leiter. 1976. Burnout. *Human Behavior* 5(9): 16–22.

Mukherjee, S., L. Rintamaki, J. L. Shucard, et al. 2022. A statistical learning approach to evaluate factors associated with post-traumatic stress symptoms in physicians: Insights from the COVID-19 pandemic. *IEEE Access* 10: 114434–14454. https://doi.org/10.1109/access.2022.3217770.

NASEM (National Academies of Sciences, Engineering, and Medicine). 2018. *Sexual Harassment of Women: Climate, Culture, and Consequences in Academic Sciences, Engineering, and Medicine*. Washington, DC: The National Academies Press. https://doi.org/10.17226/24994.

NASEM. 2019. *Taking Action against Clinician Burnout: A Systems Approach to Professional Well-Being*. Washington, DC: The National Academies Press. https://doi.org/10.17226/25521.

NASEM. 2020. *Promising Practices for Addressing the Underrepresentation of Women in Science, Engineering, and Medicine: Opening Doors*. Washington, DC: The National Academies Press. https://doi.org/10.17226/25585.

NASEM. 2021. *The Impact of COVID-19 on the Careers of Women in Academic Sciences, Engineering, and Medicine*. Washington, DC: The National Academies Press. https://doi.org/10.17226/26061.

NASEM. 2024. *Supporting Family Caregivers in STEMM: A Call to Action*. Washington, DC: The National Academies Press. https://doi.org/10.17226/27416.

Nigam, J. A., R. M. Barker, T. R. Cunningham, et al. 2023. *Vital Signs:* Health worker–perceived working conditions and symptoms of poor mental health — Quality of Worklife Survey, United States, 2018–2022. *MMWR Morbidity and Mortality Weekly Report* 72: 1197–1205. http://dx.doi.org/10.15585/mmwr.mm7244e1.

Osatuke, K., M. Leiter, L. Belton, et al. 2013. Civility, Respect and Engagement at the Workplace (CREW): A National Organization Development Program at the Department of Veterans Affairs. *Journal of Management Policies and Practices* 1(2): 25–34.

Paradis, K. C., E. A. Kerr, K. A. Griffith, et al. 2024. Burnout among mid-career academic medical faculty. *JAMA Network Open.* 7(6): e2415593. DOI: 10.1001/jamanetworkopen.2024.15593.

Pascoe, E. A., and L. Smart Richman. 2009. Perceived discrimination and health: A meta-analytic review. *Psychological Bulletin* 135(4): 531–554. https://doi.org/10.1037/a0016059.

Peck, J. A., and T. H. Porter. 2022. Pandemics and the impact on physician mental health: A systematic review. *Medical Care Research and Review* 79(6): 772–788. DOI: 10.1177/10775587221091772.

Prasad, K., C. McLoughlin, M. Stillman, et al. 2021. Prevalence and correlates of stress and burnout among US healthcare workers during the COVID-19 pandemic: A national cross-sectional survey study. *EClinicalMedicine* 35.

Rabatin, J., E. Williams, L. Baier Manwell, et al. 2016. Predictors and outcomes of burnout in primary care physicians. *Journal of Primary Care & Community Health* 7(1): 41–43.

Ripp, J., and T. Shanafelt. 2024. How should organizations be held accountable for clinician well-being? *JAMA* 332(9): 699–700. DOI: 10.1001/jama.2024.12015. PMID: 39115823.

Rudman, A., and J. P. Gustavsson. 2012. Burnout during nursing education predicts lower occupational preparedness and future clinical performance: A longitudinal study. *International Journal of Nursing Studies* 49(8): 988–1001. https://doi.org/10.1016/j.ijnurstu.2012.03.010.

Seron, C., S. S. Silbey, E. Cech, et al. 2016. Persistence is cultural: Professional socialization and the reproduction of sex segregation. *Work and Occupations* 43(2): 178–214. https://doi.org/10.1177/0730888415618728.

Taylor, C. J. 2016. "Relational by nature"? Men and women do not differ in physiological response to social stressors faced by token women. *American Journal of Sociology* 122(1): 49–89. https://doi.org/10.1086/686698.

Thaler, R. H., and C. R. Sunstein. 2008. *Nudge: Improving Decisions about Health, Wealth, and Happiness.* Yale University Press.

Thompson, M. J., D. S. Carlson, K. M. Kacmar, et al. 2020. The cost of being ignored: Emotional exhaustion in the work and family domains. *Journal of Applied Psychology* 105(2): 186.

Trinkenreich, B., F. Santos, and K. J. Stol. 2024. Predicting attrition among software professionals: Antecedents and consequences of burnout and engagement. *ACM Transactions on Software Engineering and Methodology* 33(8): 1–45. https://dl.acm.org/doi/10.1145/3691629.

WHO (World Health Organization). 2019. Burn-out an "occupational phenomenon": International Classification of Diseases. https://www.who.int/news/item/28-05-2019-burn-out-an-occupational-phenomenon-international-classification-of-diseases.

REFERENCES

Wingfield, A. H. 2010. Are some emotions marked "Whites Only"? Racialized feeling rules in professional workplaces. *Social Problems* 57(2): 251–268. https://doi.org/10.1525/sp.2010.57.2.251.

Wingfield, A. H. 2019. *Flatlining: Race, Work, and Health Care in the New Economy*. University of California Press.

Wingfield, A. H., and K. Chavez. 2020. Getting in, getting hired, getting sideways looks: Organizational hierarchy and perceptions of racial discrimination. *American Sociological Review* 85(1): 31–57. https://doi.org/10.1177/0003122419894335.

Wynn, A. T., and S. J. Correll. 2018. Puncturing the pipeline: Do technology companies alienate women in recruiting sessions? *Social Studies of Science* 48(1): 149–164. https://doi.org/10.1177/0306312718756766.

Wynn, A. T., M. Fassiotto, C. Simard, et al. 2018. Pulled in too many directions: The causes and consequences of work-work conflict. *Sociological Perspectives* 61(5): 830–849.

Appendix A

Public Meeting Agendas

COMMITTEE ON THE IMPACT OF BURNOUT ON GENDER EQUITY IN SCIENCE, ENGINEERING, AND MEDICINE

OCTOBER 1–2, 2024
HYBRID WORKSHOP

DAY 1

SESSION 1—OPEN
UNDERSTANDING BURNOUT

11:30–11:40	Welcoming Remarks **Reshma Jagsi**, Committee Chair
11:40–12:35	Understanding Burnout and Challenging Misconceptions **Christina Maslach**, University of California, Berkeley **Tait Shanafelt**, Stanford University School of Medicine
12:35–12:45	Break

12:45–1:50	Causes of Burnout and Associated Risk Factors **Youngjoo Cha**, Indiana University, Bloomington **Rene Pana-Cryan**, National Institute of Occupational Safety and Health
1:50–1:55	Break

SESSION 2—OPEN
IMPACT OF BURNOUT

1:55–3:00	Consequences of Burnout and Implications for Equity **Alden Lai**, New York University **Carolyn Porta**, University of Minnesota
3:00–4:00	Deep Dive on Burnout, Identity, and Intersectionality **Jean King**, Worcester Polytechnic Institute **Joan Y. Reede**, Harvard Medical School **José Rodriguez**, University of Utah
4:00–4:15	Summary of Day 1

DAY 2

SESSION 1—OPEN
WHAT CAN WE DO ABOUT BURNOUT?

11:00–11:10	Welcoming Remarks **Reshma Jagsi**, Committee Chair
11:10–12:15	Current and Innovative Approaches to Managing Burnout **Arla Day**, St. Mary's University **Bryant Adibe**, Princeton University
12:15–12:35	Break

12:35–1:30	Interventions to Manage Burnout: Deep Dive on Medicine **Natalia Cineas**, NYC Health and Hospitals **Liselotte Dyrbye**, University of Colorado School of Medicine **Eve Kerr**, University of Michigan Medical School **Julie Silver**, Wake Forest University School of Medicine
1:30–1:40	Break
1:40–3:35	Interactive Discussion: Imagining a Future of Greater Support
3:35–3:50	Summary of the Event

Appendix B

Understanding the Causes of Burnout and Gender and Race Disparities in STEMM: A Multilevel Approach

Youngjoo Cha, Cassie Mead

This paper was commissioned by National Academies of Sciences, Engineering, and Medicine's Committee on Women in Science, Engineering, and Medicine. Opinions and statements included in the paper are solely those of the individual authors, and are not necessarily adopted, endorsed, or verified as accurate by the committee or the National Academies of Sciences, Engineering, and Medicine.

INTRODUCTION

Many workers experience work-related stress, with 57 percent of U.S. workers experiencing emotional exhaustion and mental disengagement from work, which are both prominent symptoms of burnout (American Psychological Association, 2023). Given that burnout is strongly linked to negative physical and mental health outcomes, reduced work productivity, lower job satisfaction, and higher job turnover rates, the prevalence of burnout among the majority of the U.S. workforce is alarming (Ahola et al., 2005; Borritz et al., 2010; Ducharme et al., 2007; Melamed et al., 2006; Moen et al., 2016; Salvagioni et al., 2017; von Känel et al., 2020). Why do people experience burnout at such high rates in today's workplaces? What causes burnout, and who is most affected? How might burnout risk factors explain gender and race disparities in science, technology, engineering, mathematics, and medicine (STEMM) fields? In this paper, we provide comprehensive reviews of research that address these questions. We argue that burnout is a multilevel phenomenon that operates at the macro, meso, and micro levels and organize our reviews around this framework. While most empirical studies in the literature on burnout focus on individual-level (micro) and job and workplace (meso) factors, we also consider structural (macro) factors, which help to understand the underlying causes of burnout widespread in contemporary workplaces.

A multilevel framework is frequently employed to theorize key concepts in the social sciences, such as gender (Ridgeway and Correll, 2004) employment discrimination (Hirsh and Cha, 2008), and imprinting (Marquis and Tilcsik, 2013). In the context of burnout, a similar approach is outlined in the National Academy of Medicine's 2019 Consensus Study Report on clinician burnout, where burnout factors are categorized into: "frontline care delivery" (local contexts where clinicians- patients interactions occur), "health care organizations," or "external environment" (economic and regulatory environments). However, this framework differentiates the first two levels based on the relevance to the clinician-patient interactions, rather than the specific units in which the factors reside, as we do.

We distinguish macro-, meso-, and micro-level factors based on the contexts in which risk factors arise. Macro-level factors include (1) macroeconomic changes that have increased job demands and reduced job security; (2) cultural shifts in the valuation of work, which have raised the expectations for constant availability for work; and (3) demographic changes that have intensified work-family conflicts. These structural changes in the U.S. labor market have created a foundation for burnout risk factors operating at the meso and micro levels.

Meso-level factors operate at job and workplace levels. They include work conditions linked to a higher risk of burnout, such as increased job demands, a lack of control over work activities and schedules, and the use of communication technologies. Much of the recent literature concentrates on these meso-level factors.

Micro-level factors operate at individual and interactional levels, including workers' identification with their jobs, perceived cultural fit, interactional-level inequalities, and emotional labor. Research indicates that strong identification with work can help mitigate the effects of factors at the meso-level that make STEMM workers more susceptible to burnout than other workers (e.g., higher job demands). However, these shielding effects tend to diminish among women and minoritized workers, whose cultural fit is often questioned due to pervasive stereotypes and gendered and racialized cultural ideals in STEMM fields.

These factors interact with one another, often across different levels, moderating their effects on burnout outcomes. For example, the negative impact of increased workloads can be mitigated through workplace practices and policy redesign. The impact of workloads can also be moderated by how individuals identify with their work. In each section, we will discuss these cross-level moderating relationships.

Finally, we offer a conceptual tool to understand the effects of these factors on women and minoritized workers, categorizing burnout factors identified in the literature into two categories. First, some factors appear to be gender- and race-neutral but produce gender- and race-specific outcomes. For example, poor working conditions that contribute to burnout may seem gender- and race-neutral, since anyone who is exposed to them, regardless of their gender and race, can experience burnout. However, due to persistent gender and racial job segregation, where White men tend to occupy positions with more desirable working conditions, these factors affect disproportionately women and minoritized workers compared with their White male counterparts (Glass, 2004; Stainback and Tomaskovic-Devey, 2012; Stier and Yaish, 2014).

The second group of factors directly relates to gendered and racialized processes. These include racism and sexism that operate at the interactional level as well as workplace norms and practices grounded upon highly gendered and racialized assumptions—often implicitly favoring White men's bodies, lifestyles, and cultural images. Such dynamics produce structural disadvantages for women and minoritized workers. Experiences of discrimination and mistreatment, along with a lack of belonging, can expose these workers to a higher risk of burnout.

Many empirical studies that we discuss focus specifically on STEMM fields, while others, although not directly based on STEMM data, provide insights into general processes associated with burnout that are highly relevant to STEMM.[1] At the end of the paper, we summarize the key points and suggest directions for future research.

---

[1] Our literature review is based on three key sources: (1) influential studies in the relevant fields, (2) a literature search from select high-impact journals in sociology, human resources/management, psychology, and health, using keywords such as "burnout," "STEM," and "overwork," and (3) a snowball search of studies cited in the articles identified through (1) and (2).

WHAT CAUSES BURNOUT? MULTILEVEL APPROACH

Macro-Level Factors: Economic, Cultural and Demographic Shifts

Much of the literature identifying the causes of burnout focuses on meso- and micro-level factors. However, these factors have emerged as prominent risk factors against the backdrop of broader macrostructural shifts in the U.S. economy over the past half-century. These macro-level factors have set the stages for meso- and micro-level factors that dominate burnout research. In our view, understanding these macro-level factors is essential to grasp why burnout is so widespread in contemporary workplaces, affecting not just specific groups of workers or types of workplaces.

Macroeconomic Conditions

Research has long shown that today's workers at the upper rung of the occupational hierarchy are working longer hours than workers from a half-century ago (Cha and Weeden, 2014; Jacobs and Gerson, 2004; Kalleberg, 2011). To understand the underlying causes of rising work hours in high-skilled high-paying jobs, scholars highlight structural shifts in macroeconomic conditions in the labor market. These include globalization and downsizing, which have made jobs less secure, the compensation system that disproportionately rewards those who work long hours (e.g., tournament promotion system; Epstein et al., 1999; Landers et al., 1996), and the adoption of productivity-enhancing technologies (Beckman and Mazmanian, 2020; Perlow, 2012).

Growing global competition in product markets has led to widespread corporate restructuring in the U.S. economy. Along with the decline of unions and diffusion of shareholder value systems, these changes have fundamentally reshaped employment relations, making them less secure and more fluid (Fligstein and Shin, 2004; Kalleberg, 2011). These changes have stratified the workforce into core employees, whose job demands increased, and contingent workers, whose positions are temporary, and contract based (Kalleberg, 2001, 2011; Tomaskovic-Devey and Avent-Holt, 2019). As a result, job quality in the U.S. economy has diverged (Jacobs and Gerson, 2004; Kalleberg, 2011). Those workers who "survived" downsizing and remain as core employees enjoy relatively desirable working conditions, with higher pay, greater job autonomy, and schedule flexibility, but they often face long and intense work hours. By contrast, those who were laid off or displaced from jobs are now in more precarious employment, with lower pay, fewer job benefits and legal protections, and reduced job autonomy. The employment and financial instability experienced by contingent workers is strongly linked to poorer mental health outcomes (Glavin and Schieman, 2022).

Given the high demand for STEMM skills, a relatively high proportion of STEMM workers remain in the core sector. However, widespread downsizing has increased their workloads. Staff shortage is a widespread issue in the current economy, with even workers in noncompetitive public-sector jobs reporting frequently working beyond contracted 40-hour workweeks due to chronic staffing shortages (Lee et al., 2024). STEMM jobs are no exception. In a study of 10,184 nurses and 232,342 patients across 168 hospitals, Aiken et al. (2002) found that the major factor behind nurses' increased work hours was staff shortages. The increased workload for nurses also contributes to burnout, with each additional patient per nurse associated with a 23 percent increase in the odds of burnout. Furthermore, workplace downsizing often requires workers to learn additional skills to meet a wider range of job demands, further elevating the risk of burnout (Lebel et al., 2023).

The number of contract workers within the STEMM workforce has also been steadily rising as the economy shifts toward more flexible employment relationships (Kunda et al., 2002; Wingfield, 2019). This trend means that today's STEMM workers are less shielded from employment and financial instability than their counterparts were several decades ago. In a study of high-skilled technical contractors, Kunda et al. (2002) found that despite lucrative pay, contract workers frequently reported feeling anxious about uncertainties of their next contracts and a sense of being an "outsider," which negatively affected their psychological well-being.

These structural changes have not only increased the number of work hours but also the intensity of these hours. Using data from the 2002 National Study of Changing Workforce, Kalleberg (2011) shows that between 1977 and 2002, the proportion of workers reporting that they had too much work to do and that their jobs required that they work very fast and very hard increased significantly. Specifically, these metrics rose by 0.07 to 0.5 points on a 4-point scale.

In addition to these macrostructural changes, some scholars also highlight the diffusion of compensation systems in which workers' relative standing, rather than their absolute performance, determines their promotion chances and pay raise, for example, "up or out" systems in laws, academia, accounting, and executive pay (Biggart and O'Brien, 2010; Blair-Loy, 2003; Epstein et al., 1999; Kuhn and Lozano, 2008; Landers et al., 1996; Sharone, 2004). Under these systems, workers are pressured to provide extra evidence for their work commitment to differentiate themselves from their similarly performing colleagues, often resorting to long hours and providing around-the-clock availability for job demands.

Work hours and on-call expectations have further increased with the adoption of remote work and mobile communication technologies at work. These technologies have enabled economic activities to continue 24/7 around the globe, blurred the boundaries between work and home life, and exposed workers to a higher risk of burnout (Beckman and Mazmanian, 2020; Perlow, 2012).

Cultural Shift Toward the Ideal Worker Norm

Not only have job demands increased over the past half-century, but meanings attached to work hours have also become more normative. Across American workplaces, the prevailing view is that "ideal workers" are those who put in long hours, prioritize work above all else, and make themselves available at all times (Williams, 2001). The emergence of this ideal worker norm has pressured workers to put in more hours at work than they desire, driven both by fear of losing jobs or missing career opportunities and by a desire to meet the internalized personal standards or career goals (Blair-Loy, 2003; Lee et al., 2024). However, a large body of research indicates that the ideal worker norm can be harmful, intensifying work-life conflicts and deteriorating the health and well-being of employees (Cech and Blair-Loy, 2014; C. Collins, 2019; Kelly et al., 2010; Kleiner et al., 2015; Schieman et al., 2009; Stone, 2007; Stone and Lovejoy, 2021).

Furthermore, the emphasis of prioritizing work under strong ideal worker norms fosters a culture that devalues self-care. Experimental evidence shows that employees who leave work early for nonwork matters (e.g., childcare, personal care) are viewed negatively— seen as less committed to work, less likable, and less deserving of organizational rewards than employees who prioritize work (Sanzari et al., 2021). The study also shows that employees who leave work early for personal care reasons were viewed more negatively than those who do so for childcare needs. These findings suggest that the ideal worker norm not only pressures workers to prioritize job demands over other responsibilities but also creates a culture that neglects self-care.

The ideal worker norms are particularly pronounced in STEMM professions (Cech and Blair-Loy, 2014). STEMM workplaces often offer resources to help workers cope with increased job demands, such as paid time off and flexible work schedules, but the ideal worker norms can diminish the effectiveness of such resources. In contexts with strong ideal worker norms, taking advantage of policies designed to promote "work-life balance" is often viewed as a sign of lacking commitment to work, leading to negative evaluations of employees who use these resources (Kelly et al., 2010; J. C. Williams et al., 2013). This phenomenon, known as "flexibility stigma" (J. C. Williams et al., 2013), has been well-documented. Experimental evidence indicates that workers who use paid time off, work from home, and work flexible hours are perceived as less committed, less respected, and less deserving of promotions (Judiesch and Lyness, 1999; Munsch, 2016; Rudman and Mescher, 2013). The fear of experiencing penalties for using these policies also suppresses employee uptake (Cha and Grady, 2024; Gerstel and Clawson, 2014; Wynn and Rao, 2020). In STEMM contexts, numerous studies of healthcare workers show that taking sick leave is often seen as neglecting patient care, which is internalized by many healthcare workers, leading them to be reluctant to take time off for self-care or personal matters (Gerstel and Clawson, 2014; Kellogg, 2009).

This heightened flexibility stigma is damaging to employees' health and contributes to burnout. Cech and Blair-Loy (2014) show that among academic scientists and engineers at the top research universities, the belief that pursuing work-life balance is stigmatized within their department is associated with higher turnover intentions, lower job satisfaction, and increased experiences of work-family conflicts.

Cultural Shift Toward Intensive Parenting

Most literature focuses on increased job demands and changes in work conditions as the major contributor to workplace burnout (see the next section). However, workers' work lives are closely intertwined with their nonwork lives, and it is essential to consider family factors to fully understand the underlying causes of burnout.

Scholars have long recognized that the family is "greedy" in the same way that work is, demanding complete and undivided devotion of time and energy to meet family members' needs (Blair-Loy, 2003; Coser, 1967; Jacobs and Gerson, 2004). This normative conception is reflected in contemporary parenting practices and philosophies. Hays (1996, p. 8) argues that contemporary parenting emphasizes "child-centered, expert-guided, emotionally absorbing, labor intensive, and financially expensive" practices. Lareau (2003) similarly conceptualizes White middle-class parenting as "concerted cultivation," characterized by organized activities and interactive communication. Recent studies find that these parenting practices have become prevalent across all race and class backgrounds (Ishizuka, 2019). These contemporary parenting styles require more time and cognitive energy from parents. While the intensification of parenting is less explored in the literature on burnout, we believe that this cultural shift toward intensive parenting contributes to work-family conflicts and feelings of time deficit among working families, both of which are linked to burnout (see Kossek and Ozeki, 1999, for a review).

The intensification of parenting is likely to affect women more than men. Although "involved fatherhood" has emerged as a new cultural ideal, parenting and childrearing are still more strongly expected from and taken by women (Blair-Loy, 2003; Calarco, 2024; Daminger, 2019). Daminger (2019) shows that among middle-class couples, women handle the majority of the "cognitive labor" associated with intensive parenting, such as managing schedules, selecting childcare, and setting and monitoring children's daily routines. This gendered effect of intensive parenting norms may increase women's risk of experiencing family-to-work conflict and mental disengagement from work as a coping strategy (Aldossari and Chaudhry, 2021; Watts, 2009).

Demographic Shift in the Workforce

Another major structural source of workplace burnout is the demographic shift toward dual-earner households. Jacobs and Gerson (2004) show that the increase in work hours is more pronounced at the family level rather than at the individual level. Specifically, the joint weekly work hours among heterosexual married couples increased from 52.5 hours in 1970 to 63.1 hours by 2000, an increase of more than 10 hours. The increase in family-level work hours is largely driven by women's rising labor force participation and full-time employment (Bianchi et al., 2012; Jacobs and Gerson, 2004).

Numerous studies turn to this striking increase in work hours at the family level as a major structural source of the rising number of Americans who feel overworked, burnt out, and time pressured (Bianchi et al., 2006; Matos and Galinsky, 2011). Scholars have long argued that workplace norms and practices are built upon the implicit assumption that workers have "backstage support" (Hochschild and Machung, 1989)—a person, such as a stay-at-home spouse, who manages nonwork responsibilities, allowing workers to focus solely on their paid work. When the majority of the workforce does not fit the description of this prototype, imposing the ideals rooted in this assumption inevitably creates work-family conflicts (J. Williams, 2001).

This mismatch is more consequential for women, as most men still receive more spousal/partner support than women. Among full-time workers, many women have husbands working full-time, often with long hours, while a higher proportion of men have stay-at-home wives or wives working part-time. Among professional and managerial workers from dual-earner marriages, nearly 30 percent of women have husbands working 50 or more hours per week, compared with 13 percent of men (Cha, 2010). This disparity is especially pronounced among "super-rich couples"—those in top 1 percent in the income and wealth bracket—where the male breadwinner–female homemaker model is more common than among couples in the top 20 percent bracket (Yavorsky et al., 2023). Given that most STEMM workers are in higher income brackets, these findings suggest that STEMM women are more likely to have overworking spouses who contribute less to housework and childcare. This also means that STEMM women typically compete with STEMM men, who are generally more likely to have more spousal support.

Meso-Level Factors: Work Conditions and Practices

The impact of the structural factors discussed above manifests within specific organizational and occupational contexts, which a large body of literature examines. These meso-level factors—work conditions related to job demands and resources, along with workplace policies and practices that determine them—can moderate the effect of macro-level factors on an individual's burnout outcomes.

Job Demands

Increased job demands have been at the center of the literature. Overall, research identifies three key drivers of burnout related to job demands in high-skilled jobs: long and intensified work hours, inflexible work schedules, and increased multifunctionality of job roles (Jacobs and Winslow, 2004; Kleiner and Pavalko, 2010).

Numerous studies link long hours to negative health outcomes (e.g., Jacobs and Winslow 2004; Kleiner and Pavalko, 2010). Kleiner and Pavalko (2010) show that individuals who work between 40 and 59 hours per week report significantly higher rates of depression and poorer mental health, compared with those who work standard 40-hour work weeks. Long hours have also been identified as a major source of job dissatisfaction among academic faculty. In a large nationally representative study of full-time postsecondary faculty members, Jacobs and Winslow (2004) find that about 50 percent of men and 60 percent of women who worked more than 60 hours a week reported being either "dissatisfied" or "very dissatisfied" with their jobs, compared with 29 percent of men and 38 percent of women who worked less than 50 hours a week.

Similarly, studies find that reducing job demands in "greedy" occupations can help prevent burnout. A quasi-experiment study of surgical residents shows that restructuring the surgical resident program designed to reduce workloads improved burnout outcomes (Hutter et al., 2006). Specifically, 1 year after the program changes—reducing on-call duties from every third night to every fourth night, allowing calls from home, and implementing cross-covering—the average burnout score among surgical residents, measured by the Maslach Burnout Inventory, decreased approximately 20 percent, moving from "high" (29.1) to "medium" (23.1).

Work-Work Conflict

An emerging body of literature identifies multiple roles and tasks required in a job as an important source of mental strain among high-skilled workers. For example, academic faculty often juggle between competing demands from multiple job functions—research, teaching, and administrative service. Wynn et al. (2018) introduce the concept of "work-work conflict," to describe the strain that these inter-role conflicts create, which they find to be a major factor associated with burnout and lower job satisfaction among physicians and faculty in an academic medical center.

Another related source of inter-role conflict arises from being part of multiple teams in the workplace. A study of knowledge workers at a large research organization shows that multiple team memberships, especially switching between project teams, are associated with higher-level job stress and emotional exhaustion, resulting in a 34 percent increase in turnover rates (van de Brake et al., 2024).

Women and minoritized academic faculty are more prone to this inter-role conflict due to higher likelihood of holding joint affiliations and taking on cross-department assignments. In a study of an R1 university, Tian and Smith (2024) found that Black assistant professors were 2.08 times more likely to have dual appointments than their White counterparts. This disparity is also linked to lower retention rates among Black professors compared with their White peers.

Hidden Work

Some work activities of STEMM workers are often less visible and are seen merely "extra," yet occupy much of their already tight schedules. Tasks categorized under "service" in academic sciences include a wide range of responsibilities, including administrative service for their department and university, additional leadership roles within universities or professional organizations, discipline-specific service, professional networking, and public outreach. One study finds that faculty spend on average about 9 hours per week in these service activities (Guarino and Borden, 2017).

Women and minoritized workers are more likely to take on this "unseen" work than their White men counterparts. Guarino and Borden (2017) find that women faculty spend on average 0.6 more hours per week than men. A study analyzing 33,456 resident physicians' evaluation records across eight U.S. hospitals shows that women attending physicians spend more time on providing more detailed and constructive feedback to medical residents than men attending physicians (Nelson et al., 2023).

Women and minoritized workers also frequently take on multiple administrative roles or serve on taskforce committees related to efforts to expand STEMM access, in addition to their regular job duties. The increased service load is a risk factor for burnout among these workers. In the essay that appeared in Molecular Biology of the Cell, Trejo (2020) argues that the rise of the DEI initiatives in academic institutions increases the service burden of minority faculty, which she describes as a new form of the "minority tax."

Technology

The adoption of remote work and communication technologies has enhanced worker productivity and provided flexibility in when and where employees work (Kalleberg, 2016). At the same time, however, mobile technologies also increase the permeability of work and blurred the lines between work and home life. Work does not stop when workers leave their office, since employers, coworkers, and clients can reach them outside of business hours. Remote work technologies can also encourage employees who fully embrace a "workaholic" mentality to work even more. This boundary spanning has been shown to increase feelings of guilt and work-family conflicts, particularly among women (Glavin et al., 2011; Kossek et al., 2006).

Based on ethnographies of nine families with school-age children, Beckman and Mazmanian (2020) show that communication technologies exacerbate feelings of being perpetually behind and lacking control, while reinforcing myths of the ideal worker and ideal parents. Similarly, a case study analyzing detailed communication logs and surveys from 74 workers across three departments (engineering, marketing, and technical writers) finds that the time employees spend on emails is positively associated with perceptions of overload—emotional exhaustion, burnout, stress, and frustration from work (Barley et al., 2011). However, the author notes that time spent on emails reflects larger structural problems, such as workplace norms that create time pressure and an inefficient structure of work. That is, the volume of emails is a symptom of burnout rather than its cause.

Types of Tasks

Repetitive and routinized tasks are recognized as important stressors, so engaging in less routinized and high-creativity tasks in STEMM jobs can help alleviate some of the burnout risks (Schieman and Young, 2010). However, while those who engage with creative work are less likely to report work-related stress, the burnout-reducing effects of creative tasks can diminish in many professional occupations, because creative tasks often involve frequent boundary spanning and multitasking, which are risk factors of burnout (Schieman and Young, 2010).

Moreover, technology adoption and the rise of big data have increased the prevalence of repetitive and detail-oriented tasks in science and technical occupations. Bruns and Lingo (2024) show that this increase in "tedious" work results in time drain, disengagement, and information overload among academic scientists. These tasks are often assigned to younger, lower-ranked workers, whom other research has identified as being a high-risk group for burnout (e.g., Marchand et al., 2018).

Control Over Work Activities

Another important dimension that determines the quality of work is whether employees have control over work activities (Kalleberg, 2011). This is often defined as the extent to which employees can exercise autonomy or discretion in how to perform their jobs. The literature identifies inability to influence decision-making or plan one's own work activities as important stressors that increase the risk of burnout (Karasek, 1979; Maslach and Leiter, 2008; Maslach et al., 2001). Conversely, providing workers with job control can help mitigate this risk. In a study of Italian healthcare workers, higher perceived job control was associated with lower levels of exhaustion among those reporting high workload (Portoghese et al., 2014). More broadly, however, high-skilled professional and managerial occupations tend to offer greater job autonomy compared with lower-skilled jobs. In this context, tasks commonly performed in most STEMM jobs are less associated with burnout risk.

Inflexible Schedules

The literature indicates that inflexible hours are major risk factors for burnout. Duffee and Willis (2023) show that the unpredictable nature of ambulance paramedics' jobs limits their control over work schedules, which is a major predictor of high job stress.

However, organizational practices that give employees more control over work schedules, such as flextime, remote work, and paid time off, can help to prevent burnout. Studies of information technology (IT) employees at Fortune 500 companies show that workplace initiatives granting employees greater control over their work schedules reduce burnout and psychological distress (Kelly et al., 2011, 2014; Moen et al., 2016). Notably, these interventions did not reduce employees' work hours, suggesting that it is not the number of hours worked but rather how those hours are structured that changed employees' psychological health outcomes. Similarly, a study of healthcare workers found that adjusting work schedules in ways to support employees' nonwork demands resulted in higher quality of patient care outcomes (Kossek et al., 2020).

Moderating Relationships: The Role of Job Demands and Resources in STEMM

Much of the literature investigating the role of working conditions emphasizes the moderating relationships among job conditions that often offset each other's effects. The upshot of these ideas is that while higher job demands can negatively impact workers' well-being, job resources can buffer some of these adverse effects ("job demands-resources model"). More specifically, research identifies managerial support, job authority, job autonomy, creative tasks, higher earnings, and schedule control as important resources that help mitigate burnout (Bakker and Demerouti, 2007; Crawford et al., 2010; Karasek, 1979; Schieman et al., 2009).

Workplace support is consistently shown to be highly influential for workers' engagement, psychological well-being, and outcomes in the work-family interface (Ducharme and Martin, 2000; Moen et al., 2016; O'Connor and Cech, 2018; Walsh, 2013). A study based on a national survey of hospital employees in England shows that while burnout rates are high among doctors, perceptions of burnout are contingent upon organizational support: specifically, coworkers' support for women and family-friendly work culture and management support for men (Walsh, 2013). Similarly, O'Connor and Cech (2018) show that coworkers' and supervisors' support moderate the negative relationship between perceived flexibility stigma and job satisfaction and work-life conflicts. Ducharme and Martin (2000) find that both affective (emotional) support and instrumental (tangible aid) support were positively associated with job satisfaction.

Another strand of research turns to the role of job autonomy and schedule flexibility as a key resource that can mitigate the "harms" of long hours (De Moortel et al., 2017; Kaduk et al., 2019; Kelly et al., 2011, 2014; Kesavan et al., 2022). Van Yperen and Hagedoorn (2003) show that higher levels of job autonomy and control over work schedules significantly reduce the negative impact of high job demands on fatigue among nurses. A series of workplace intervention studies consistently show that providing employees with schedule control is the key to improving employees' health, including burnout, depression, sleep, and work-life conflicts (Kelly et al., 2011; Moen et al., 2011, 2016).

However, the broader literature suggests that the effects of flexible work policies are contingent upon other factors. Empirical evidence regarding the ability of flexible work practices to mitigate burnout and improve employee outcomes has been mixed (see Kelly et al., 2008, for review). This inconsistency is partly because strong ideal worker norms that stigmatize employees who use these policies lead to underutilization of these resources (Blair-Loy, 2003; Cha and Grady, 2024; Munsch, 2016; Schieman et al., 2009). Additionally, the financial cost incurred from using these policies—such as unpaid time off or paid leave with lower wage replacement rate—can further inhibit their use (Thébaud and Pedulla, 2022). This implies that for these policies to achieve their intended outcomes of preventing burnout and improving employee well-being, they must be accompanied by additional organizational support.

Some research finds that the efficacy of these policies is selective. Koltai and Schieman (2015) show that for workers with low socioeconomic status (SES), job autonomy and schedule flexibility help mitigate the effect of job pressure on anxiety. For those with high SES, by contrast, greater autonomy and schedule flexibility exacerbate this relationship. Related research introduces the concept of "stress of higher status" to explain this paradoxical pattern (e.g., Schieman et al., 2009). These scholars argue that workers in higher-status jobs face stronger normative pressure to demonstrate high-level work commitment, which serves as a unique stressor in these higher-status jobs. This, in turn, leads to a paradoxical pattern in which workers in higher-status jobs experience higher-level work permeability, despite having access to more job resources that could reduce burnout, such as greater temporal flexibility and control over their work activities.

In the context of STEMM jobs, these offsetting relationships between job demands and resources provide a useful framework for understanding burnout risks. Many STEMM jobs are characterized by long work hours, high time pressure, and large job demands. At the same time, however, they have greater access to job resources that could buffer the impact of these risk factors, such as higher job and financial security, more predictable work schedules, and better work-family policies (Blair-Loy and Cech, 2022; Cha and Grady, 2024; Schieman et al., 2009). However, the stronger ideal worker norms therein often inhibit the utilization of these resources. This implies that providing resources while minimizing the stigma and creating an organizational culture that promotes the utilization of these resources is a key to preventing burnout among workers in STEMM fields.

MICRO AND INTERACTIONAL-LEVEL: WORK IDENTITY, CULTURAL FIT, INTERACTIONAL INEQUALITY, EMOTIONAL LABOR

Work Identity and Meaningful Work

Strong identification with work can shield workers from burnout. A study of 555 nurses shows that while high job demands were associated with fatigue from work, these nurses also had high-level intrinsic motivation.

Other workers in high-status jobs, such as corporate executives, engineers, and investment bankers, similarly view work as their "calling," "passion project," and what makes their life "worthwhile" (Blair-Loy, 2003; E. Cech, 2021). This work identity and intrinsic motivation shield these workers from burnout. Many women executives in Blair-Loy (2003) expressed challenges of fast-paced and highly competitive jobs, but they were also strongly identified with and inspired by work. One of her interviewees expressed, "This profession gives me, in a lot of ways, a real piece of me, and the longer you do it, the more it gives you. . . . It's been enormously good for me and not just financially. I mean, in terms of who I think and I know I am" (p. 11). Similarly, Dill et al. (2016) show that acute care hospital nurses who express high intrinsic (e.g., following their passion) and extrinsic motivation (e.g., for career success) show better health and job outcomes. They are also less likely to experience burnout and are less likely to leave their jobs, compared with those who have prosocial motivation (i.e., desire to help others).

The "meaningful" work serves as an important moderator in burnout-producing processes. Based on a meta-analysis of 55 studies, Crawford et al. (2010) show that not all high job demands lead to burnout, and instead, only job demands accompanied by tasks conflicting with their identities, such as role conflicts, role ambiguity, and organizational politics, are negatively associated with job engagement. By contrast, job demands involving tasks that individuals view as meaningful and important to them do not result in job disengagement. Similarly, in a study of employees from 21 European countries, De Moortel et al. (2017) show that not all long hours lead to negative health outcomes among men, but instead, only "involuntary" long hours—additional hours that employees were forced to put in—are negatively associated with their well-being outcomes.

However, Bredehorst et al. (2024) find that managing passion could also be a challenge. Using 30 days of daily diaries of individuals, the authors find that higher passion on one day is associated with higher emotional exhaustion the next day. Cech (2021) also warns that employees' inclination to view their efforts to meet the job demands as a reflection of their passion can be an exploitation logic, in which employees "voluntarily" put in long hours for the benefit of employers, often at the expense of employees' own personal well-being and health.

While some studies view work identification as a predictor for burnout outcomes (Blair-Loy, 2003; Cech, 2021; Cech et al., 2011), other scholars view strong work identification as an outcome of good working conditions. In a study of women finance executives, Blair-Loy (2003) argues that a strong sense of dedication to jobs, employers, and professions is intertwined with reward systems. That is, employees who demonstrate complete allegiance are rewarded with large salary increases, promotions, and larger responsibilities that require longer work hours and more emotional energy to jobs. Focusing on these goals gives these workers a "rush of adrenaline" (p. 30) and "a sense of transcendence" (p. 32), which shields them from burnout. Simply put, economic reward systems and cultural recognition of work can also create a sense of strong work identification. Kalleberg (2011) similarly argues that favorable job conditions—higher earnings, generous employee benefits, job autonomy, and schedule flexibilities—can mold what we consider "intrinsic rewards," one's subjective experiences as meaningful and interesting jobs. By the same logic, poor working conditions can make workers lose their strong sense of commitment to work. Yavaş (2024) shows that overloaded job demands, lacking work-life balance, and feeling alienated at work led high-power elite white-collar employees to ask an existential question, "What am I doing with my life?" (p. 762), which ultimately led them to leave their jobs.

Cultural Fit

A strong identification with work can be influenced by cultural beliefs about stereotypical traits and skills associated with ideal employees in STEMM fields. Research has shown that while an increasing number of women select STEMM majors, women are less likely than men to pursue careers relevant to their majors. Using the National Science Foundation's Scientists and Engineers Statistical Data System, Sassler et al. (2023) show that among computer science degree holders, 66 percent of men with computer science degrees have jobs in STEM, but only 52 percent of women do.

Several studies offer explanations for this "gendered persistence" in STEMM careers. Based on longitudinal surveys of engineering students from four colleges, E. Cech et al. (2011) show that female students are more likely than men to believe that they lack expertise and career fit to pursue engineering careers. This lower "professional role confidence" is a strong predictor of women's lower rate in pursuing engineering careers. In a follow-up study, the same authors show that women's lower professional confidence often results from professional socialization in college engineering programs (Seron et al., 2016). During orientation, coursework and team projects, and internships, women frequently encounter stereotypes, are relegated to supporting roles, and receive fewer opportunities to develop technical skills. This gendered socialization in turn contributes to their lower "professional role confidence" as engineers.

Studies find that employees' self-assessed fit with their jobs and professions impacts their job satisfaction and their persistence. In a study of technical employees across seven Silicon Valley firms, Wynn and Correll (2017) show that women are less likely than men to perceive themselves as fitting the image of successful tech employees. The authors also show that this self-assessed "cultural" and "skill" alignment is a strong predictor of their intention to leave. In another study, these authors observed that during recruiting sessions, company representatives use images, languages, and behaviors that reinforce gender stereotypes, exhibiting men presenters taking the technical roles while women presenters take supporting roles, and often emphasizing masculine geek cultures (Wynn and Correll, 2018). The authors argue that these recruitment strategies work as gendered cultural signals about who belongs in the tech industry, further alienating women.

A separate stream of the literature examines how beliefs on the role of beliefs in meritocracy and objectivity of STEMM can undermine efforts to promote equality (Blair-Loy and Cech, 2022; Doerr et al., 2021). Blair-Loy and Cech (2022) demonstrate that strong beliefs in objectivity in science and engineering often prevent STEM faculty from recognizing unequal outcomes and structural barriers faced by women and minoritized scholars. This phenomenon is well-documented elsewhere, illustrated by the concept "paradox of meritocracy" (Castilla and Benard, 2010): a phenomenon that when individuals perceive the system as meritocratic, they are less vigilant about the effects of institutionalized biases, and consequently, become more prone to those biases than individuals who believe that the system is unjust.

Moreover, the concepts of "scientific excellence" and "merit" may seem "objective," but these ideals are constructed around the values and attributes of White heterosexual men (e.g., assertiveness, self-promotion), thereby perpetuating cultures and norms that disadvantage women and racial and sexual minority workers. The belief in meritocracy is also widely accepted by women and minoritized STEM workers, influencing their self-assessed career fit. Doerr et al. (2021) show that despite experiencing marginalization in their engineering careers, women engineers from diverse ethnoracial backgrounds often endorse the idea that gender is irrelevant in engineering and the field operates on meritocratic principles.

Related literature shows how the "abstract" and disembodied notion of the worker, constructed around White heterosexual men, their bodies, and their lifestyles (Acker, 1990), creates structural disadvantages for women and minoritized workers in STEMM. Women's experiences tied to motherhood are largely hidden in the workplace and considered what women need to manage privately to maintain a "professional" appearance. In a study of graduate students in science and engineering programs, Thébaud and Taylor (2021) find that motherhood is broadly seen as undermining their professional legitimacy as scientists and engineers. In her autoethnography, Haynes (2024) speaks about how managerialism is highly tied to masculine norms in academic leadership, and how the pressures assimilated to these norms lead many women academics to experience burnout.

Recent empirical studies document how women's bodily experiences, such as pregnancy, lactation, and menopause, are often disregarded in the professional workspace and are considered something to hide, which can lead to feelings of exclusion, emotional exhaustion, perceived discrimination, and burnout (Little et al., 2015; Steffan and Loretto, 2024; Watts, 2009). Little et al. (2015) show nearly all professional women they interviewed reported concerns about their professional images from the early stages of their pregnancy. Many of these women used strategies of detaching themselves from pregnancy, such as keeping the pace of work and avoiding asking for special accommodations. The authors find that women who used these strategies reported significantly lower levels of burnout, perceived discrimination, and turnover rate than women who did not. This may appear good news at first glance, as it seems to suggest that individual strategies of "hiding" pregnancy are effective. However, the underlying implication is troubling, as the subtle implication is that women who did embrace their pregnant identity at work experienced significantly higher rates of burnout, perceived discrimination, and turnover. Simply put, without the individual effort to conceal their pregnancy, pregnant workers face a higher risk of burnout and marginalization at work.

Interactional Inequality

Studies find that workplace interaction is an important source of burnout (Beck et al., 2022; Cardador et al., 2022; W. Hall et al., 2019; W. M. Hall et al., 2015; Haynes, 2024; Maslach and Leiter, 2008; Nelson et al., 2023; Wingfield and Chavez, 2020). These scholars identify several key mechanisms contributing to burnout in the international processes, including challenges of being a token (or a numerical minority), status beliefs and stereotypes, and discrimination.

In a classic study of women and men in a large corporation, Kanter (1977) argues that being a numerical minority brings numerous challenges for women in male-dominated workspaces. They include hypervisibility, increased scrutiny on their work performance, being seen through stereotypical lenses, and pressure to conform to men-centered sexist cultures. Subsequent work has linked these challenges to psychological well-being and job outcomes in broader contexts (Jackson et al., 1995; Taylor, 2016). Using a laboratory study, Taylor (2016) shows that being the only man or woman in a mixed-gender group elevates the stress hormone levels for both genders. Jackson et al. (1995) find that Black leaders across business, politics, and media in predominantly White workspaces experience higher-level stress, with heightened visibility identified as a major driver.

Another strand of research shows that women and minoritized workers experience disadvantages in small group interactions because they are widely perceived as "lower status" groups (Ridgeway, 2011, 2014). As members of a lower-status group, their work competency is questioned, and their contribution is often underappreciated, compared with their White men counterparts. The sense of being underappreciated has been linked to a host of burnout-related outcomes, including feelings of discouragement and injustice, lower job satisfaction, and decreased psychological well-being, work disengagement, and higher turnover rates (Beck et al., 2022; W. Hall et al., 2019; W. M. Hall et al., 2015; Haynes, 2024; Pascoe and Smart Richman, 2009).

The associations between perceived racial discrimination and psychological well-being outcomes are well established (King et al., 2023; Muñoz and Villanueva, 2022; Pascoe and Smart Richman, 2009). A study of 374 Black employees across the United States shows that experiencing microaggressions is positively associated with burnout (King et al., 2023). A review article on Latino/a faculty in STEM documents a clear pattern that those who experience discrimination experience negative psychological health outcomes (Muñoz and Villanueva, 2022). W. Hall et al. (2019) show these stressors are conveyed through everyday interactions. Based on a study of engineering workers in Canada and graduate students in STEM in North American universities, the authors show that having conversations with their male colleagues who display less acceptance of women in the workplace are strongly associated with burnout among STEM women.

Emotional Labor

In her study of flight attendants and bill collectors, Hochschild (1983) introduced the concept of "emotional labor"—the management and display of emotions in the workplace. This concept inspired numerous studies to investigate the nature and consequences of such labor. While much of the work has been focused on service jobs, such as restaurant work, nail salon workers, retail clerks, and childcare workers (Godwyn, 2006; Kang, 2003; Macdonald and Sirianni, 1996), recent research shows that emotional labor is also a prominent aspect of high-skilled managerial and professional occupations (see Wharton, 2009, for a review).

Specifically, emotional labor has been used to understand the psychological well-being of healthcare workers (Cottingham and Erickson, 2020; Erickson and Grove, 2008). Cottingham and Erickson (2020) show that care nurses often experience a complex range of emotions, such as worry, anger, sadness, and frustration, due to the interactive nature of their jobs with patients. However, they are expected to suppress, manage, and display these emotions in limited ways. Data from 48 acute care hospital nurses show that the challenges of managing emotions arising from demanding interactions with doctors and patients led to physical and psychological symptoms, such as headaches, insomnia, and depression. Based on a survey of more than 3,000 women RNs (registered nurses) and nursing aids in France, Jolivet et al. (2010) found that poor interpersonal relationships between workers are associated with higher depressive scores among nurses. Stokar (2024) shows that negative patient outcomes give physicians and nurses a "sense of failure," which increases the rate of burnout and traumatic stress.

Scholars also point to gendered and racialized "feeling rules," which may increase the emotional strain among women and minoritized workers (R. Collins, 2004; Pierce, 1996; Wingfield, 2010, 2021). In a study of legal professionals, Pierce (1996) shows that while litigators are expected to use anger and aggressiveness as litigation tactics, these behaviors are often viewed more negatively when exhibited by women attorneys. This different feeling rules can create additional cognitive labor. Harlow (2003) shows that Black professors engage in additional emotional work during interactions with students to navigate through negative racial stereotypes of being less intelligent.

Given that technical expertise required in STEMM fields are less aligned with traits that women and Black and Hispanic workers are stereotypically viewed to possess, the emotional and cognitive labor fighting for stereotypes while expressing emotions can make their work life doubly challenging.

IMPLICATIONS FOR GENDER AND RACE DISPARITIES

So far, we have reviewed academic research that identifies burnout risk factors at macro, meso, and micro levels. In this section, we revisit key findings to understand how these factors reinforce gender and race disparities in STEMM. We offer a conceptual tool to categorize these factors into two categories: (1) "disparate" risk factors and (2) gender- and race-specific risk factors.

First, some factors we reviewed appear to be gender- and race-neutral at first glance. Many of the poor working conditions (e.g., long hours, lack of autonomy, schedule control) are good examples of this, as they affect whoever is exposed to it, regardless of gender and race. However, when combined with persistent gender and race segregation in jobs—women and racial minorities disproportionately work in lower-skilled, lower-quality, and lower-paying jobs, compared with White men—these seemingly gender- and race-neutral factors produce gender- and race-specific patterns, in which more women and minoritized workers are exposed to these conditions. For example, emotional labor is more intense among nurses than among doctors, while a higher proportion of women is found among nurses than doctors. Consequently, more women than men are exposed to emotional labor.

Higher-status occupations and higher-performing organizations offer more job resources (e.g., job autonomy, schedule flexibilities) that help to prevent burnout (Davis and Kalleberg, 2006). And women and minoritized workers are underrepresented in these occupations and organizations (Glass, 2004; Hodges, 2020). By analyzing texts from 155 work groups appearing in 162 published ethnographies, Crowley (2012) shows that work groups consisting of predominantly men were designed to offer higher-level autonomy, creativity, meaningfulness, and satisfaction. By contrast, work groups consisting of predominantly women were run with more coercive arrangement, using more direct supervision rather than offering autonomy.

Second, some factors more directly speak to gendered and racialized processes that create systematic disadvantages for women and minoritized workers. These factors include race and gender biases that operate at the micro level through everyday interactions and are institutionalized as norms and practices at the meso level. This strand of research demonstrates that the gendered notion of the ideal workers and gendered and racialized cultural ideals of the STEMM workers leads to a lack of cultural fit for women and minoritized workers. Interactional inequalities based on stereotypes lead to underappreciation of the contribution made by women and minoritized workers and raise doubts about their work competency. These processes are strong predictors of gender-specific and race-specific burnout factors.

SUMMARY AND CONCLUSION

In the contemporary workplace, an increasing number of people report exhaustion from work, time pressure, and work-family conflicts. These phenomena have been linked to poorer physical and psychological health, lower job satisfaction, and higher turnover rates. In this paper, we review academic research that identifies sources of burnout in STEMM fields. In so doing, we argue that burnout is an outcome produced through multilevel processes at macro (macroeconomic, cultural, and demographic changes), meso (workplace and job factors), and micro (identities and interactional inequality) levels and review relevant studies in this organizing frame.

First, we began by introducing macro-level changes, which created structural conditions making everyone in the economy prone to burnout. From this perspective, the rise of burnout is an outcome of macrostructural shifts that occurred in the U.S. economy over the last half-century. We discussed how increased global competition and market pressures have increased job demands for high-skilled workers, including STEMM workers, while decreasing job insecurity and working conditions for low-skilled workers. These economic changes were also accompanied by cultural shifts that have intensified work and parenting norms. The rise in workplace expectations for around-the-clock availability, facilitated by mobile communication technologies, has increased the spillover of work into family life. Concurrently, the emergence of intensive parenting norms, which require greater effort and time commitment to family care, has led many employees to experience heightened work-family conflicts. Demographic shifts toward dual-earner households have dramatically raised work hours at the family level than at the individual level.

Second, much of the research literature on burnout focuses on workplace and job factors that have become more pronounced because of macro-level changes. Most notably, increased job demands have been identified as a major source of burnout among high-skilled workers. That said, the impact of job demands is contingent upon job resources available to individual workers. When workers have more control over work activities and schedules, and receive better support from management and coworkers, the negative effects of job demands can be mitigated. Similarly, tasks that are less routinized and require higher-level creativity can also help alleviate the adverse effects of high job demands among high-skilled workers, such as STEMM workers.

Third, at the micro level, identities and interactions play important roles in creating or reducing mental exhaustion at work. Gender and race biases result in interactional disadvantages for women and minority workers: these workers are seen as less competent and suitable for STEMM fields. This creates feelings of discouragement and injustice and diminishes their sense of belonging. An emerging body of literature examines the embodied nature of work, particularly institutionalized practices and norms that implicitly or explicitly assume White heterosexual masculinity. Workplace practices and norms built upon the notion that the ideal type of workers embodies the characteristics, cultural values, and lifestyles of White heterosexual men can disadvantage workers who do not fit this mold. This perceived lack of fit can in turn increase burnout.

Many STEMM workers are employed in high-performing well-resourced organizations. Their work lives are centered on competitive, fast-paced, and overloaded job demands. Despite this, STEMM workers are generally part of relatively privileged groups, who enjoy higher earnings, job security, and job resources that can help buffer the impact of higher job demands. However, a prevailing occupational norm that valorizes "overwork," and stigmatizes workers who seek work-life balance or utilize organizational resources to achieve it can put these workers at a higher risk of burnout. Occupational values emphasizing "objectivity" and "scientific expertise" can also hinder efforts to address deeply institutionalized gender- and race-based biases within STEMM fields. In our view, these more covert forms of bias, which are hidden in STEMM education, curriculum, cultures, and compensation systems, are less explored in the literature, which are promising avenues for future research.

The 2020 COVID-19 pandemic brought several important changes in individuals' work life. Many people worked from home during this time, and many workers wish to keep such flexibility in the post-pandemic years (Parker et al., 2022). Some scholars suspect that the pandemic experience has also reshaped employees' relationship with work. A record number of people left jobs (the Great Resignation), and some have become disengaged from work without quitting entirely (quiet quitting). The alarming signs of burnout during the pandemic have elevated mental health and well-being concerns to a national priority (U.S. Department of Health and Human Services, 2024). How will these changes impact STEMM workers in the post-pandemic era? While we have gained cultural momentum in raising awareness of burnout as a social issue, our reviews suggest that structural changes in work and a shift away from the toxic ideal worker norms are essential to fundamentally address the problem in STEMM and beyond.

REFERENCES

Acker, J. (1990). Hierarchies, Jobs, Bodies: A Theory of Gendered Organizations. Gender & Society, 4(2), 139–158. https://doi.org/10.1177/089124390004002002.

Ahola, K., Honkonen, T., Isometsä, E., Kalimo, R., Nykyri, E., Aromaa, A., & Lönnqvist, J. (2005). The Relationship between Job-Related Burnout and Depressive Disorders—Results from the Finnish Health 2000 Study. Journal of Affective Disorders, 88(1), 55–62. https://doi.org/10.1016/j.jad.2005.06.004.

Aiken, L. H., Clarke, S. P., Sloane, D. M., Sochalski, J., & Silber, J. H. (2002). Hospital Nurse Staffing and Patient Mortality, Nurse Burnout, and Job Dissatisfaction. JAMA, 288(16), 1987–1993. https://doi.org/10.1001/jama.288.16.1987.

Aldossari, M., & Chaudhry, S. (2021). Women and Burnout in the Context of a Pandemic. Gender, Work & Organization, 28(2), 826–834. https://doi.org/10.1111/gwao.12567.

American Psychological Association. (2023). 2023 Work in America Survey: Workplaces as Engines of Psychological Health and Well-Being. https://www.apa.org/pubs/reports/work-in-america/2023-workplace-health-well-being.

Bakker, A. B., & Demerouti, E. (2007). The Job Demands-Resources Model: State of the Art. Journal of Managerial Psychology, 22(3), 309–328. https://doi.org/10.1108/02683940710733115.

Barley, S. R., Meyerson, D. E., & Grodal, S. (2011). E-mail as a Source and Symbol of Stress. Organization Science, 22(4), 887–906. https://doi.org/10.1287/orsc.1100.0573.

Beck, M., Cadwell, J., Kern, A., Wu, K., Dickerson, M., & Howard, M. (2022). Critical Feminist Analysis of STEM Mentoring Programs: A Meta-Synthesis of the Existing Literature. Gender, Work & Organization, 29(1), 167–187. https://doi.org/10.1111/gwao.12729.

Beckman, C. M., & Mazmanian, M. (2020). Dreams of the Overworked: Living, Working, and Parenting in the Digital Age. Stanford University Press. http://ebookcentral.proquest.com/lib/iub-ebooks/detail.action?docID=6173725.

Bianchi, S. M., Casper, L. M., & King, R. B. (2006). Work, Family, Health, and Well-Being. Routledge.

Bianchi, S. M., Sayer, L. C., Milkie, M. A., & Robinson, J. P. (2012). Housework: Who Did, Does or Will Do It, and How Much Does It Matter? Social Forces, 91(1), 55–63. https://doi.org/10.1093/sf/sos120.

Biggart, L., & O'Brien, M. (2010). Uk Fathers' Long Work Hours: Career Stage or Fatherhood? Fathering, 8(3), 341–361. https://doi.org/10.3149/fth.0803.341.

Blair-Loy, M. (2003). Competing Devotions: Career and Family among Women Executives. Harvard University Press. https://doi.org/10.4159/9780674021594.

Blair-Loy, M., & Cech, E. A. (2022). Misconceiving Merit. University of Chicago Press.

Borritz, M., Christensen, K. B., Bültmann, U., Rugulies, R., Lund, T., Andersen, I., Villadsen, E., Diderichsen, F., & Kristensen, T. S. (2010). Impact of Burnout and Psychosocial Work Characteristics on Future Long-Term Sickness Absence. Prospective Results of the Danish PUMA Study Among Human Service Workers. Journal of Occupational and Environmental Medicine, 52(10), 964. https://doi.org/10.1097/JOM.0b013e3181f12f95.

Bredehorst, J., Krautter, K., Meuris, J., & Jachimowicz, J. M. (2024). The Challenge of Maintaining Passion for Work over Time: A Daily Perspective on Passion and Emotional Exhaustion. Organization Science, 35(1), 364–386. https://doi.org/10.1287/orsc.2023.1673.

Bruns & Lingo (2024). Tedious Work: Developing Novel Outcomes with Digitization in the Arts and Sciences. Administrative Science Quarterly, 69(1), 39–79. https://doi.org/10.1177/00018392231208190

Calarco, J. (2024). Holding It Together. Portfolio/Penguin. https://www.penguinrandomhouse.com/books/697130/holding-it-together-by-jessica-calarco/.

Cardador, M. T., Hill, P. L., & Salles, A. (2022). Unpacking the Status-Leveling Burden for Women in Male-Dominated Occupations. Administrative Science Quarterly, 67(1), 237–284. https://doi.org/10.1177/00018392211038505.

Castilla, E. J., & Benard, S. (2010). The Paradox of Meritocracy in Organizations. Administrative Science Quarterly, 55(4), 543–676. https://doi.org/10.2189/asqu.2010.55.4.543.

Cech, E. (2021). The Trouble with Passion: How Searching for Fulfillment at Work Fosters Inequality. University of California Press.

Cech, E. A., & Blair-Loy, M. (2014). Consequences of Flexibility Stigma Among Academic Scientists and Engineers. Work and Occupations, 41(1), 86–110. https://doi.org/10.1177/0730888413515497.

Cech, E., Rubineau, B., Silbey, S., & Seron, C. (2011). Professional Role Confidence and Gendered Persistence in Engineering. American Sociological Review, 76(5), 641–666. https://doi.org/10.1177/0003122411420815.

Cha, Y. (2010). Reinforcing Separate Spheres: The Effect of Spousal Overwork on Men's and Women's Employment in Dual-Earner Households. American Sociological Review, 75(2), 303–329. https://doi.org/10.1177/0003122410365307.

Cha, Y., & Grady, R. K. (2024). Overwork and the Use of Paid Leave and Flexible Work Policies in U.S. Workplaces. Social Science Research, 121, 103006. https://doi.org/10.1016/j.ssresearch.2024.103006.

Cha, Y., & Weeden, K. A. (2014). Overwork and the Slow Convergence in the Gender Gap in Wages. American Sociological Review, 79(3), 457–484. https://doi.org/10.1177/0003122414528936.

Collins, C. (2019). Making Motherhood Work: How Women Manage Careers and Caregiving. Princeton University Press. https://doi.org/10.1515/9780691185156.

Collins, R. (2004). Rituals of Solidarity and Security in the Wake of Terrorist Attack. Sociological Theory, 53–86.

Coser, L. A. (1967). Greedy Organisations. European Journal of Sociology / Archives Européennes de Sociologie, 8(2), 196–215. https://doi.org/10.1017/S000397560000151X.

Cottingham, M. D., & Erickson, R. J. (2020). The Promise of Emotion Practice: At the Bedside and Beyond. Work and Occupations, 47(2), 173–199. https://doi.org/10.1177/0730888419892664.

Crawford, E. R., LePine, J. A., & Rich, B. L. (2010). Linking Job Demands and Resources to Employee Engagement and Burnout: A Theoretical Extension and Meta-Analytic Test. Journal of Applied Psychology, 95(5), 834–848. https://doi.org/10.1037/a0019364.

Crowley, M. (2012). Gender, the Labor Process and Dignity at Work Gender Inequality. Social Forces, 91(4), 1209–1238.

Daminger, A. (2019). The Cognitive Dimension of Household Labor. American Sociological Review, 84(4), 609–633. https://doi.org/10.1177/0003122419859007.

Davis, A. E., & Kalleberg, A. L. (2006). Family-Friendly Organizations? Work and Family Programs in the 1990s. Work and Occupations, 33(2), 191–223. https://doi.org/10.1177/0730888405280446.

De Moortel, D., Thévenon, O., De Witte, H., & Vanroelen, C. (2017). Working Hours Mismatch, Macroeconomic Changes, and Mental Well-being in Europe. Journal of Health and Social Behavior, 58(2), 217–231. https://doi.org/10.1177/0022146517706532.

Dill, J., Erickson, R. J., & Diefendorff, J. M. (2016). Motivation in Caring Labor: Implications for the Well-Being and Employment Outcomes of Nurses. Social Science & Medicine, 167, 99–106. https://doi.org/10.1016/j.socscimed.2016.07.028.

Doerr, K., Riegle-Crumb, C., Russo-Tait, T., Takasaki, K., Sassler, S., & Levitte, Y. (2021). Making Merit Work at the Entrance to the Engineering Workforce: Examining Women's Experiences and Variations by Race/Ethnicity. Sex Roles, 85(7), 422–439. https://doi.org/10.1007/s11199-021-01233-6,

Ducharme, L. J., Knudsen, H. K., & Roman, P. M. (2007). Emotional Exhaustion and Turnover Intention in Human Service Occupations: The Protective Role of Coworker Support. Sociological Spectrum, 28(1), 81–104. https://doi.org/10.1080/02732170701675268.

Ducharme, L. J., & Martin, J. K. (2000). Unrewarding Work, Coworker Support, and Job Satisfaction: A Test of the Buffering Hypothesis. Work and Occupations, 27(2), 223–243. https://doi.org/10.1177/0730888400027002005.

Duffee, B., & Willis, D. B. (2023). Paramedic Perspectives of Job Stress: Qualitative Analysis of High-Stress, High-Stakes Emergency Medical Situations. Social Science & Medicine, 333, 116177. https://doi.org/10.1016/j.socscimed.2023.116177.

Epstein, C. F., Seron, C., Oglensky, B., & Sauté, R. (1999). The Part-time Paradox: Time Norms, Professional Life, Family and Gender. Routledge. https://doi.org/10.4324/9781315811352.

Erickson, R. J., & Grove, W. J. C. (2008). Why Emotions Matter: Age, Agitation, and Burnout Among Registered Nurses. Online Journal of Issues in Nursing, 13(1), 1–12. https://doi.org/10.3912/OJIN.Vol13No01PPT01.

Fligstein, N., & Shin, T.-J. (2004). The Shareholder Value Society: A Review of the Changes in Working Conditions and Inequality in the United States, 1976 to 2000. In Social Inequality (pp. 401–432). Russell Sage Foundation.

Gerstel, N., & Clawson, D. (2014). Unequal Time: Gender, Class, and Family in Employment Schedules. Russell Sage Foundation. https://muse-jhu-edu.proxyiub.uits.iu.edu/pub/207/monograph/book/33240.

Glass, J. (2004). Blessing or Curse?: Work-Family Policies and Mother's Wage Growth Over Time. Work and Occupations, 31(3), 367–394. https://doi.org/10.1177/0730888404266364.

Glavin, P., & Schieman, S. (2022). Dependency and Hardship in the Gig Economy: The Mental Health Consequences of Platform Work. Socius, 8, 23780231221082414. https://doi.org/10.1177/23780231221082414.

Glavin, P., Schieman, S., & Reid, S. (2011). Boundary-Spanning Work Demands and Their Consequences for Guilt and Psychological Distress. Journal of Health and Social Behavior, 52(1), 43–57. https://doi.org/10.1177/0022146510395023.

Godwyn, M. (2006). Using Emotional Labor to Create and Maintain Relationships in Service Interactions. Symbolic Interaction, 29(4), 487–506. https://doi.org/10.1525/si.2006.29.4.487.

Guarino, C. M., & Borden, V. M. H. (2017). Faculty Service Loads and Gender: Are Women Taking Care of the Academic Family? Research in Higher Education, 58(6), 672–694. https://doi.org/10.1007/s11162-017-9454-2.

Hall, W. M., Schmader, T., & Croft, E. (2015). Engineering Exchanges: Daily Social Identity Threat Predicts Burnout Among Female Engineers. Social Psychological and Personality Science, 6(5), 528–534. https://doi.org/10.1177/1948550615572637.

Hall, W., Schmader, T., Aday, A., & Croft, E. (2019). Decoding the Dynamics of Social Identity Threat in the Workplace: A Within-Person Analysis of Women's and Men's Interactions in STEM. Social Psychological and Personality Science, 10(4), 542–552. https://doi.org/10.1177/1948550618772582.

Harlow, R. (2003). "Race Doesn't Matter, but...": The Effect of Race on Professors' Experiences and Emotion Management in the Undergraduate College Classroom. Social Psychology Quarterly, 66(4), 348–363. https://doi.org/10.2307/1519834.

Haynes, K. (2024). Resisting Sexisms, Aggression, and Burnout in Academic Leadership: Surviving in the Gendered Managerial Academy. Gender, Work & Organization, 1–17. https://doi.org/10.1111/gwao.13137.

Hays, S. (1996). The Cultural Contradictions of Motherhood. Yale University Press.

Hochschild, A. (1983). The Managed Heart. University of California Press. https://www.ucpress.edu/books/the-managed-heart/paper.

Hochschild, A., & Machung, A. (1989). The Second Shift: Working Families and the Revolution at Home. Penguin.

Hodges, L. (2020). Do Female Occupations Pay Less but Offer More Benefits? Gender & Society, 34(3), 381–412. https://doi.org/10.1177/0891243220913527.

Hutter, M. M., Kellogg, K. C., Ferguson, C. M., Abbott, W. M., & Warshaw, A. L. (2006). The Impact of the 80-Hour Resident Workweek on Surgical Residents and Attending Surgeons: Annals of Surgery, 243(6), 864–875. https://doi.org/10.1097/01.sla.0000220042.48310.66.

Ishizuka, P. (2019). Social Class, Gender, and Contemporary Parenting Standards in the United States: Evidence from a National Survey Experiment. Social Forces, 98(1), 31–58. https://doi.org/10.1093/sf/soy107.

Jackson, P. B., Thoits, P. A., & Taylor, H. F. (1995). Composition of the Workplace and Psychological Well-Being: The Effects of Tokenism on America's Black Elite*. Social Forces, 74(2), 543–557. https://doi.org/10.1093/sf/74.2.543.

Jacobs, J. A., & Gerson, K. (2004). Understanding Changes in American Working Time: A Synthesis. In Fighting for Time: Shifting Boundaries of Work and Social Life. Russell Sage Foundation.

Jacobs, J. A., & Winslow, S. E. (2004). Overworked Faculty: Job Stresses and Family Demands. The ANNALS of the American Academy of Political and Social Science, 596(1), 104–129. https://doi.org/10.1177/0002716204268185.

Jolivet, A., Caroly, S., Ehlinger, V., Kelly-Irving, M., Delpierre, C., Balducci, F., Sobaszek, A., De Gaudemaris, R., & Lang, T. (2010). Linking Hospital Workers' Organisational Work Environment to Depressive Symptoms: A Mediating Effect of Effort–Reward Imbalance? The ORSOSA Study. Social Science & Medicine, 71(3), 534–540. https://doi.org/10.1016/j.socscimed.2010.04.003.

Judiesch, M. K., & Lyness, K. S. (1999). Left Behind? The Impact of Leaves of Absence on Managers' Career Success. Academy of Management Journal, 42(6), 641–651.

Kaduk, A., Genadek, K., Kelly, E. L., & Moen, P. (2019). Involuntary vs. Voluntary Flexible Work: Insights for Scholars and Stakeholders. Community, Work & Family, 22(4), 412–442. https://doi.org/10.1080/13668803.2019.1616532.

Kalleberg, A. L. (2001). Organizing Flexibility: The Flexible Firm in a New Century. British Journal of Industrial Relations, 39(4), 479–504. https://doi.org/10.1111/1467-8543.00211.

Kalleberg, A. L. (2011). Good Jobs, Bad Jobs: The Rise of Polarized and Precarious Employment Systems in the United States, 1970s-2000s. Russell Sage Foundation.

Kalleberg, A. L. (2016). Good Jobs, Bad Jobs. In The SAGE Handbook of the Sociology of Work and Employment (pp. 111–128). SAGE Publications, Limited. http://ebookcentral.proquest.com/lib/iub-ebooks/detail.action?docID=4531683.

Kang, M. (2003). The Managed Hand: The Commercialization of Bodies and Emotions in Korean Immigrant–Owned Nail Salons. Gender & Society, 17(6), 820–839. https://doi.org/10.1177/0891243203257632.

Kanter, R. M. (1977). Some Effects of Proportions on Group Life: Skewed Sex Ratios and Responses to Token Women. American Journal of Sociology, 82(5), 965–990. https://doi.org/10.1086/226425.

Karasek, R. A. (1979). Job Demands, Job Decision Latitude, and Mental Strain: Implications for Job Redesign. Administrative Science Quarterly, 24(2), 285–308. https://doi.org/10.2307/2392498.

Kellogg, K. C. (2009). Operating Room: Relational Spaces and Microinstitutional Change in Surgery. American Journal of Sociology, 115(3), 657–711. https://doi.org/10.1086/603535.

Kelly, E. L., Ammons, S. K., Chermack, K., & Moen, P. (2010). Gendered Challenge, Gendered Response: Confronting the Ideal Worker Norm in a White-Collar Organization. Gender & Society, 24(3), 281–303. https://doi.org/10.1177/0891243210372073.

Kelly, E. L., Kossek, E. E., Hammer, L. B., Durham, M., Bray, J., Chermack, K., Murphy, L. A., & Kaskubar, D. (2008). Getting There from Here: Research on the Effects of Work–Family Initiatives on Work–Family Conflict and Business Outcomes. Academy of Management Annals, 2(1), 305–349. https://doi.org/10.5465/19416520802211610.

Kelly, E. L., Moen, P., Oakes, J. M., Fan, W., Okechukwu, C., Davis, K. D., Hammer, L. B., Kossek, E. E., King, R. B., Hanson, G. C., Mierzwa, F., & Casper, L. M. (2014). Changing Work and Work-Family Conflict: Evidence from the Work, Family, and Health Network. American Sociological Review, 79(3), 485–516. https://doi.org/10.1177/0003122414531435.

Kelly, E. L., Moen, P., & Tranby, E. (2011). Changing Workplaces to Reduce Work-Family Conflict: Schedule Control in a White-Collar Organization. American Sociological Review, 76(2), 265–290. https://doi.org/10.1177/0003122411400056.

Kesavan, S., Lambert, S. J., Williams, J. C., & Pendem, P. K. (2022). Doing Well by Doing Good: Improving Retail Store Performance with Responsible Scheduling Practices at the Gap, Inc. Management Science, 68(11), 7818–7836. https://doi.org/10.1287/mnsc.2021.4291.

King, D. D., Fattoracci, E. S. M., Hollingsworth, D. W., Stahr, E., & Nelson, M. (2023). When Thriving Requires Effortful Surviving: Delineating Manifestations and Resource Expenditure Outcomes of Microaggressions for Black Employees. Journal of Applied Psychology, 108(2), 183–207. https://doi.org/10.1037/apl0001016.

Kleiner, S., & Pavalko, E. K. (2010). Clocking In: The Organization of Work Time and Health in the United States. Social Forces, 88(3), 1463–1486. https://doi.org/10.1353/sof.0.0301.

Kleiner, S., Schunck, R., & Schömann, K. (2015). Different Contexts, Different Effects?: Work Time and Mental Health in the United States and Germany. Journal of Health and Social Behavior, 56(1), 98–113. https://doi.org/10.1177/0022146514568348.

Koltai, J., & Schieman, S. (2015). Job Pressure and SES-contingent Buffering: Resource Reinforcement, Substitution, or the Stress of Higher Status? Journal of Health and Social Behavior, 56(2), 180–198. https://doi.org/10.1177/0022146515584151.

Kossek, E. E., Lautsch, B. A., & Eaton, S. C. (2006). Telecommuting, Control, and Boundary Management: Correlates of Policy Use and Practice, Job Control, and Work–Family Effectiveness. Journal of Vocational Behavior, 68(2), 347–367. https://doi.org/10.1016/j.jvb.2005.07.002.

Kossek, E. E., & Ozeki, C. (1999). Bridging the Work—Family Policy and Productivity Gap: A Literature Review. Community, Work & Family, 2(1), 7–32. https://doi.org/10.1080/13668809908414247.

Kossek, E. E., Rosokha, L. M., & Leana, C. (2020). Work Schedule Patching in Health Care: Exploring Implementation Approaches. Work and Occupations, 47(2), 228–261. https://doi.org/10.1177/0730888419841101.

Kuhn, P., & Lozano, F. (2008). The Expanding Workweek? Understanding Trends in Long Work Hours among U.S. Men, 1979–2006. Journal of Labor Economics, 26(2), 311–343. https://doi.org/10.1086/533618.

Kunda, G., Barley, S. R., & Evans, J. (2002). Why Do Contractors Contract? The Experience of Highly Skilled Technical Professionals in a Contingent Labor Market. ILR Review, 55(2), 234–261. https://doi.org/10.1177/001979390205500203.

Landers, R. M., Rebitzer, J. B., & Taylor, L. J. (1996). Rat Race Redux: Adverse Selection in the Determination of Work Hours in Law Firms. The American Economic Review, 86(3), 329–348.

Lareau, A. (2003). Unequal Childhoods: Class, Race, and Family Life. In Inequality in the 21st Century. Routledge.

Lebel, R. D., Yang, X., Parker, S. K., & Kamran-Morley, D. (2023). What Makes You Proactive Can Burn You Out: The Downside of Proactive Skill Building Motivated by Financial Precarity and Fear. Journal of Applied Psychology, 108(7), 1207–1222. https://doi.org/10.1037/apl0001063.

Lee, J. J., Kelley, K., Mead, C., & Cha, Y. (2024). 'It's Just My Personality.' How Employees Make Sense of Their Long Work Hours in a Supportive Workplace. Community, Work & Family, 1–21. https://doi.org/10.1080/13668803.2024.2396600.

Little, L. M., Smith Major, V., Hinojosa, A. S., & Nelson, D. L. (2015). Professional Image Maintenance: How Women Navigate Pregnancy in the Workplace. Academy of Management Journal, 58(1), 8–37. https://doi.org/10.5465/amj.2013.0599.

Macdonald, C. L., & Sirianni, C. (1996). Working in the Service Society. Temple University Press.

Marchand, A., Blanc, M.-E., & Beauregard, N. (2018). Do Age and Gender Contribute to Workers' Burnout Symptoms? Occupational Medicine, 68(6), 405–411. https://doi.org/10.1093/occmed/kqy088.

Maslach, C., & Leiter, M. P. (2008). Early Predictors of Job Burnout and Engagement. Journal of Applied Psychology, 93(3), 498–512. https://doi.org/10.1037/0021-9010.93.3.498.

Maslach, C., Schaufeli, W. B., & Leiter, M. P. (2001). Job Burnout. Annual Review of Psychology, 52, 397–422. https://doi.org/10.1146/annurev.psych.52.1.397.

Matos, K., & Galinsky, E. (2011). Workplace Flexibility in the United States: A Status Report. Families and Work Institute.

Melamed, S., Shirom, A., Toker, S., Berliner, S., & Shapira, I. (2006). Burnout and Risk of Cardiovascular Disease: Evidence, Possible Causal Paths, and Promising Research Directions. Psychological Bulletin, 132(3), 327–353. https://doi.org/10.1037/0033-2909.132.3.327.

Moen, P., Kelly, E. L., Fan, W., Lee, S.-R., Almeida, D., Kossek, E. E., & Buxton, O. M. (2016). Does a Flexibility/Support Organizational Initiative Improve High-Tech Employees' Well-Being? Evidence from the Work, Family, and Health Network. American Sociological Review, 81(1), 134–164. https://doi.org/10.1177/0003122415622391.

Moen, P., Kelly, E. L., Tranby, E., & Huang, Q. (2011). Changing Work, Changing Health: Can Real Work-Time Flexibility Promote Health Behaviors and Well-Being? Journal of Health and Social Behavior, 52(4), 404–429. https://doi.org/10.1177/0022146511418979.

Muñoz, J. A., & Villanueva, I. (2022). Latino STEM Scholars, Barriers, and Mental Health: A Review of the Literature. Journal of Hispanic Higher Education, 21(1), 3–16. https://doi.org/10.1177/1538192719892148.

Munsch, C. L. (2016). Flexible Work, Flexible Penalties: The Effect of Gender, Childcare, and Type of Request on the Flexibility Bias. Social Forces, 94(4), 1567–1591. https://doi.org/10.1093/sf/sov122.

Nelson, L. K., Brewer, A., Mueller, A. S., O'Connor, D. M., Dayal, A., & Arora, V. M. (2023). Taking the Time: The Implications of Workplace Assessment for Organizational Gender Inequality. American Sociological Review, 88(4), 627–655. https://doi.org/10.1177/00031224231184264.

O'Connor, L. T., & Cech, E. A. (2018). Not Just a Mothers' Problem: The Consequences of Perceived Workplace Flexibility Bias for All Workers. Sociological Perspectives, 61(5), 808–829. https://doi.org/10.1177/0731121418768235.

Parker, K., Horowitz, J. M., & Minkin, R. (2022, February 16). COVID-19 Pandemic Continues to Reshape Work in America. Pew Research Center. https://www.pewresearch.org/social-trends/2022/02/16/covid-19-pandemic-continues-to-reshape-work-in-america/.

Pascoe, E. A., & Smart Richman, L. (2009). Perceived Discrimination and Health: A Meta-Analytic Review. Psychological Bulletin, 135(4), 531–554. https://doi.org/10.1037/a0016059.

Perlow, L. A. (2012). Sleeping with Your Smartphone: How to Break the 24/7 Habit and Change the Way You Work. Harvard Business Press.

Pierce, J. L. (1996). Gender Trials: Emotional Lives in Contemporary Law Firms. University of California Press.

Ridgeway, C. L. (2011). Framed by Gender: How Gender Inequality Persists in the Modern World. Oxford University Press.

Ridgeway, C. L. (2014). Why Status Matters for Inequality. American Sociological Review, 79(1), 1–16. https://doi.org/10.1177/0003122413515997.

Rudman, L. A., & Mescher, K. (2013). Penalizing Men Who Request a Family Leave: Is Flexibility Stigma a Femininity Stigma? Journal of Social Issues, 69(2), 322–340. https://doi.org/10.1111/josi.12017.

Salvagioni, D. A. J., Melanda, F. N., Mesas, A. E., González, A. D., Gabani, F. L., & Andrade, S. M. de. (2017). Physical, Psychological and Occupational Consequences of Job Burnout: A Systematic Review of Prospective Studies. PLOS ONE, 12(10), e0185781. https://doi.org/10.1371/journal.pone.0185781.

Sanzari, C. M., Dennis, A., & Moss-Racusin, C. A. (2021). Should I Stay or Should I Go?: Penalties for Briefly De-Prioritizing Work or Childcare. Journal of Applied Social Psychology, 51(4), 334–349. https://doi.org/10.1111/jasp.12738.

Sassler, S. L., Smith, K. E., & Michelmore, K. (2023). Cohort Differences in Occupational Retention among Computer Science Degree Holders: Reassessing the Role of Family. Sociological Perspectives, 66(6), 1060–1083. https://doi.org/10.1177/07311214231195024.

Schieman, S., Glavin, P., & Milkie, M. A. (2009). When Work Interferes with Life: Work-Nonwork Interference and the Influence of Work-Related Demands and Resources. American Sociological Review, 74(6), 966–988. https://doi.org/10.1177/000312240907400606.

Schieman, S., & Young, M. (2010). The Demands of Creative Work: Implications for Stress in the Work–Family Interface. Social Science Research, 39(2), 246–259. https://doi.org/10.1016/j.ssresearch.2009.05.008.

Seron, C., Silbey, S. S., Cech, E., & Rubineau, B. (2016). Persistence Is Cultural: Professional Socialization and the Reproduction of Sex Segregation. Work and Occupations, 43(2), 178–214. https://doi.org/10.1177/0730888415618728.

Sharone, O. (2004). Engineering Overwork: Bell-Curve Management at a High-Tech Firm. In Fighting For Time: Shifting Boundaries of Work and Social Life (pp. 191–218). Russell Sage Foundation.

Stainback, K., & Tomaskovic-Devey, D. (2012). Documenting Desegregation: Racial and Gender Segregation in Private Sector Employment Since the Civil Rights Act. Russell Sage Foundation.

Steffan, B., & Loretto, W. (2024). Menopause, Work and Mid-Life: Challenging the Ideal Worker Stereotype. Gender, Work & Organization. https://doi.org/10.1111/gwao.13136.

Stier, H., & Yaish, M. (2014). Occupational Segregation and Gender Inequality in Job Quality: A Multi-Level Approach. Work, Employment and Society, 28(2), 225–246. https://doi.org/10.1177/0950017013510758.

Stokar, Y. N. (2024). Sense of Failure in End of Life Care: Perspectives from Physicians and Nurses. Social Science & Medicine, 348, 116805. https://doi.org/10.1016/j.socscimed.2024.116805.

Stone, P. (2007). Opting Out?: Why Women Really Quit Careers and Head Home. University of California Press.

Stone, P., & Lovejoy, M. (2021). Opting Back In: What Really Happens When Mothers Go Back to Work. University of California Press.

Taylor, C. J. (2016). "Relational by Nature"? Men and Women Do Not Differ in Physiological Response to Social Stressors Faced by Token Women. American Journal of Sociology, 122(1), 49–89. https://doi.org/10.1086/686698.

Thébaud, S., & Pedulla, D. S. (2022). When Do Work-Family Policies Work? Unpacking the Effects of Stigma and Financial Costs for Men and Women. Work and Occupations, 49(2), 229–263. https://doi.org/10.1177/07308884211069914.

Thébaud, S., & Taylor, C. J. (2021). The Specter of Motherhood: Culture and the Production of Gendered Career Aspirations in Science and Engineering. Gender & Society, 35(3), 395–421. https://doi.org/10.1177/08912432211006037.

Tian, T. Y., & Smith, E. B. (2024). Stretched Thin: How a Misalignment Between Allocation and Valuation Underlies the Paradox of Diversity Achievement in Higher Education. Administrative Science Quarterly, 00018392241247744. https://doi.org/10.1177/00018392241247744.

Tomaskovic-Devey, D., & Avent-Holt, D. (2019). Relational Inequalities: An Organizational Approach. Oxford University Press.

Trejo, J. (2020). The Burden of Service for Faculty of Color to Achieve Diversity and Inclusion: The Minority Tax. Molecular Biology of the Cell, 31(25), 2752–2754. https://doi.org/10.1091/mbc.E20-08-0567.

U.S. Department of Health and Human Services. (2024, August 28). U.S. Surgeon General Issues Advisory on the Mental Health and Well-Being of Parents [News Release]. https://www.hhs.gov/about/news/2024/08/28/us-surgeon-general-issues-advisory-mental-health-well-being-parents.html.

van de Brake, H. J., van der Vegt, G. S., & Essens, P. J. M. D. (2024). More Than Just a Number: Different Conceptualizations of Multiple Team Membership and Their Relationships with Emotional Exhaustion and Turnover. Journal of Applied Psychology, 109(5), 714–729. https://doi.org/10.1037/apl0001168.

Van Yperen, N. W., & Hagedoorn, M. (2003). Do High Job Demands Increase Intrinsic Motivation or Fatigue or Both? The Role of Job Control and Job Social Support. Academy of Management Journal, 46(3), 339–348. https://doi.org/10.5465/30040627.

von Känel, R., Princip, M., Holzgang, S. A., Fuchs, W. J., van Nuffel, M., Pazhenkottil, A. P., & Spiller, T. R. (2020). Relationship between Job Burnout and Somatic Diseases: A Network Analysis. Scientific Reports, 10(1), 18438. https://doi.org/10.1038/s41598-020-75611-7.

Walsh, J. (2013). Gender, the Work-Life Interface and Wellbeing: A Study of Hospital Doctors. Gender, Work & Organization, 20(4), 439–453. https://doi.org/10.1111/j.1468-0432.2012.00593.x.

Watts, J. H. (2009). 'Allowed into a Man's World' Meanings of Work–Life Balance: Perspectives of Women Civil Engineers as 'Minority' Workers in Construction. Gender, Work & Organization, 16(1), 37–57. https://doi.org/10.1111/j.1468-0432.2007.00352.x.

Wharton, A. S. (2009). The Sociology of Emotional Labor. Annual Review of Sociology, 35, 147–165. https://doi.org/10.1146/annurev-soc-070308-115944.

Williams, J. (2001). Unbending Gender: Why Family and Work Conflict and What To Do About It. Oxford University Press.

Williams, J. C., Blair-Loy, M., & Berdahl, J. L. (2013). Cultural Schemas, Social Class, and the Flexibility Stigma. Journal of Social Issues, 69(2), 209–234. https://doi.org/10.1111/josi.12012.

Wingfield, A. H. (2010). Are Some Emotions Marked "Whites Only"? Racialized Feeling Rules in Professional Workplaces. Social Problems, 57(2), 251–268. https://doi.org/10.1525/sp.2010.57.2.251.

Wingfield, A. H. (2019). Flatlining: Race, Work, and Health Care in the New Economy. University of California Press.

Wingfield, A. H. (2021). The (Un)Managed Heart: Racial Contours of Emotion Work in Gendered Occupations. Annual Review of Sociology, 47(Volume 47, 2021), 197–212. https://doi.org/10.1146/annurev-soc-081320-114850.

Wingfield, A. H., & Chavez, K. (2020). Getting In, Getting Hired, Getting Sideways Looks: Organizational Hierarchy and Perceptions of Racial Discrimination. American Sociological Review, 85(1), 31–57. https://doi.org/10.1177/0003122419894335.

Wynn, A. T., & Correll, S. J. (2017). Gendered Perceptions of Cultural and Skill Alignment in Technology Companies. Social Sciences, 6(2), Article 2. https://doi.org/10.3390/socsci6020045.

Wynn, A. T., & Correll, S. J. (2018). Puncturing the Pipeline: Do Technology Companies Alienate Women in Recruiting Sessions? Social Studies of Science, 48(1), 149–164. https://doi.org/10.1177/0306312718756766.

Wynn, A. T., Fassiotto, M., Simard, C., Raymond, J. L., & Valantine, H. (2018). Pulled in Too Many Directions: The Causes and Consequences of Work-Work Conflict. Sociological Perspectives, 61(5), 830–849. https://doi.org/10.1177/0731121418774568.

Wynn, A. T., & Rao, A. H. (2020). Failures of Flexibility: How Perceived Control Motivates the Individualization of Work–Life Conflict. ILR Review, 73(1), 61–90. https://doi.org/10.1177/0019793919848426.

Yavaş, M. (2024). White-Collar Opt-Out: How "Good Jobs" Fail Elite Workers. American Sociological Review, 89(4), 761–788. https://doi.org/10.1177/00031224241263497.

Yavorsky, J. E., Keister, L. A., Qian, Y., & Thébaud, S. (2023). Separate Spheres: The Gender Division of Labor in the Financial Elite. Social Forces, 102(2), 609–632. https://doi.org/10.1093/sf/soad061.

Appendix C

Job Burnout: Consequences for Individuals, Organizations, and Equity

Alden Yuanhong Lai, Kenneth Z. Wee, Erin E. Sullivan, Amber L. Stephenson, Mark Linzer

This paper was commissioned by National Academies of Sciences, Engineering, and Medicine's Committee on Women in Science, Engineering, and Medicine. Opinions and statements included in the paper are solely those of the individual authors, and are not necessarily adopted, endorsed, or verified as accurate by the committee or the National Academies of Sciences, Engineering, and Medicine.

INTRODUCTION

Burnout is generally defined as "a state of exhaustion in which one is cynical about the value of one's occupation and doubtful of one's capacity to perform" (Maslach et al., 1997, p. 20). Maslach and Leiter (2022; p. 72) cautioned that when the mismatches between what organizations require of workers and what workers need to perform their jobs are not addressed, workers experience a "lack of control, insufficient rewards, breakdown of community, absence of fairness and value conflicts" at work, which can in turn lead to burnout. At a time when more than half of workers in certain occupations (e.g., physicians, applied psychologists) are reporting some form of burnout (Shanafelt et al., 2022; McCormack et al., 2018), understanding the range of consequences and the implications of this occupational phenomenon is long overdue.

As part of the program by the National Academies of Sciences, Engineering, and Medicine's Committee on Women in Science, Engineering, and Medicine (SEM), this paper seeks to highlight the consequences of burnout among the SEM occupations and their implications for equity. We conducted systematic literature searches across all three SEM occupations to synthesize evidence for the paper. It is organized into the following sections to reflect the consequences of burnout at multiple levels of workers' lives and our society. First, we highlight the individual consequences of burnout on health and quality of life, including mental health, cognitive function, and substance use, showing the array of consequences that burnout produces among SEM workers as individuals. Second, we highlight the occupational consequences, including decreased job satisfaction and increased turnover. Third, we highlight the consequences for organizations, showing how most attention has been paid to the impact of burnout on service quality. Fourth, although the literature here is comparatively scanter, we highlight the consequences of burnout for society at large, including greater use of, and spending on, healthcare. Finally, we highlight the implications of our findings for equity, including how burnout affects groups disproportionately by sex, age, race, job tenure, and job roles.

Overall, this paper shows that the consequences of burnout are pervasive among SEM occupations, with important implications for equity. It provides several recommendations. First, future research seeking to understand the impact of burnout should focus more on the consequences of burnout for organizations and society at large. Second, because burnout disproportionately affects women SEM workers and workers who are early in their careers, those groups deserve additional, and targeted, support from both leaders and institutions. Third, more attention is needed to understand how burnout affects the lived experiences of workers in underrepresented racial and ethnic groups, including the prevalence, consequences, and measures (i.e., how and when these groups choose to report burnout at work). Fourth, because most of the literature on burnout has concentrated on its effects on those working in medicine and healthcare, more research on the effects of burnout on those in the fields of science and engineering is both needed and warranted. Finally, despite some research gaps, we know enough about burnout to take action to ameliorate its consequences, including the conduct of high-quality interventions, especially for women SEM workers and those who are early in their careers.

APPENDIX C

METHODS

Evidence synthesis was conducted from July to September 2024. Our literature search took on a three-stage process to gather and synthesize the evidence. Because burnout has been so extensively studied, the first stage involved a review-of-reviews approach, where we focused on identifying review articles (e.g., systematic, narrative, meta-analysis) on burnout and its consequences across SEM fields. A reference librarian searched the databases of PsycINFO, MedLine, Web of Science, and IEEE Xplore using relevant search terms. We screened the resulting 6,459 articles and, from them, identified 98 articles for full-text review during this stage. Our exclusion criteria were nonresearch articles (e.g., opinion editorials); articles that did not investigate burnout; articles that did not investigate the consequences of burnout; and articles that did not focus on workers in SEM. An overwhelming portion of the articles produced in this first stage were based in medicine or healthcare, in comparison to science and engineering. We therefore conducted a second search for articles studying burnout in the fields of science or engineering specifically, but without restricting our search to review articles. This second search produced an additional 1,090 articles, from which we identified 35 articles for full-text review. We applied the same set of exclusion criteria at this stage. For this paper, we focused primarily on evidence from SEM workers based in the United States, although we cite studies conducted elsewhere if and where relevant. When reviewing articles in full text, we sought to extract the following information: research question/aim; whether the article was based in the field of science, engineering, or medicine; whether the article focused on individual and/or organizational outcomes; the type and number of participants; the measures of burnout being used; the consequences of burnout studied; and whether particular groups or subgroups at higher risk of experiencing consequences of burnout (i.e., equity issues) were described. In the third and final stage, we also performed backward and forward reference searches for 15 key articles (e.g., Schaufeli et al., 2009).

RESULTS

We make two notes about the results section. First, because the majority of studies used variants of the Maslach Burnout Inventory to measure and analyze burnout, the findings are occasionally specific to one or all of the subscales of the instrument (i.e., emotional exhaustion, depersonalization or cynicism, and reduced professional accomplishment or reduced professional efficacy).[1] In this paper, we distinguish among the three subscales of the Maslach Burnout Inventory, where relevant to the reporting of our findings. These distinctions, in turn, facilitate a more nuanced understanding of the consequences of burnout. Second, because most of the studies are neither longitudinal nor randomized in design, our discussions of their results are necessarily limited to describing associations. We suggest causation only in certain instances, such as when there is a dose-response relationship.

UNPACKING BURNOUT CONSEQUENCES

Individual Health and Quality of Life Consequences

The individual consequences of burnout refer to indicators of individual functioning, health, and well-being. Studies across physicians, nurses, dentists, and healthcare workers in general show that burnout is associated with reduced levels of physical health, of mental health, and of the quality-of-life for individual workers (see Box C-1). Workers experiencing burnout also report higher levels of anxiety and depression. The evidence of links between burnout and substance use and suicide ideation are, however, more mixed. Research has also documented an association between burnout and poorer cognitive function, especially the impact of burnout on memory. Finally, some studies have positioned burnout as a cumulative process in which individual-level consequences accumulate and become increasingly severe over time.

Mental Health

The relationship among burnout, anxiety, and depression as the individual manifestations of burnout has been the consequence documented most frequently in the literature (e.g., Ryan et al., 2023; Kratkze et al., 2022; Johnson et al., 2022). In a review of physicians, Ryan et al.'s (2023) review reported that 45 studies that examined the relationship between burnout and depression found a significant association, with correlations

---

[1] Broadly, *emotional exhaustion* refers to the depletion of emotional resources, *cynicism* refers to the distancing of oneself from work and developing negative attitudes toward work, and *reduced professional efficacy* refers to the tendency to evaluate one's work as negative. For a discussion on the terms and subscales, see Bakker et al. (2002) and Leiter and Schaufeli (1996).

BOX C-1
Summary of Individual, Occupational, Organizational, and Societal Consequences of Burnout Highlighted in This Paper

Individual:
Somatized symptoms (e.g., headaches, neck pain, body pain)
Physical health conditions (e.g., gastrointestinal infections, respiratory infections)
Mental health conditions (e.g., depression, anxiety, post-traumatic stress disorder, mood disturbances)
Appetite and sleep
Alcohol and medication use
Chronic fatigue
General quality-of-life and professional quality-of-life
Cognitive function (e.g., executive functioning, attention, memory)
Suicidal ideation

Organizational:
Reduced job satisfaction
Absenteeism
Intention to leave job and profession
Regretting career choice
Dropping out of training programs/engagement in professional development
Professionalism (e.g., irritability)
Work ability

Occupational:
Service quality (e.g., self-perceived errors, patient-reported care satisfaction, weaker patient safety culture)
Resources (e.g., social support, performance feedback) for workers reporting to burned out leaders
Financial costs due to turnover and reduced hours

Societal:
Healthcare use and spending (e.g., more referrals to specialists and hospitalizations, greater opioid and antibiotic prescriptions)
Change of service providers

between r = 0.41 and r = 0.74. Additionally, all 12 studies that examined the relationship between burnout and anxiety found a significant association, with correlations of approximately r = 0.46. Similar results were found among trainees (Kratzke et al., 2022; Johnson et al., 2022). Mukherjee et al. (2022) found that burnout was the second-best predictor of post-traumatic stress syndrome, after depression. Yang and Hayes (2020) reviewed the literature on burnout among psychotherapists and reported that burnout is related to physical well-being as well as their psychological well-being, including anxiety, depression, secondary traumatic stress, and psychological distress. Overall, workers who experience burnout, including physicians and nurses, also report poorer health, chronic fatigue, and lower levels of general quality-of-life and professional quality-of-life (Williams et al., 2020; Friganovic et al., 2017).

Substance Use

The evidence is mixed as to substance use among those experiencing burnout at work (Johnson et al., 2022; Ryan et al., 2023; Kratze et al., 2022; Williams et al., 2020). The majority of reviews report that workers experiencing burnout are more likely to engage in substance use, including psychiatric medications and alcohol. Ryan et al.'s (2023) review of physicians found that, of 16 studies that examined the relationship between burnout and substance use, only 1 found a significant association. The authors suggested the mixed findings to be a function of two factors. First, studies examining substance use often employ different measurement tools, making it challenging to draw consistent conclusions across studies. Second, substance use is often a comorbid outcome of both burnout and other mental health conditions (e.g., depression) and results differ depending on whether such confounding factors have been sufficiently considered (Ryan et al., 2023).

Suicide Ideation

A small number of papers have described higher levels of suicidal ideation among physicians, veterinarians, and trainees who experience burnout (e.g., Ryan et al., 2023; Ishak et al., 2013). Ishak et al.'s (2013) review of nine papers found that 45 to 71 percent of medical students experienced burnout and that those experiencing burnout are 2–3 times more likely to have experienced suicidal ideation in the past. Additionally, the authors observed that, although emotional exhaustion, depersonalization, and reduced professional efficacy all significantly predicted suicidal ideation, depersonalization had the strongest effect, even after controlling for depression. Ryan et al.'s (2023) review showed a significant association between burnout and suicidal ideation among physicians, with Ishak et al. (2013) showing similar findings among medical students.

Cognitive Function

Some reviews have evaluated the effect of burnout on workers and trainees' cognitive function—comprising executive functioning, attention, and memory (Renaud & Lacroix, 2023; Deligkaris et al., 2014; Gavelin et al., 2022). For example, Saxena (2024) concluded that among 513 science, technology, engineering, and mathematics students, burnout was associated with mind-wandering (i.e., not focusing on tasks on hand). However, certain methodological challenges, such as not controlling for confounding factors or not including more severe cases of burnout in the subject pool, have prevented researchers from drawing more definitive conclusions about the effect of burnout on cognitive functioning (Deligkaris et al., 2014). The strongest evidence to date is the effect of burnout on memory. Renaud and Lacroix's (2023) review reported that burnout had a strong association with memory performance, with workers experiencing burnout exhibiting both poorer prospective memory and delayed memory. Gavelin et al. (2022) noted that burnout had a small but significant effect on working memory. On the other hand, evidence of the effect of burnout on executive functioning (with the subcomponents of inhibiting, switching, and updating), and the effect of burnout on attention, are more mixed. Inhibition is the ability to control one's attention, behavior, or thinking by preventing distraction or the use of learned reflexes; switching is the ability to change perspectives when needed; and updating is the ability to refresh information that is relevant to the goal at hand (Renaud & Lacroix, 2023). For example, although Renaud and Lacroix's (2023) review found that burnout had a medium effect on switching and updating, Gavelin et al.'s (2022) review found that burnout affected both switching and inhibiting but not updating.

Viewing Individual Consequences of Burnout as a Cumulative Process

Some studies have conceptualized burnout as a cumulative process in which individual-level consequences become increasingly severe (Peck & Porter, 2022; Williams et al., 2020). These studies used the

Burnout Cascade Framework, which first emerged from occupational studies (Weber & Jaekel-Reinhard, 2000). Based on this framework, workers initially experience a burst of activity, but once this hyperactivity subsides, both activity and productivity decline. This pattern of decreased activity resonates with findings reported by existing reviews of how workers who experience the onset of burnout often seek to conserve resources, and therefore, reduce participation in professional growth or develop intentions to leave their job (e.g., Williams et al., 2020). In the later stages of the Burnout Cascade Framework, the consequences become more severe: workers begin to experience emotional, social, and psychosomatic malaise. The final stage of the framework points to diseases and harm to self. Specifically, Williams et al.'s (2020) work has highlighted the eight stages of burnout and their consequences as follows:

1. *Hyperactivity*: an initial period of high levels of activity, as evidenced by putting more effort into work to address increasing demands
2. *Exhaustion*: once hyperactivity subsides, a period of exhaustion in the form of fatigue and loss of energy
3. *Reduced activity*: a period of reduced capability and productivity in the form of disengagement
4. *Emotional reactions*: experiences of anxiety and fear
5. *Breakdowns*: experiences of impaired cognition, lack of motivation, and depression
6. *Degradation*: social isolation and physical withdrawal
7. *Psychosomatic*: psychosomatic symptoms including insomnia, headaches, gastro-intestinal disorders
8. *Despair*: chronic physical disorders, serious illnesses, or suicide

OCCUPATIONAL CONSEQUENCES

The occupational consequences of burnout are twofold: one, they refer to how one feels about their job and work environment; two, they refer to aspects of one's job performance in an organization or career advancement in their field (see Box C-1). A majority of studies in this area document that burnout predicts one's willingness to leave their job. Comparatively fewer studies have looked at how burnout predicts one's willingness to leave their profession or field entirely (c.f. Dall'Ora et al., 2020); we located two studies that show burnout is related to nurses' plans to leave the nursing profession entirely.

Overall, research highlights several occupational consequences of burnout, including lower job satisfaction, absenteeism, and reduced professionalism, productivity, and commitment to the organization.

Intention to Leave

Research has most commonly documented a relationship between burnout and SEM workers' plans to leave their job (e.g., Kratzke et al., 2022; Williams et al., 2020; Dewa et al., 2014). Ford et al. (2013) studied 287 information technology professionals employed by a university and found that emotional exhaustion and disengagement together explained approximately 53 percent of the variance in their turnover plans. A study of 360 engineers in India investigated the effect of emotional exhaustion on plans to leave and reported that emotional exhaustion mediates the relationship between role stress (i.e., stress from work stemming from role ambiguity, role conflict, and role overload) and plans to leave (Hazeen & Umarani, 2022). Indeed, a systematic review of 92 articles on information technology professionals, including software engineers, reported that planning to leave is the most studied and frequent consequence of burnout in the field (Tulili et al., 2023), citing studies conducted both in and outside the United States (e.g., Moore, 2000; Shropshire & Kadlec, 2012; Shih et al., 2013). In medicine, Hodkinson et al.'s (2022) meta-analysis of approximately 240,000 physicians found those who are burned out are 3 times more likely to plan to leave their jobs or regret their career choice. In a recent systematic review and meta-analysis, de Vries et al. (2024) reported that burnout was a primary determinant of nurses and physicians' plans to leave their job and profession during the COVID-19 pandemic. Specifically, the meta-analysis revealed that 38 percent of nurses intended to leave their jobs (pooled prevalence across 18 studies) and that 28 percent of nurses intended to leave the profession entirely (pooled prevalence across 16 studies). Fewer studies have examined the intention to leave the job and profession among physicians—de Vries et al. (2024) found only three and two studies, respectively—but those studies reported that 29 percent of physicians planned to leave their job and 24 percent planned to leave the profession entirely. Kratzke et al.'s (2022) review of surgical residents found that residents experiencing burnout are more likely to consider leaving residency, while Skillman and Tom's (2022) study showed that acute care nurses experiencing burnout are likely to leave the nursing profession altogether, with effort-reward imbalance as the strongest predictor. Ishak et al. (2013)

noted that medical students who are experiencing burnout are more likely to drop out of medical school. Locatelli et al. (2015) studied healthcare workers and found that employee voice, or the degree to which participants felt that they were included in decision-making or that their opinions were heard, may make them less likely to leave. The study found that healthcare workers with lower burnout scores and lower intention to leave their jobs tend to report that employees' concerns were more represented in organizational decision-making.

Job and career turnover can be challenging to assess in research, especially in cross-sectional studies, because participants are often lost to follow-up. Longitudinal research designs can therefore be helpful in better understanding the impact of burnout on one's job or career trajectories, although such studies are rare. Barthauer et al. (2020) studied German academic scientists (Ph.D. candidates and postdoctoral fellows) who took part in a time-lagged online survey at three points of time (1-year intervals from 2014 to 2016). The study examined the relationship between burnout and career turnover plans among German scientists from fields such as economics, engineering, information technology, natural sciences, mathematics, social sciences, and humanities. The results indicated that burnout is positively related to career turnover plans, but this relationship is mediated by perceived internal marketability and career satisfaction. In particular, academic scientists in science and mathematics were more likely to consider leaving their careers ($r = 0.11$, $p < 0.05$), while those in economics, engineering, and information technology were less likely ($r = -0.15$, $p < 0.01$). Additionally, those who had completed their Ph.D. and those with long-term contracts reported lower burnout and turnover plans, with significant negative correlations ($r = -0.11$, $p < 0.05$ for Ph.D. status, $r = -0.20$, $p < 0.01$ for contract status). Additionally, we located one longitudinal mixed-methods study that offered counterintuitive results on burnout and career change. Cherniss (1992) studied human service professionals (i.e., public health nursing, public law, mental health, teaching) over a period of 12 years, and found that professionals who experienced burnout within the first year of their career were less likely to experience a career change over the next decade. The author provided two possible explanations: that professionals who experience burnout earlier in their careers may be more reluctant to switch careers later to avoid having to go through a similar, negative experience again, or that experiencing burnout in the early stage of one's career can lead to greater investment in and commitment to their profession. Although this study yielded contrasting results, it had a small sample size (only 25 human service professionals) and was conducted between the 1970s and the 1980s.

Professionalism, Productivity, and Commitment

Burnout among workers has been linked to decreased professionalism and productivity at work. Hodkinson et al.'s (2022) meta-analysis showed that physicians experiencing burnout are twice as likely to show decreased professionalism at work. To illustrate examples of reduced professionalism, Zheng et al.'s (2018) study of a group of surgeons in China, for example, showed that they were prone to displaying irritability at work. Separately, Williams et al.'s (2020) review noted that physicians are less likely to engage in professional development when burned out. Dewa et al.'s (2014) review further showed that burnout among physicians was significantly associated with reduced ability to work, defined as "the degree to which a worker is physically and mentally able to cope with the demands at work" (Ruitenberg et al., 2012, p. 2), a finding that was echoed by Hodkinson et al. (2022). Studies among nurses document similar trends: Jun et al.'s (2021) review reported that burnout among nurses, especially emotional exhaustion, is negatively associated with both commitment to the organization and productivity. These findings are supported by other studies (Edwards & Burnard, 2003; Friganovic et al., 2017; Torlak et al., 2021). Separately, a study of 824 human service workers (which included hospital and homecare workers) in Denmark observed that workers who were in the highest quartile for burnout scores were absent from work due to sickness an average of 13.6 days a year, compared with an average of 5.4 days for workers with the lowest quartile of burnout scores, even after adjusting for socioeconomic, family, health, and lifestyle factors (Borritz et al., 2006).

Beyond medicine, we located a 2003 study focused on burnout among Australian civil engineers, 92 percent of whom were men. Although the study highlighted that engineers derived a sense of accomplishment from the social value of their work, it also noted that cynicism was linked to dissatisfaction with pay and promotion and that both cynicism and emotional exhaustion were significant predictors of turnover plans (Lingard, 2003). However, many engineers experiencing burnout remained in their jobs due to a perceived lack of better alternatives, raising concerns about underperformance in the construction industry. Additionally, we located two studies that examined the effects of burnout on organizational commitment among information services directors in the United States (Sethi et al., 1999) and software developers in India (Singh et al., 2012). In a sample of 312 information services directors in the United States, burnout was positively correlated with role stressors, with emotional exhaustion negatively impacting affective commitment (emotional attachment to the organization) but increasing continuance commitment (staying due to economic and social costs) (Sethi et al., 1999). Meanwhile, an Indian study of 372 software developers found that burnout decreased commitment to both the organization and to interpersonal relationships but, paradoxically, improved job performance (Singh et al., 2012); thus, software developers experiencing high burnout may perform better. Burnout among software developers was also associated with frequent job-hopping (average professional experience among software developers in their past job(s) is less than 2 years), work-family conflicts, and lower quality of life (Singh et al., 2012).

ORGANIZATIONAL CONSEQUENCES

Organizational consequences related to burnout refer to constructs that are linked to an organization's performance or attainment of valued goals. Most research on burnout and its impact on organizations has centered on healthcare organizations and their service delivery performance (see Box C-1).

Service Quality

A body of literature has focused on examining the quality of healthcare as an organizational consequence of burnout among medical providers (Mossburg & Dennison Himmelfarb, 2021; Rathert et al., 2018; Salyers et al., 2017; Johnson et al., 2022; Mangory et al., 2021; Rabatin et al., 2016; Tawfik et al., 2019; NASEM, 2019). A 2019 report on clinician burnout from the National Academies noted that the combination of the many consequences of burnout, including absenteeism, sub-optimal performance, and reduced effort have "a major impact on the ability of healthcare organizations to maintain an adequate professional workforce" (NASEM, 2019; pg. 71). However, higher-quality studies, including randomized trials and the use of a standardized and consistent set of outcomes, are needed to more accurately determine the magnitude of the relationship between worker burnout and service quality. Tawfik et al.'s (2019) review of the literature over a 25-year period with more than 240,000 healthcare professionals, for example, concluded that burnout was related to decreased quality of care in 58 studies, although they did not find this relationship in 50 studies. Rathert et al.'s (2018) review found that the association between physician burnout and medical errors was significant only in studies that measured physicians' perceptions, with no associations found in studies that used objective measures of medical errors, such as chart reviews or clinical records. Rabatin et al. (2016) could not confirm a correlation between burnout and the quality of healthcare outcomes when objective measures were used. However, numerous studies have documented associations between worker burnout and a range of quality-of-care indicators, including unsolicited patient complaints, patient dissatisfaction, hospital-acquired infections, and post-discharge recovery time, suggesting that it is important to consider the quality of care as an important potential consequence of burnout (Cimiotti et al., 2012; Halbesleben & Rathert, 2008; Trockel et al., 2022; Welle et al., 2020). Scholars have offered two perspectives in light of the mixed findings. First, our inability to draw more definitive conclusions is in part because of the variability with which the quality of care is defined (e.g., medical errors, safety culture, patient outcomes, patient satisfaction) and measured (e.g., clinical records, self-perceptions) (Dewa et al., 2017; Hall et al., 2016; Humphries et al., 2014). Second, an overly strong focus on the relationship between burnout among healthcare workers and quality of care can mislead stakeholders at-large into thinking that burnout is causing decreases in service quality, when healthcare workers are using their personal resources against organizational pressures to prevent harm to patients or decreases in the quality of care. Indeed, scholars have suggested that healthcare professionals act as buffers between adverse work conditions and patient care (Linzer et al., 2009; Wallace & Lemaire, 2009).

Nevertheless, there is consensus that burnout in workers affects service quality generally, especially when subjective or self-reported measures are used (e.g., Salyers et al., 2016; Owoc et al., 2022; Steffey et al., 2023). In a meta-analysis, Owoc et al. (2022) reported that 34 to 77 percent of physicians experience burnout and that these physicians are approximately 3 times more likely to make self-perceived errors, findings similar to a study of veterinarians (Steffey et al., 2023). Reviews have also found significant negative associations between burnout among healthcare professionals and perceptions of the culture of patient safety (e.g., Garcia et al., 2019; Mossburg & Dennison Himmelfarb, 2021). Garcia et al.'s (2019) systematic review and meta-analysis found that burnout among healthcare professionals reduces the incidence of actions taken to promote patient safety. Hall et al. (2016), in their review, concluded that the majority of studies show that clinician burnout is associated with medical errors, and they cautioned that objective measures, like chart reviews or clinical records, may not be sensitive enough to capture the extent to which burnout is affecting the quality of care. Indeed, Humphries et al. (2014) suggested that the quality of care should be divided into two components when evaluating the effect by burnout: technical (e.g., clinical elements such as diagnosis and treatment) and interpersonal (e.g., communication, respect, and time spent with patients). The authors suggested that healthcare professionals experiencing burnout are more likely to neglect the interpersonal dimension than the technical dimension (Khazen et al., 2022).

Researchers have also examined the differential effects of the three subscales of the Maslach Burnout Inventory on service quality. Overall, depersonalization and emotional exhaustion among physicians predict more self-reported medical errors, whereas professional accomplishment serves as a protective factor (Dewa et al., 2017; Salyers et al., 2016). For example, Shanafelt et al. (2010) reported that physicians experiencing higher depersonalization and emotional exhaustion are significantly more likely to report higher odds of a major medical error in the past 3 months, but those with higher professional accomplishment report lower odds. Rathert et al. (2018) documented similar findings for patient-reported care satisfaction, where patients were less satisfied with their care and experienced longer postdischarge recovery times when their physicians were experiencing higher levels of depersonalization (see also Hall et al., 2016). The effect of the magnitude of depersonalization versus emotional exhaustion on service quality has generated mixed findings. While Owoc et al.'s (2022) meta-analysis and Dewa et al.'s (2017) review found that depersonalization had a stronger impact than emotional exhaustion on self-perceived errors, Salyers et al.'s (2016) review reached a contrary conclusion: that emotional exhaustion is the stronger predictor. Jun et al. (2021) demonstrated that emotional exhaustion among nurses is the best predictor of decreased quality of care, patient safety, and patient satisfaction. Researchers have suggested that, because of reduced levels of empathy, feelings of depersonalization and emotional exhaustion are likely not allowing healthcare professionals to be attentive to patients' needs and to be patient centered in their communication, therefore affecting service quality (Garcia et al., 2019; Rathert et al., 2018; Wilkinson et al., 2017).

Interestingly, some studies reveal a cyclical effect between burnout and medical errors. West et al. (2006, 2009) documented, for example, that burnout leads to errors, which can in turn exacerbate burnout among medical residents. Studies that examine such cyclical effects remain rare, but they should be pursued to expand our understanding in this area.

Financial Costs

Several studies have sought to document the financial costs of burnout. For example, Han et al. (2019) provided a conservative cost-estimate of the impact of physician burnout, which was $7,600 per employed physician at the organizational level, and $4.6 billion at the national level annually, largely due to turnover and reduced clinical hours. Separately, Muir et al. (2022) estimated that hospitals that do not have burnout reduction programs in place for nurses incur burnout-related costs that amount to $16,736 per nurse per year, while hospitals with burnout reduction programs in place incur lower costs of $11,592—savings that approximate $5,000 per nurse per year. Muir et al.'s (2023) study highlights the "business case" of burnout reduction programs for workers, where efforts to reduce burnout are not only beneficial for employees, but also financially beneficial (among other dimensions) for organizations. Indeed, Cunningham et al. (2024) highlight that because the high cost and scale of turnover among nurses—existing studies suggest a range of $46,100–$88,000 per nurse, with approximately 19 percent of nurses planning to leave their jobs within 6 months—are much more significant than the cost of reducing burnout, there is a strong business case for organizations and leaders to protect workers from burnout.

Leader Burnout and Its Impact on Others

Within an organization, burnout among leaders can affect those who report to them, indicating a trickle-down effect among leaders and workers. Huang et al.'s (2016) study found that burnout among software developer leaders is negatively associated with changes in workers' resources at work, including decreases in autonomy, social support, performance feedback, professional development, self-efficacy, self-esteem, and optimism. The authors documented such changes over a 6-month period and that these changes were in turn associated with burnout among the workforce. A study of an academic medical center documented that approximately 10 percent of the variation in leadership behavior was associated with physician leaders' own levels of burnout (Shanafelt et al., 2020). While not focused on SEM workers, a multilevel analysis of 442 workers in 68 teams in child daycare centers in Germany demonstrated similar findings: That is, when leaders' workload was high, workers perceived lower levels of support from their leaders, which in turn correlated with higher levels of emotional exhaustion among the workers (Stein et al., 2020).

SOCIETAL CONSEQUENCES

Comparatively less research has focused on the broader societal consequences of burnout among SEM workers (see Box 1). Some studies outside the United States point to the impact of burnout on greater healthcare spending by society as a whole, such as more referrals to specialists and more hospitalizations. One study of 136 primary care physicians in Israel showed that physician burnout is associated with higher rates of referral for diagnostic imaging, specialist health services, and nurse-sensitive treatments (Kushnir et al., 2014). Nørøxe et al. (2019a) showed that, in a Danish cohort of more than 460,000 patients seen by 392 general practitioners, physician burnout was associated with a 19 percent greater likelihood of hospitalization among patients, due to a lack of appropriate interventions in primary care.

Other studies have sought to document different forms of the societal consequences of burnout. These consequences range from patient-initiated change of primary care physicians (which reflects poorer patient experiences) to greater physician prescription of opioids and antibiotics. For example, Nørøxe et al. (2019b) documented that in a Danish cohort of more than 550,000 patients seen by 409 general practitioners, patients are 24 percent more likely to change their doctors—unrelated to a change of address—when their general practitioners experienced depersonalization and 40 percent more likely to change their doctors when their general practitioners experienced reduced professional accomplishment. The authors explained that when physicians are experiencing burnout, they may exhibit less empathetic concern for patients or have longer waiting times for consultations, which can strain the patient-doctor relationship. Another study in the United Kingdom of a sample of 351 general practitioners showed that increases in emotional exhaustion and depersonalization were associated with 19 percent and 10 percent greater likelihood, respectively, of prescriptions of strong opioids (Hodkinson et al., 2023). The same study also showed that increases in emotional exhaustion and depersonalization among physicians are associated with 19 percent and 24 percent greater likelihood, respectively, of prescriptions of strong antibiotics.

DOSE-RESPONSE RELATIONSHIPS BETWEEN BURNOUT AND CONSEQUENCES

In our review of the literature, we located a handful of studies that have described dose-response relationships between burnout and its consequences. Peterson (2008) concluded that self-rated health, anxiety, and depression among healthcare workers increased in order of the following: workers that were not burned out, disengaged, exhausted, and burned out. Additionally, Kim et al. (2011) showed that higher rates of burnout among social workers are associated with faster deterioration in physical health over a 1-year period. In a study of approximately 1,600 general employees (across technology, academia, and administration), Toker and Biron (2012) found that physical activity attenuates the effect of burnout on depression in a dose-response manner. The authors observed that increases in job burnout and depression were the strongest in workers that did not report engaging in any physical activity, while the correlation was the weakest, to the point of nonsignificance, for workers that reported the highest levels of physical activity.

LONGER-TERM EFFECTS OF BURNOUT

We located at least two studies that described the time periods in which the consequences of burnout occur (or continue to occur). Although most of the studies neglected to use time series designs, thereby limiting the ability to track outcomes over time, they are nonetheless important in understanding how long the consequences of burnout persist. Hillhouse et al. (2000) reported that emotional exhaustion predicted mood disturbance in medical residents over a period of 1 year, and Hakanen and Schaufeli (2012) reported that burnout predicted depressive symptoms and life dissatisfaction among Finnish dentists over a period of 7 years.

BURNOUT CONSEQUENCES AND IMPLICATIONS FOR EQUITY

Differences by Sex

The consequences of burnout differ by factors such as sex, race, age, job tenure, and even job roles (see Box C-2). Most evidence to date on differences by sex has, however, focused on disparities in terms of prevalence or

BOX C-2
Summary of the Equity-Based Consequences of Burnout Highlighted in This Report

Differences in Outcomes by Sex:
Physical health conditions differ by gender (e.g., burnout associated with musculoskeletal disorders in women; increased risk of coronary/cardiovascular disease in women)
Mental health conditions differ by gender (e.g., higher stress, lower emotional well-being, greater fear and worry, and more significant anxiety than men)
Decreased resilience, diminished perception of success at work, greater for women compared with men
Less job satisfaction for women than men
Women are more likely to intend to leave job or reduce hours
Women are more likely to engage in certain coping mechanisms than men (e.g., counseling or seeking domestic support)

Differences in Outcomes by Race:
Underrepresented minorities experience higher exhaustion-related burnout, but are less likely to experience disengagement
Underrepresented minorities experience higher reported burnout with the experience of racial/ethnic microaggressions
Associations of burnout with poor diet and lack of sleep for Black students; associations of burnout with stress about grades and publishing by Asian students
Skin color showed inverse correlation with quality of life (e.g., physical and financial security, recreation, home life, healthcare, transportation)
Underrepresented minorities experience higher stress but lower burnout, though a large number of "Prefer Not to Identify" participants suggests concerns for metrics and perceived lack of safety when reporting burnout

Differences in Outcomes by Age/Tenure:
Younger and less experienced workers experience more severe consequences
Early-career professionals reported higher stress, depression, and mental health outcomes
Less tenure within an organization associated with lower intention to stay when feeling burned out
Late-career stages may have better coping skills as a function of experience
Association between burnout and low professionalism strongest in physicians in training

predictive factors. For example, a longitudinal study of radiology residents found that individual resilience predicts lower burnout, and that although women and men residents did not differ on resilience levels at baseline (i.e., the start of residency), women residents' resilience decreased significantly over a period of 3 years. Additionally, studies have also shown that women physicians reported higher stress, lower emotional well-being, greater fear and worry, and more significant anxiety, both at home and in interpersonal relationships (e.g., Peck & Porter, 2022). The focus on disparities in terms of prevalence or predictive factors is similar in engineering—in a matched-pair study of 102 engineers, women engineers who experienced burnout were more likely to see themselves as less successful at work, while this effect did not hold for engineers who were men (Etzion, 1988). Etzion's (1988) study, although less recent, also described that women engineers who experienced burnout were more likely to place importance on success "outside of work," suggesting the challenges for women engineers to achieve or integrate success in both work and nonwork (e.g., family) domains.

Among the studies that have examined disparities in terms of consequences, studies have shown that both health and health behaviors differ by sex. While not specific to the SEM workforce, Ahola et al.'s (2008) study on a nationally representative worker population in Finland found that burnout was associated with musculoskeletal disorders in women and cardiovascular diseases in men, even after controlling for other factors. In two studies of the general worker population in Israel who underwent a health examination, burnout predicted triglyceride levels as well as inflammation biomarkers in women employees, suggesting an association with increased risk for coronary or cardiovascular-related diseases (Shirom et al., 1997; Toker et al., 2005). When compared with men, women physicians and surgeons were at a higher risk of increased alcohol consumption as a function of burnout (Gold et al., 2016; Oreskovich et al., 2012; Templeton et al, 2019). Likewise, women physicians were 2.27 times more likely to die by suicide than women in other professions (Schernhammer & Colditz, 2004) or to experience suicidal ideation as a function of depression and burnout (LaFaver et al., 2018). Women physicians also had a higher suicide rate ratio than physicians who were men (1.76 versus 1.05; Zimmerman et al., 2024).

There are also differences between women and men in the consequences of burnout beyond health and health behaviors, although the evidence is more mixed. For instance, Klein (2010) observed that burnout was significantly associated with therapeutic and diagnostic errors in men, but not women, surgeons in Germany. However, in a study of patients in Sweden,

Gavelin et al. (2022) found no evidence of moderating effects of gender on the relationship between clinical burnout and cognitive impairment, suggesting that some cognitive outcomes of burnout may be consistent for men and women.

When considering work-related outcomes and coping mechanisms, women had higher odds of intending to leave a job, with Apple et al. (2023) showing 51.4 percent of women, compared with 42.4 percent of men, intending to depart among a sample of U.S. healthcare workers. Likewise, there were indications that women family physicians, in particular (Eden et al., 2020), and physicians inclusive of all specialties (Lyubarova et al., 2023) were more likely to reduce work hours, particularly to accommodate work-life balance. Women were also more likely to hire domestic help or talk to a therapist than men (Eden et al., 2020). Coping strategies were different among women in science; Lee and Riach (2024) identified three cognitive pathways through which these women navigate burnout: combative, regenerative, and promissory. More specifically, women using the "combative" ritual navigated burnout by resisting the status quo and asserting personal agency. Women using the "regenerative" ritual coped through reconciling and compromising. Lastly, women in the "promissory" frame coped through utilizing mental framings that showed movement away from the burnout experience (e.g., put burnout behind them). The identification of these cognitive pathways highlights the diverse ways in which women navigate burnout, with each approach reflecting different coping strategies and responses to workplace stress. These observations emphasize the need for organizations to recognize the varied emotional and cognitive processes in which women engage when experiencing burnout, because tailored interventions that acknowledge these differences may be more effective in addressing burnout and promoting well-being in the long term.

While there were differences in consequences of burnout by sex, it should also be noted that the prevalence of burnout among men, compared with women, is widely established in the literature. Women in primary care were more likely to report burnout (Apaydin et al., 2021) and women physicians and engineers tended to report higher levels of burnout than men (Marshall et al., 2020; Ronen & Pines, 2008). Mehta et al. (2019) found that women cardiologists reported burnout more frequently than men (31 percent vs. 24 percent). Similarly, Cullen et al. (2021) surveyed cardiovascular program directors and reported that women were less satisfied with their jobs and experienced higher stress levels than men, and that men reported higher rates of enjoyment without burnout (43 percent vs. 13 percent), though this finding must be cautiously interpreted due to the smaller sample size of women in the study (22 women vs. 78 men). Women veterinarians showed early signs of burnout more frequently than veterinarians who were men (Elkins, 1992, in Platt et al., 2012), and women biosafety lab technicians in China had a higher job burnout detection rate (Lu et al., 2021). In physicians, women had 60 percent higher odds of being burned out than men (McMurray et al., 2000), and that gap has persisted over time (Linzer et al., 2020) with burnout being almost twice as high for women physicians in some studies (Linzer et al., 2024). The differences in prevalence are also true for women engineers, who reported higher levels of burnout than engineers who were men (Ronen & Pines, 2008).

The differences in burnout prevalence by sex may be due to higher expectations for spending more time by women physicians. These gendered expectations may contribute to higher burnout rates in multiple fields (Linzer & Harwood, 2018). Indeed, research on clinician-scientists indicates that gendered expectations of women at work and at home are imposing significant mental burden and stress on women (Szczygiel et al., 2024). Some studies suggested that burnout rates are highest in nonbinary respondents and nurses when compared with other health workers (e.g., Prasad et al., 2021). Also, the role of the organizational environment should not be overlooked, as it is associated with the experience of burnout. Women in SEM fields who are exposed to environments that challenge their professional identity (e.g., science is seen as a men's occupation), and where the environments are unwelcoming or hostile toward women, experience higher levels of burnout (Jensen & Deemer, 2019).

Differences by Race

Literature that examined the differential consequences of burnout by race was sparse. In a systematic review, Lawrence et al. (2022) noted the wide variation in burnout among underrepresented minorities in medicine, although studies examining prevalence yielded inconsistent findings. When examining medical students whose races are underrepresented in medicine, O'Marr et al. (2022) indicated that underrepresented minorities tended to be in the top quartile of exhaustion-related burnout but were less likely to experience disengagement from burnout. In a study of sexist and racial/ethnic microaggressions against women physicians, women physicians who identified as racial minorities and experienced racial/ethnic microaggressions were more likely to report burnout, though the consequences were not examined (Sudol et al., 2021). In examining the intersection of burnout, gender, and racial identity, this result suggests women physicians who identified as racial/ethnic minorities who had a compound experience of microaggressions that were both racist and sexist had a higher likelihood of experiencing burnout compared with racial/ethnic–minority (OR, 1.60; 95% CI, 1.01-2.42; $P = 0.05$) and White physicians who were men (OR, 2.50; 95% CI, 1.51-4.14; $P = 0.001$; Sudol et al., 2021). In an examination of medical student burnout, Briggs et al. (2023) discovered that Black medical students reported that their experience of burnout was influenced more by poor diet and lack of sleep, whereas Asian medical students reported stress over residency, grades, and publishing pressures. In either case, as it was a cross-sectional survey, the authors did not attempt to claim causality. In examining the association between various facets of burnout and quality-of-life domains in Brazil, Pai et al. (2022) found an inverse relationship between depersonalization, skin color, and the environmental domain of quality-of-life. In the study, environmental indicators of quality-of-life included physical and financial security, recreation, home life, healthcare, and transportation.

Alternatively, in an examination of planned turnover among healthcare workers during COVID-19, Mercado et al. (2022) found that identifying as a person of color was associated with higher stress levels but lower burnout, a finding contrary to their hypothesis. This finding was also found in Prasad et al.'s (2021) study of coping with COVID-19, where persons of color were found to experience higher levels of stress but significantly lower burnout. These findings may have been explained in part by the large number (13.9 percent) of respondents who preferred not to identify (PNTI) race or ethnicity, a group that had substantially and significantly higher burnout rates (e.g., 42 percent burnout in Black respondents vs. 62 percent in those who PNTI). These data raised the question whether many persons of color do not find burnout surveys to be safe spaces to report burnout using standard metrics, thus making a case for a deeper look at burnout metrics and survey construction that would allow a fuller understanding of the lived experiences of minoritized groups and, indeed, of all survey respondents. Linzer et al. (forthcoming) suggest numerous reasons why those within healthcare systems who feel vulnerable may not perceive surveys as safe spaces in which to report burnout and propose ways to improve perceived survey safety and to provide convincing evidence that action will be taken to rectify adverse work conditions, if identified.

Some scholars assert that the lower rates of burnout reported by racial and ethnic minorities, particularly on the metrics of depersonalization and exhaustion, is further support for the potentially protective effects of delivering healthcare in a culturally diverse community, and that it is an asset to the healthcare system, as it could mitigate known effects of burnout, including turnover and poor quality of care (Douglas et al., 2021).

Differences by Age and Job Tenure

Research underscores significant variations in burnout outcomes based on age and job tenure, with younger and less experienced workers often experiencing more severe consequences. While there is evidence, for example, that mid-career cardiologists had worse levels of burnout than early- or later-stage professionals (Mehta et al., 2019), data on the consequences that have been reported for early-stage professionals is far more limited. Burnout has been shown to predict mental health outcomes for newly qualified nurses in several studies (Rudman & Gustavsson, 2011; Laschinger et al., 2015; Dall'Ora et al., 2020). Cullen et al. (2021) observed that early-career professional cardiology fellowship directors reported higher levels of stress than did their mid- and late-career counterparts. Furthermore, those in late-career stages experienced more enjoyment without burnout, while early-career individuals were more likely to consider resignation. In a study of early-career construction management professionals, Franz et al. (2023) observed that emotional exhaustion and cynicism among early-career professionals were similar to mid-to-late career professionals, but also that professional efficacy dimension was higher in the early-career group, suggesting a discrepancy of experiences across the dimensions of burnout. Research in technology also seems to suggest a U-curve of occupational consequences of burnout based on one's tenure in the organization: One study of more than 13,000 software professionals at a global information technology firm showed that new employees (< 6 months) had higher intention to stay compared with employees who had worked for 1–3 years at the organization, but also that employees who had 1–3 years of tenure were less inclined to stay when feeling burned out, compared with employees who had worked for more than 5 years (Trinkenreich et al., 2024). These findings raise two possibilities: that those in late-career stages have developed better coping skills as a function of experience or that there is a "survivor effect" among people who did not leave their jobs. Nurses who perceived more prominent levels of organizational politics, which might be more immediately experienced by those newer to the environment, also reported more burnout (Dall'Ora et al., 2020). Likewise, Peck and Porter (2022) and West et al. (2018) both found that younger, less experienced workers had higher rates of stress and depression, indicating that early-career stages are particularly vulnerable to emotional burnout outcomes. For instance, the relationship between burnout and patient safety events was most pronounced in younger physicians (20–30 years old), whereas the link between burnout and low professionalism was weakest in physicians aged 50 years or older (Hodkinson et al., 2022). Furthermore, a link between burnout and low professionalism was greatest in physicians in training, residents, and those working in emergency medicine or intensive care (Hodkinson et al., 2022).

Differences by Job Role

The literature revealed differences in consequences of burnout by job role, with a particular emphasis in healthcare, as driven by clinical responsibilities and patient interactions. According to Peck and Porter (2022), physicians were less likely to experience nervousness or anxiety compared with other healthcare workers; they exhibited fewer symptoms of depression than did nurses. Nurses working in COVID-19 wards, on the other hand, reported significantly higher workload changes compared with physicians and scored higher in the three dimensions of burnout: exhaustion, deterioration of relationships, and work efficacy. These observations are consistent with de Vries et al.'s (2024) systematic review and meta-analysis, which revealed that nurses are more likely to have the intention to leave their job and profession (38 percent and 28 percent, respectively) compared with physicians (29 percent and 24 percent, respectively).

When comparing physicians to physicians, Mukherjee et al. (2022) observed that 30.8 percent of frontline physicians fell in the high-risk category compared with only 21.3 percent of second-line physicians, described by the authors as those who did not directly treat COVID-19 patients. Similarly, 10.5 percent of frontline compared with 5 percent of second-line physicians reported high levels of Post Traumatic Stress Symptoms (PTSS). Burnout was the second-highest predictor of PTSS for frontline physicians. Additionally, the relationship between burnout and patient safety incidents was most pronounced in physicians working in emergency medicine given the critical nature of the work (Hodkinson et al., 2022). Indeed, a cross-sectional study of 11,743 nurses across 60 magnet hospitals in the United States reported that emergency nurses are significantly more likely to report burnout, job dissatisfaction, and intention to leave compared with other inpatient nurses who worked in the same hospital (Turnbach et al., 2024). A separate study of 221 hospitals in New York and Illinois documented that 58 percent of emergency nurses experienced high levels of burnout, and 27 percent intended to leave their jobs (Muir et al., 2023). In comparing primary care practitioners who specialize in women's health and primary care practitioners in general practice, burnout was higher in the former (55 percent compared with 47 percent), though there was no significant difference in intent to leave by provider type (Apaydin et al., 2021). These discrepancies can be due to gendered expectations for women physicians to spend more time listening during care delivery (Linzer and Harwood, 2018).

Beyond healthcare, we identified one study on Australian cybersecurity professionals that found that women security consultants reported higher levels of emotional exhaustion compared with their counterparts who were men (approximately 28 percent vs. 13 percent; Reeves et al., 2024). Gender and job role were significant predictors of emotional exhaustion, but not of depersonalization or professional efficacy. The study authors posited that women in cybersecurity, particularly in consultant roles, experienced higher burnout levels, possibly due to poor cultural fit in a men-dominated industry characterized by stereotypes, harassment, and lack of flexible work options.

DISCUSSION

This report shows that the consequences of burnout are both pervasive and consequential—they impact SEM workers at the individual, occupational, organizational, and societal levels and pose important implications for equity. At the individual level, we find evidence of lower cognitive function, poorer mental health, and substance use and suicidal ideation among some occupational groups. At the occupational level, we find consensus on the impact of burnout on one's intention to leave their jobs, and lower levels of professionalism, productivity, and commitment to the organization. At the organization level, we find a robust body of literature on the consequences of burnout on self-reported service quality, as well as pronounced estimates of financial costs related to personnel turnover and reduced working hours. While findings at the societal level are scanter, researchers have demonstrated how burnout among healthcare workers can be linked to greater healthcare use and spending as a whole. A handful of studies have also demonstrated a dose-response relationship between burnout and its consequences, suggesting the utility of conceptualizing burnout as a stage-like process with varying levels of severity that warrant different types and intensities of intervention at each stage. In terms of equity, we report striking gender differences in the health and health behaviors between women and men SEM workers, although the knowledge to date has focused on disparities in prevalence and predictive factors. We also raise issues and concerns surrounding SEM workers who identify with underrepresented racial and ethnic groups, who are younger and/or have less organizational tenure, and who are in certain job roles, such as being on the frontlines of care delivery.

We organize this discussion as follows. First, we synthesize areas in the burnout literature that represent existing evidence of the consequences of burnout and their implications for equity. We suggest these areas as blocks of foundational knowledge that can inform current research and practice, including interventions, on burnout. Second, we synthesize the perceived research gaps. Third, we discuss the implications of our findings for action—by both researchers and practitioners—in the future. Finally, we discuss the limitations and strengths of the report.

EXISTING EVIDENCE

Our findings suggest that there is already a strong knowledge base of the individual- and occupational-level consequences of burnout, and that research seeking to expand this array will have less impact when compared with research focusing on organizational- and societal-level consequences. Most of the published knowledge on burnout, however, is concentrated in medicine and the healthcare setting. This disproportion is plausibly due to differences in the nature of work between workers in medicine and workers in science and engineering. Maslach and Leiter (2016) and others have described burnout among the "caring professions" (i.e., healthcare, social work, education, and counseling) due to key characteristics these professions share, namely, the emotionally demanding nature of the work, the tendency for these emotional demands to lead to compassion fatigue (Figley, 1995), as well as workplace characteristics such as high workload (Demerouti et al., 2001), underappreciation (Stillman et al., 2024), or moral distress (Epstein & Hamric, 2009; Rushton et al., 2015). In addition to emotional demands, healthcare professionals like physicians, nurses, and other frontline workers also face intense requirements such as working long hours and at times the pressures of having to make life-or-death decisions (NASEM, 2019). In contrast, engineering and science professions are often viewed as highly technical and problem-solving oriented, with fewer emotional demands and emotional labor than the caring professions (Rasoal et al., 2012). Additionally, science and engineering disciplines focus on productivity and achievement, which may obfuscate burnout, or lead to it being underresearched. As Singh et al. (2012) demonstrated, there was a paradoxical relationship between burnout and improved job performance, meaning software developers experiencing high burnout may actually perform better. By comparison, the day-to-day tasks and work of the caring professions have more immediate concerns for human health, safety, and well-being—both of the professionals and of the people they care for—which may have driven substantial research interest in the field of medicine.

Our findings suggest that early-career SEM workers are particularly vulnerable to the consequences of burnout. Younger workers, and those with less tenure in the organization, face greater risks from burnout, which impacts their mental health, job satisfaction, and performance (Cullen et al., 2021; Hodkinson et al., 2022). This effect may be due to newness in the profession, feelings of being overwhelmed, and/or having fewer mechanisms for coping with stress at work (Dyrbye & Shanafelt, 2016; Satterfield & Becerra, 2010; Zhou et al., 2020). Additionally, early-career SEM workers may feel pressured to "prove" themselves or feel that they have less control over the situation, making them more susceptible to working longer hours and meeting high expectations (Shanafelt & Noseworthy, 2017). The constant pressure to perform and succeed, especially in highly competitive fields, can lead to a cycle of chronic stress (e.g., Rice et al., 2015). Without adequate support systems, mentorship, or opportunities for professional development, early-career SEM workers may struggle, and fail, to balance personal well-being with career ambitions (Dyrbye et al., 2019). Over time, this imbalance can exacerbate burnout symptoms, contributing to decreased productivity, lower retention rates, and even early exits from their chosen profession (Cullen et al., 2021; Trinkenreich et al., 2024). As a result, organizations and institutions must prioritize mental health resources, work-life balance initiatives, and mentorship programs to mitigate burnout and to support the long-term success of early-career professionals (Ripp et al., 2017; Shen et al., 2022).

Our findings also highlight that differences among occupations, work responsibilities, and work settings drive, in part, differences in the consequences of burnout. As a result, some SEM workers are at a higher risk of burnout and require more attention to burnout prevention and mitigation efforts than others. High-stress environments like healthcare or emergency response require quick, high-risk decision-making, and can often lead to severe emotional exhaustion (e.g., Hodkinson et al., 2022). Indeed, in our review of the literature, job roles that require a frontline presence were associated with higher burnout than job roles for non-frontline presence. Frontline workers in healthcare were encountering acute burnout specifically from direct patient interaction (Mukherjee et al., 2022). Moreover, differences exist even among frontline workers (e.g., physicians vs. nurses), suggesting that interventions will require tailoring to each occupational group (Peck & Porter, 2022). These differences exist because work conditions related to burnout and its mediators (e.g., feeling valued by the organization) vary by role. For example, Mallick et al. (2024) showed that, among cardiology physicians, a sense of meaning and purpose directly reduced their burnout, but among nurses and other clinical staff, a sense of feeling valued was most effective in reducing burnout. The mechanisms surrounding a sense of value had repercussions for staff turnover: physicians were the most vulnerable, leaving the practice within 1–5 years, while other clinical staff were the most vulnerable to leaving the practice within 16–20 years. These differences reflect how different types of roles and workers experience burnout and its consequences differently, with a different set of work conditions surrounding the outcome of burnout and its varied consequences. More research across varied disciplines and worker roles will be meaningful in expanding our understanding of these relationships and patterns.

RESEARCH GAPS

Regarding equity, differences in burnout consequences associated with factors such as sex, race, age, job tenure, and job role have emerged in the literature. The differences between men and women in both the prevalence and severity of burnout are striking. These findings may be associated with women having dual and often competing pressures of professional and personal responsibilities, being sought to take on "invisible" work not counting toward promotion, career development or income, and gendered expectations for greater listening while being allotted similar amounts of time for care as men (Linzer & Harwood, 2018; Ramas et al., 2021). For example, women experience unique challenges related to pregnancy, childbirth, and returning to work with lactation needs, to which men are not susceptible (Chesak et al., 2020). Highlighting the link between childcare stress and burnout, Harry et al. (2022) determined that healthcare workers facing high levels of childcare stress were 80–90 percent more likely to experience burnout, compared with those facing lower levels of childcare stress. Additionally, the study revealed that workers in underrepresented racial and ethnic groups had a 40 to 50 percent higher likelihood of reporting childcare stress than were White respondents, while women had a 22 percent higher likelihood of reporting it than were men with children. These figures suggest that SEM workers who are women, in underrepresented racial and ethnic groups, and have childcare responsibilities are the most at risk for the consequences of burnout. At the same time, addressing gender disparities in the experience and outcomes of burnout is crucial, especially as growing evidence, such as from Miyawaki et al. (2024), indicates that care by women physicians is associated with better clinical outcomes, including lower patient mortality. To avoid these gender disparities in burnout, workplaces must take intentional steps to reduce burnout through work redesign and acknowledgement of all work. Likewise, organizations can reduce gender disparities in burnout by offering more comprehensive support for childcare, eldercare, and pregnancy-related needs, including flexible work schedules and enhanced policies that can support a more equitable work environment.

When considering differences by race, there are some studies that suggest higher prevalence of burnout among ethnic and racial minorities (e.g., Armstrong & Reynolds, 2020), whereas others have posited that workers who identify as a racial or ethnic minority are less likely to provide identifying data, therefore making it challenging to fully understand the lived experience of underrepresented groups and what and how they choose to report (e.g., Linzer et al., forthcoming; Prasad et al., 2021). Single-item measures of adverse work experiences (e.g., negative experiences by race or gender; see Audi et al., 2021) show promise as a means of directly asking different genders, races, and cultures about their lived experiences. In this study, results of adverse work experiences correlated with burnout metrics. The authors therefore suggest that burnout may be viewed by many as a vulnerable outcome, suggesting "weakness" on the part of the individual who is burned out. Such feelings of vulnerability may make people who identify in racial and ethnic minority groups feel unsafe by reporting experiences of burnout. Current research on the reporting of compromising integrity and moral injury (LeClaire et al., 2022), where injury is linked to an outcome as a result of organizational actions and not necessarily perceived as a personal failing, may be worthy of future investigations to see when SEM workers in different gender, racial, and ethnic groups feel more comfortable identifying various detrimental work-related outcomes.

IMPLICATIONS FOR ACTION AND FUTURE RESEARCH

This paper has several implications for both action and for future research. Regarding action, there has been a lack of urgency to correct burnout findings despite the overwhelming evidence that the consequences are wide, deep, and serious. In particular, gender differences have been known for more than 20 years, and these should be made visible, followed, and addressed (Van Emmerik, 2002; Leiter et al., 2001; Vermeulen & Mustard, 2000). Proposals have been advanced, including adjusting for differential workloads and expectations (e.g., Linzer & Harwood, 2018; Lyubarova et al., 2023). Similarly, better metrics for understanding the lived experiences of those from racially and ethnically minoritized groups need to be developed through improved survey design, better perceived safety when participating in surveys, and qualitative and mixed-methods studies to listen to those in these groups and those who do not identify race or gender and learn how to better ask about and then understand and improve their work lives. To better include underrepresented groups who may prefer not to identify race and ethnicity on traditional surveys, researchers could benefit by adopting more inclusive and nuanced racial categories, emphasizing confidentiality to alleviate the fear of bias, and by employing community-based participatory methods (Linzer et al., forthcoming). Collaborating with trusted community leaders, members of the communities, and organizations can facilitate trust and engender a more natural space in which participants can share their experiences of burnout at work without feelings of individual vulnerability or weakness.

Additionally, new and more inclusive metrics may be required to understand what burnout means to workers in science and engineering, given that most published knowledge on burnout has been concentrated in medicine and the healthcare setting. Citing two surveys among software engineers, Tulili (2023) suggested that 80 percent were experiencing burnout in 2021, although data on the consequences of burnout among engineers is sparse. The wide spectrum of ways in which workers experience burnout appears to require newer, more nuanced approaches as we seek to include workers in studies of distress at work and how to improve job quality and work environments. In healthcare, for example, there is emerging evidence that moral injury as an outcome of adverse work conditions is a construct that connects strongly with a variety of worker roles and backgrounds (e.g., Dean et al., 2024). Using constructs like moral injury may therefore complement our understanding of the prevalence, antecedents, and consequences of burnout. Separately, cluster-randomized control trials of varying degrees of complexity (e.g., the Multiphase Optimization Strategy, or Sequential, Multiple Assignment, Randomized Trial; Collins, 2018; Kidwell & Almirall, 2023) can also be quickly implemented, supported at organizational and institutional levels with sufficient funding, and then published and advanced, through organizational learning approaches, to move the field ahead and alleviate the degree of human suffering we have demonstrated here (Greene et al., 2012). There is a universality among fields for what produces stress in humans who work (e.g., Karasek et al., 1981), and thus what can be done to improve it. We urge attention to these factors (e.g., time pressure, lack of control in the workplace, chaotic environments, and unsupportive organizational cultures) in the design of future intervention studies and actions.

In general, more research is needed to link the mechanisms of worker burnout with its organizational and societal consequences. Studies should focus on understanding the organizational and societal contexts in which human capital is being eroded or lost. There are areas replete with opportunity to deepen our understanding of worker burnout and its broader effects. One potential area to explore is the domino effect of burnout among leaders and how their well-being affects the employees they manage (e.g., Huang et al., 2016). This cascading effect can reveal how leader burnout contributes to increased stress, disengagement, and exhaustion among other outcomes experienced by the employees who report to them. These processes may also perpetuate a cycle of exhaustion within organizations, yielding harmful consequences like absenteeism and attrition, particularly in highly demanding fields like SEM. Understanding these dynamics could reveal how burnout creates organizational inefficiencies, hinders organizational efforts made to improve burnout, or even contributes to broader workforce shortages. Additionally, there should be longitudinal studies following the career trajectories of SEM workers who choose to leave their job or profession, and whether and how these workers choose to return. Consequently, future studies can then better track the effect of turnover with metrics that are beyond financial in nature, such as on the talent pipeline within the profession or field. Studies should also consider exploring the degree to which burnout among SEM workers influences creativity, innovation, or other desired aspects within an organization.

LIMITATIONS AND STRENGTHS

Our synthesis of the evidence has several limitations worth noting. Although 7,549 total articles were screened, it became clear that there is a relative scarcity of research in the fields of science and engineering, along with great variety in the approaches used to assess burnout outcomes. Furthermore, little research has been done to differentiate the consequences of burnout based on gender identity or race/ethnic identity, which limited our understanding of how burnout may have disparate effects on different populations. Additionally, the minimal presence of randomized controlled trials or longitudinal studies has relegated many results to assessments of correlation without the ability to assert causation or more robust linkages.

Simultaneously, our synthesis of the evidence has several strengths. We employed a multilevel, systematic approach using a review-of-reviews, as well as relevant nonreview articles, examining burnout at the individual, organization, and societal levels. This approach provided a comprehensive view of the impact of burnout at each of those levels. Our work was enriched by a multidisciplinary team of scholars in the field, ensuring depth and expertise throughout the process. We also adopted a horizon-focused perspective, considering the implications of our findings for future research and, ultimately, interventions that may help to address the continually growing problem of burnout. Importantly, we prioritized equity, aiming to use and advance the findings to foster a diverse and sustainable workforce in the fields of science, engineering, and medicine. Finally, the consequences of burnout, which to our knowledge are being systematically tabulated for the first time, offers a valuable resource to guide future inquiries, innovations, and, most importantly, improvements in the field for those working in SEM occupations.

CONCLUSION

The consequences of burnout are pervasive in SEM occupations, with important implications for equity. More research is needed on the organizational- and societal-level consequences of burnout in science and engineering. SEM workers who are women, early-careerists, and in underrepresented racial and ethnic groups require more research and both attention and support from institutions and their leaders. Although there are some gaps in our knowledge, we know enough to better support disproportionately affected groups and to address burnout and its consequences, especially for women SEM workers. We suggest that the time to take action against the consequences of burnout is now.

REFERENCES

Ahola, K, Kivimaki, M, Honkonen, T, Virtanen M., Koskinen, S., Vahtera, J., & Lonnqvist, J. (2008). Occupational burnout and medically certified sickness: a population-based study of Finnish employees. Journal of Psychosomatic Research, 64(2), 185–193.

Apaydin, E. A., Rose, D. E., Yano, E. M., et al. (2021). Burnout among primary care healthcare workers during the COVID-19 pandemic. Journal of Occupational and Environmental Medicine, 63(8), 642–645.

Apple, R., O'Brien, E., Daraiseh, N., et al. (2023). Gender and intention to leave healthcare during the COVID-19 pandemic among U.S. healthcare workers: A cross sectional analysis of the HERO registry. PLoS One, 18(6), 1–13.

Armstrong, M., & Reynolds, K. (2020). Assessing burnout and associated risk factors in medical students. Journal of the National Medical Association, 112(6), 597–601.

Audi, C., Poplau, S., Freese, R., Heegaard, W., & Linzer, M. (2021). Negative experiences due to gender and/or race: A component of burnout in women providers within a safety-net hospital. Journal of General Internal Medicine, 36(3), 840–842.

Bakker, A. B., Demerouti, E., & Schaufeli, W. B. (2002). Validation of the Maslach burnout inventory-general survey: An internet study. Anxiety, Stress & Coping, 15(3), 245–260.

Barthauer, L., Kaucher, P., Spurk, D., & Kauffeld, S. (2020). Burnout and career (un) sustainability: Looking into the blackbox of burnout triggered career turnover intentions. Journal of Vocational Behavior, 117, 103334.

Briggs, L. G., Riew, G. J., Kim, N. H., et al. (2023). Racial and gender differences in medical student burnout: A 2021 national survey. Mayo Clinic Proceedings, 98(5), 723–735.

Borritz, M., Rugulies, R., Christensen, K. B., Villadsen, E., & Kristensen, T. S. (2006). Burnout as a predictor of self-reported sickness absence among human service workers: Prospective findings from three year follow up of the PUMA study. Occupational and Environmental Medicine, 63(2), 98–106.

Cherniss, C. (1992). Long-term consequences of burnout: An exploratory study. Journal of Organizational Behavior, 13(1), 1–11.

Chesak, S. S., Cutshall, S., Anderson, A., Pulos, B., Moeschler, S., & Bhagra, A. (2020). Burnout among women physicians: A call to action. Current Cardiology Reports, 22(7), 1–9.

Cimiotti, J. P., Aiken, L. H., Sloane, D. M., & Wu, E. S. (2012). Nurse staffing, burnout, and health care-associated infection. American Journal of Infection Control, 40(6), 486–490.

Collins, L. M. (2018). Optimization of Behavioral, Biobehavioral, and Biomedical Interventions: The Multiphase Optimization Strategy (MOST). Germany: Springer International Publishing.

Cullen, M. W., Damp, J. B., Soukoulis, V., Keating, F. K., Abudayyeh, I., Auseon, A., et al. (2021). Burnout and well-being among cardiology fellowship program directors. Journal of the American College of Cardiology, 78(17), 1717–1726.

Cunningham, T., Caza, B., Hayes, R., Leake, S., & Cipriano, P. (2024). Design health care systems to protect resilience in nursing. Nursing Outlook, 72(1), 101999.

de Vries, N., Maniscalco, L., Matranga, D., Bouman, J., & de Winter, J. P. (2024). Determinants of intention to leave among nurses and physicians in a hospital setting during the COVID-19 pandemic: A systematic review and meta-analysis. PLoS One, 19(3), 1–21.

Dall'Ora, C., Ball, J., Reinius, M. & Griffiths, P. (2020). Burnout in nursing: a theoretical review. Human Resources for Health,18(41), 1–17.

Dean, W., Morris, D., Llorca, P.-M., et al. (2024). Moral injury and the global health workforce crisis. New England Journal of Medicine, 391(9), 782–785.

Deligkaris, P., Panagopoulou, E., Montgomery, A.J., & Masoura, E. (2014). Job burnout and cognitive functioning: A systematic review. Work and Stress 28(2): 107–123.

Demerouti, E., Bakker, A. B., Nachreiner, F., & Schaufeli, W. B. (2001). The job demands-resources model of burnout. Journal of Applied Psychology, 86(3), 499–512.

Dewa, C. S., Loong, D., Bonato, S., Thanh, N.X., & Jacobs, P. (2014). How does burnout affect physician productivity? A systematic literature review. BMC Health Services Research 14(325), 1–10.

Dewa, C. S., Loong, D., Bonato, S. & Trojanowski, L. (2017). The relationship between physician burnout and quality of healthcare in terms of safety and acceptability: a systematic review. BMJ Open, 7(6), 1–16.

Douglas, M., Coman, E., Eden, A. R., Abiola, S., & Grumbach, K. (2021). Lower likelihood of burnout among family physicians from underrepresented racial-ethnic groups. The Annals of Family Medicine, 19(4), 342–350.

Dyrbye, L. N., Shanafelt, T.D., Sinsky, C.A., Cipriano, P., Bhatt, J., Ommaya, A., West, C.P., & Meyers, D. (2019). Burnout among healthcare professionals: A call to explore and address this underrecognized threat to safe, high-quality care. National Academy of Medicine Discussion Paper.

Dyrbye, L., & Shanafelt, T. (2016). A narrative review on burnout experienced by medical students and residents. Medical Education, 50(1), 132–149.

Eden, A. R., Jabbarpour, Y., Morgan, Z. J., Wilkinson, E., & Peterson, L. E. (2020). Burnout among family physicians by gender and age. The Journal of the American Board of Family Medicine, 33(3), 355–356.

Edwards, D. & Burnard, P. (2003). A systematic review of stress and stress management interventions for mental health nurses. Journal of Advanced Nursing, 42(2): 169–200.

Epstein, E. G., & Hamric, A. B. (2009). Moral distress, moral residue, and the crescendo effect. Journal of Clinical Ethics, 20(4), 330–342.

Etzion, D. (1988). The experience of burnout and work-non-work success in male and female engineers: A matched-pairs comparison. Human Resources Management, 27(2), 163–179.

Figley, C. R. (1995). Compassion fatigue: Coping with secondary traumatic stress disorder in those who treat the traumatized. Brunner/Mazel.

Ford, V. F., Swayze, S., & Burley, D. L. (2013). An exploratory investigation of the relationship between disengagement, exhaustion and turnover intention among IT professionals employed at a university. Information Resources Management Journal, 26(3), 55–68.

Franz, B., Wang, T., & Issa, R. R. (2023). Exploration of burnout in early-career construction management professionals in the USA. Engineering, Construction and Architectural Management, 30(3), 1061–1079.

Friganovic, A., Kovacevic, I., Illic, B., Zulec, M., Kriksic, V., & Bile, C.G. (2017). Healthy settings in hospital: how to prevent burnout syndrome in nurses: literature review. Acta Clinica Croatica, 56(2), 292–298.

Garcia, C.d.L., de Abreu, L.C., Ramos, J.L.S., de Castro, C.F.D., Smiderle, F.R.N., dos Santos, J.A., Bezerra, I.M.P. (2019). Influence of burnout on patient safety: Systematic review and meta-analysis. Medicina, 55(9), 55–67.

Gavelin, H. M., Domellöf, M. E., Åström, E., Nelson, A., Launder, N. H., Neely, A. S., & Lampit, A. (2022). Cognitive function in clinical burnout: A systematic review and meta-analysis. Work & Stress, 36(1), 86–104.

Gold, K. J., Andrew, L. B., Goldman, E. B., & Schwenk, T. L. (2016). "I would never want to have a mental health diagnosis on my record": A survey of female physicians on mental health diagnosis, treatment, and reporting. General Hospital Psychiatry, 43, 51–57.

Greene, S. M., Reid, R. J., & Larson, E. B. (2012). Implementing the learning health system: From concept to action. Annals of Internal Medicine, 157(3), 207–210.

Hakanen, J. J., & Schaufeli, W. B. (2012). Do burnout and work engagement predict depressive symptoms and life satisfaction? A three-wave seven-year prospective study. Journal of Affective Disorders, 141(2-3), 415–424.

Halbesleben, J. R., & Rathert, C. (2008). Linking physician burnout and patient outcomes: Exploring the dyadic relationship between physicians and patients. Health Care Management Review, 33(1), 29–39.

Hall, L. H., Johnson, J., Watt, I., Tspia, A. & O'Connor, D.B. (2016). Healthcare staff wellbeing, burnout, and patient safety: A systematic review. PLoS One, 11(7), 1–12.

Han, S., Shanafelt, T. D., Sinsky, C. A., Awad, K. M., Dyrbye, L. N., Fiscus, L. C., et al. (2019). Estimating the attributable cost of physician burnout in the United States. Annals of Internal Medicine, 170(11), 784–790.

Harry, E. M., Carlasare, L. E., Sinsky, C. A., Brown, R. L., Goelz, E., Nankivil, N., & Linzer, M. (2022). Childcare stress, burnout, and intent to reduce hours or leave the job during the COVID-19 pandemic among US health care workers. JAMA Network Open, 5(7), 1–12.

Hazeen Fathima, M., & Umarani, C. (2022). A study on the impact of role stress on engineer intention to leave in Indian construction firms. Scientific Reports, 12(1), 17576.

Hillhouse, J. J., Adler, C. M., & Walters, D. N. (2000). A simple model of stress, burnout and symptomatology in medical residents: A longitudinal study. Psychology, Health & Medicine, 5(1), 63–73.

Hodkinson, A., Zhou, A., Johnson, J., Geraghty, K., Riley, R., Zhou, A., Panagopoulou, E., Chew-Graham, C.A., Peters, D., Esmail, A, & Panagiotti, M. (2022). Associations of physician burnout with career engagement and quality of patient care: Systematic review and meta-analysis. BMJ, 378, 1–15.

Hodkinson, A., Zghebi, S. S., Kontopantelis, E., et al. (2023). The association of strong opioids and antibiotics prescribing with general practitioner burnout. British Journal of General Practice, 73(733), e634–e643.

Huang, J., Wang, Y., Wu, G., & You, X. (2016). Crossover of burnout from leaders to followers: A longitudinal study. European Journal of Work and Organizational Psychology, 25(6), 849–861.

Humphries, N., Morgan, K., Conry, M.C., McGowan, Y., Montgomery, A., & McGee, H. (2014). Quality of care and health professional burnout: Narrative literature review. International Journal of Health Care Quality Assurance 27(4): 293–307.

IsHak, W., Nikravesh, R., Lederer, S., Perry, R., Ogunyemi, D., & Bernstein, C. (2013). Burnout in medical students: A systematic review. The Clinical Teacher, 10(4), 242–245.

Jensen, L. E., & Deemer, E. D. (2019). Identity, campus climate, and burnout among undergraduate women in STEM fields. Career Development Quarterly, 67(2), 96–109.

Johnson, J., Al-Ghunaim, T. A., Biyani, C. S., Montgomery, A., Morley, R., & O'Connor, D. B. (2022). Burnout in surgical trainees: A narrative review of trends, contributors, consequences and possible interventions. Indian Journal of Surgery, 1–10.

Jun, J., Ojemeni, M.M., Kalamani, R., Tong, J., & Crecelius, M.L. (2021). Relationship between nurse burnout, patient and organizational outcomes: Systematic review. International Journal of Nursing Studies, 119, 1–11.

Karasek, R., Baker, D., Marxer, F., Ahlborn, A., & Theorell. T. (1981). Job decision latitude, job demands, and cardiovascular disease: A prospective study of Swedish men. American Journal of Public Health, 71(7), 694–705.

Khazen, M., Sullivan, E., Arabadjis, S., et al. (2022). How does work environment relate to diagnostic quality? A prospective, mixed methods study in primary care. BMJ Open, 1–10.

Kidwell, K. M., & Almirall, D. (2023). Sequential, multiple assignment, randomized trial designs. JAMA, 329(4), 336–337.

Kim, H. J., Ji, J., & Kao, D. 2011. Burnout and physical health among social workers: A three-year longitudinal study. Social Work, 56(3), 258–68

Klein, J., Grosse Frie, K., Blum, K., & von dem Knesebeck, O. (2010). Burnout and perceived quality of care among German clinicians in surgery. International Journal for Quality in Health Care, 22(6), 525–530.

Kratzke, I. M., Woods, L. C., Adapa, K., Kapadia, M. R., & Mazur, L. (2022). The sociotechnical factors associated with burnout in residents in surgical specialties: A qualitative systematic review. Journal of Surgical Education, 79(3), 614–623.

Kushnir, T., Greenberg, D., Madjar, N., Hadari, I., Yermiahu, Y., & Bachner, Y. G. (2014). Is burnout associated with referral rates among primary care physicians in community clinics? Family Practice, 31(1), 44–50.

LaFaver, K., Miyasaki, J. M., Keran, C. M., et al. (2018). Age and sex differences in burnout, career satisfaction, and well-being in US neurologists. Neurology 91(20), e1928–e1941.

Laschinger, H. K. S., Borgogni, L., Consiglio, C., & Read, E. (2015). The effects of authentic leadership, six areas of worklife, and occupational coping self-efficacy on new graduate nurses' burnout and mental health: A cross-sectional study. International Journal of Nursing Studies, 52(6), 1080–1089.

Lawrence, J. A., Davis, B. A., Corbette T., et al. (2022). Racial/ethnic differences in burnout: A systematic review. Journal of Racial Ethnic Health Disparities, 9(1), 257–269.

LeClaire, M., Poplau, S., Linzer, M., Brown, R., & Sinsky, C. (2022). Compromised integrity, burnout, and intent to leave the job in critical care nurses and physicians. Critical Care Explorations, 4(2), e0629.

Lee, M. Y., & Riach, K. (2024). Beyond the brink: STEM women and resourceful sensemaking after burnout. Journal of Organizational Behavior, 45(3), 477–496.

Leiter, M. P., Frizzell, C., Harvie, P., & Churchill, L. (2001). Abusive interactions and burnout: Examining occupation, gender, and the mediating role of community. Psychology & Health, 16(5), 547–563.

Leiter, M. P., & Schaufeli, W. B. (1996). Consistency of the burnout construct across occupations. Anxiety, Stress, and Coping, 9(3), 229–243.

Lingard, H. (2003). The impact of individual and job characteristics on burnout among civil engineers in Australia and the implications for employee turnover. Construction Management & Economics, 21(1), 69–80.

Linzer, M., Baier Manwell, L., Williams E., et al. (2009). Working conditions in primary care: Physician reactions and care quality. Annals of Internal Medicine, 151(1), 28–36.

Linzer, M., & Harwood, E. (2018). Gendered expectations: Do they contribute to high burnout among female physicians? Journal of General Internal Medicine, 33(6), 963–965.

Linzer, M., Johnson, D., Stillman, M., & Goelz, E. (forthcoming). Potential implications of the large number of respondents who prefer not to identify gender or race on burnout surveys. Journal of Health Care for the Poor and Underserved.

Linzer, M., Mallick S., Shah, P., et al. (2024). Resident worklife and wellness through the late phase of the pandemic: A mixed methods national survey study. BMC Medical Education, 24.

Linzer, M., Smith, C., Hingle, S., et al. (2020). Evaluation of work satisfaction, stress, and burnout among US internal medicine physicians and trainees. JAMA Network Open, 3(10), e2018758.

Locatelli, S. M., & LaVela, S. L. (2015). Professional quality of life of veterans affairs staff and providers in a patient-centered care environment. The Health Care Manager, 34(3), 246–254.

Lu, Y., Liu, Q., Yan, H., Gao, S., & Liu, T. (2021). Job burnout and its impact on work ability in biosafety laboratory staff during the COVID-19 epidemic in Xinjiang. BMC Psychiatry, 21, 1–13.

Lyubarova, R., Salman, L., & Rittenberg, E. (2023). Gender differences in physician burnout: Driving factors and potential solutions. The Permanente Journal, 27(2), 130–136. doi: 10.7812/TPP/23.023.

Mallick. S., Douglas, P. S., Shroff, G. R., et al. (2024). Work environment, burnout, and intent to leave current job among cardiologists and cardiology health care workers: Results from the National Coping with COVID Survey. JAHA, 13(18).

Marshall, A. L., Dyrbye, L. N., Shanafelt, T. D., et al. (2020). Disparities in burnout and satisfaction with work-life integration in US physicians by gender and practice setting. Academic Medicine, 95(9), 1435–1443.

Maslach, C., & Leiter, M. P. (2016). Understanding the burnout experience: Recent research and its implications for psychiatry. World Psychiatry, 15(2), 103–111.

Maslach, C., & Leiter, M. P. (2022). The burnout challenge: Managing people's relationships with their jobs. Harvard University Press.

Maslach, C., Jackson, S. E., & Leiter, M. P. (1997). Maslach burnout inventory. Scarecrow Education.

McCormack, H. M., MacIntyre, T. E., O'Shea, D., Herring, M. P., & Campbell, M. J. (2018). The prevalence and cause(s) of burnout among applied psychologists: A systematic review. Frontiers in Psychology, 9, 1897.

McMurray, J. E., Linzer, M., Konrad, T. R., Douglas, J., Shugerman, R., Nelson, K., & SGIM Career Satisfaction Study Group. (2000). The work lives of women physicians: Results from the physician work life study. Journal of General Internal Medicine, 15, 372–380.

Mehta, L. S., Fisher, K., Rzeszut, A. K., Lipner, R., Mitchell, S., Dill, M., et al. (2019). Current demographic status of cardiologists in the United States. JAMA Cardiology, 4(10), 1029–1033.

Mercado, M., Wachter, K., Schuster, R. C., Mathis, C. M., Johnson, E., Davis, O. I., & Johnson-Agbakwu, C. E. (2022). A cross-sectional analysis of factors associated with stress, burnout and turnover intention among healthcare workers during the COVID-19 pandemic in the United States. Health & Social Care in the Community, 30(5), e2690–e2701.

Miyawaki, A., Jena, A. B., Rotenstein, L. S., & Tsugawa, Y. (2024). Comparison of hospital mortality and readmission rates by physician and patient sex. Annals of Internal Medicine, 177(5), 598–608.

Moore, J. E. (2000). One road to turnover: An examination of work exhaustion in technology professionals. MIS Quarterly, 24(1), 141–168. http://dx.doi.org/10.2307/3250982.

Mossburg, S. E., & Dennison Himmelfarb, C. (2021). The association between professional burnout and engagement with patient safety culture and outcomes: A systematic review. Journal of Patient Safety, 17(8), 1307–1319.

Muir, K. J., Sloane, D. M., Aiken, L. H., Hovsepian, V., & McHugh, M. D. (2023). The association of the emergency department work environment on patient care and nurse job outcomes. Journal of the American College of Emergency Physicians Open, 4(5), e13040. doi: 10.1002/emp2.13040.

Mukherjee, S., Rintamaki, L., Shucard, J. L., Wei, Z., Carlasare, L. E., & Sinsky, C. A. (2022). A statistical learning approach to evaluate factors associated with post-traumatic stress symptoms in physicians: Insights from the COVID-19 pandemic. IEEE Access, 10, 114434–114454.

NASEM (National Academies of Sciences, Engineering, and Medicine); National Academy of Medicine; Committee on Systems Approaches to Improve Patient Care by Supporting Clinician Well-Being. (2019). Taking action against clinician burnout: A systems approach to professional well-being. Washington, DC: National Academies Press. Ch. 4, Factors Contributing to Clinician Burnout and Professional Well-Being. Available at https://www.ncbi.nlm.nih.gov/books/NBK552615/.

Nørøxe, K. B., Pedersen, A. F., Carlsen, A. H., et al. (2019a). Mental well-being, job satisfaction and self-rated workability in general practitioners and hospitalisations for ambulatory care sensitive conditions among listed patients: A cohort study combining survey data on GPs and register data on patients. BMJ Quality & Safety, 28, 997–1006.

Nørøxe, K. B., Vedsted, P., Bro, F., Carlsen, A. H., & Pedersen, A. F. (2019). Mental well-being and job satisfaction in general practitioners in Denmark and their patients' change of general practitioner: A cohort study combining survey data and register data. BMJ Open, 9(11), 1–8.

O'Marr, J. M., Chan, S. M., Crawford, L., Wong, A. H., Samuels, E., & Boatright, D. (2022). Perceptions on burnout and the medical school learning environment of medical students who are underrepresented in medicine. JAMA Network Open, 5(2), 1–12.

Oreskovich, M. R., Kaups, K. L., Balch, C. M., et al. (2012). Prevalence of alcohol use disorders among American surgeons. Archives of Surgery, 147(2), 168–174.

Owoc, J., Manczak, M., Jablonska, M., Tombarkiewicz, M., Olszewski, R. (2022). Association between physician burnout and self-reported errors: Meta-analysis. Journal of Patient Safety, 18(1), 180–188.

Pai, D. D., Olino, L., Eich, L., Lautenchleger, R., Fernandes, M. N. D. S., & Tavares, J. P. (2022). Factors associated with the quality of life of multi-professional health residents. Revista Brasileira de Enfermagem, 75(6), e20210541.

Peck, J. A., & Porter, T.H. (2022). Pandemics and the impact on physician mental health: A systematic review. Medical Care Research and Review 79(6): 772-788.

Peterson, U., Demerouti, E., Bergström, G., Åsberg, M., & Nygren, Å. (2008). Work characteristics and sickness absence in burnout and nonburnout groups: A study of Swedish health care workers. International Journal of Stress management, 15(2), 153.

Platt, B., Hawton, K., Simkin, S., Dean, R., & Mellanby, R.J. (2012). Suicidality in the veterinary profession. Crisis, 33(5), 1–10.

Prasad, K., McLoughlin, C., Stillman, M., et al. (2021). Prevalence and correlates of stress and burnout among US healthcare workers during the COVID-19 pandemic: A national cross-sectional survey study. EClinicalMedicine, 35.

Rabatin, J., Williams, E., Baier Manwell, L., Schwartz, M. D., Brown, R. L., & Linzer, M. (2016). Predictors and outcomes of burnout in primary care physicians. Journal of Primary Care & Community Health, 7(1), 41–43.

Ramas, M. E., Webber, S., Braden, A. L., Goelz, E., Linzer, M., & Farley, H. (2021). Innovative wellness models to support advancement and retention among women physicians. Pediatrics, 148(2).

Rasoal, C., Danielsson, H., & Jungert, T. (2012). Empathy among students in engineering programmes. European Journal of Engineering Education, 37(5), 427–435.

Rathert, C., Williams, E., & Linhart, H. (2018). Evidence for the quadruple aim: A systematic review of the literature on physician burnout and patient outcomes. Medical Care, 56(12), 976–984.

Reeves, A., Pattinson, M., & Butavicius, M. (2024). The sleepless sentinel: Factors that predict burnout and sleep quality in cybersecurity professionals. Information & Computer Security, 32(4), 477–491.

Renaud, C., & Lacroix, A. (2023). Systematic review of occupational burnout in relation to cognitive functions: Current issues and treatments. International Journal of Stress Management, 30(2), 109–127.

Rice, K. G., Ray, M. E., Davis, D. E., DeBlaere, C., & Ashby, J. S. (2015). Perfectionism and longitudinal patterns of stress for STEM majors: Implications for academic performance. Journal of Counseling Psychology, 62(4), 718–731.

Ripp, J. A., Privitera, M. R., West, C. P., Leiter, R., Logio, L., Shapiro, J., & Bazari, H. (2017). Well-being in graduate medical education: A call for action. Academic Medicine 92(7), 914–917.

Ronen, S., & Malach Pines, A. (2008). Gender differences in engineers' burnout. Equal Opportunities International, 27(8), 677–691.

Rudman, A., & Gustavsson, J. P. (2011). Early-career burnout among new graduate nurses: A prospective observational study of intra-individual change trajectories. International Journal of Nursing Studies, 48(3), 292–306.

Ruitenburg, M. M., Frings-Dresen, M. H., & Sluiter, J. K. (2012). The prevalence of common mental disorders among hospital physicians and their association with self-reported work ability: A cross-sectional study. BMC Health Services Research, 12, 1–7.

Rushton, C. H., Batcheller, J., Schroeder, K., & Donohue, P. (2015). Burnout and resilience among nurses practicing in high-intensity settings. American Journal of Critical Care, 24(5), 412–420.

Ryan, E., Hore, K., Power, J., & Jackson, T. (2023). The relationship between physician burnout and depression, anxiety, suicidality and substance abuse: A mixed methods systematic review. Frontiers in Public Health, 11, 1–21.

Salyers, M. P., Bonfils, K.A., Luther, L., Firmin, R.L., White, D.A., Adams, E.L., Rollins, A.L. (2017). The relationship between professional burnout and quality and safety in healthcare: A meta-analysis. Journal of General Medicine, 32(4), 475–482.

Satterfield, J. M., & Becerra, C. (2010). Developmental challenges, stressors and coping strategies in medical residents: A qualitative analysis of support groups. Medical Education, 44(9), 908–916.

Saxena, M. (2024). Burnout and attention failure in STEM: The role of self-control and the buffer of mindfulness. International Journal of Environmental Research and Public Health, 21(8), 1000.

Schaufeli, W. B., Leiter, M. P., & Maslach, C. (2009). Burnout: 35 years of research and practice. Career Development International, 14(3), 204–220.

Schernhammer, E. S., & Colditz, G. A. (2004). Suicide rates among physicians: A quantitative and gender assessment (meta-analysis). American Journal of Psychiatry, 161(12), 2295–2302.

Sethi, V., Barrier, T., & King, R. C. (1999). An examination of the correlates of burnout in information systems professionals. Information Resources Management Journal (IRMJ), 12(3), 5–13.

Shanafelt, T. D., Balch, C. M., Bechamps, G., Russell, T., Dyrbye, L., Satele, D., et al. (2010). Burnout and medical errors among American surgeons. Annals of Surgery, 251(6), 995–1000.

Shanafelt, T. D., & Noseworthy, J. H. (2017). Executive leadership and physician well-being: Nine organizational strategies to promote engagement and reduce burnout. Mayo Clinic Proceedings, 92(1), 129–146.

Shanafelt, T. D., Makowski, M. S., Wang, H., Bohman, B., Leonard, M., Harrington, R. A., Minor, L., & Trockel, M. (2020). Association of burnout, professional fulfillment, and self-care practices of physician leaders with their independently rated leadership effectiveness. JAMA Network Open, 3(6), 1–11.

Shanafelt, T. D., West, C. P., Dyrbye, L. N., et al. (2022). Changes in burnout and satisfaction with work-life integration in physicians during the first 2 years of the COVID-19 pandemic. Mayo Clinic Proceedings, 97(12), 2248–2258.

Shen, M. R., Tzioumis, E., Andersen, E., Wouk, K., McCall, R., Li, W. Girdler, S., & Malloy, E. (2022). Impact of mentoring on academic career success for women in medicine: A systematic review. Academic Medicine 97(3), 444–458.

Shih, S.P., Jiang, J. J., Klein, G., & Wang, E. (2013). Job burnout of the information technology worker: Work exhaustion, depersonalization, and personal accomplishment, Information & Management, 50(7), 582–589.

Shirom, A., Westman, M., Shamai, O., & Carel, R. S. (1997). Effects of work overload and burnout on cholesterol and triglycerides levels: The moderating effects of emotional reactivity among male and female employees. Journal of Occupational Health Psychology, 2(4), 275.

Shropshire, J., & Kadlec, C. (2012). I'm leaving the IT field: The impact of stress, job insecurity, and burnout on IT professionals. International Journal of Information and Communication Technology Research, 2(1).

Singh, P., Suar, D., & Leiter, M. P. (2012). Antecedents, work-related consequences, and buffers of job burnout among Indian software developers. Journal of Leadership & Organizational Studies, 19(1), 83–104.

Skillman, D. and R. Toms (2022). Factors influencing nurse intent to leave acute care hospitals: A systematic literature review. The Journal of nursing administration 52(12): 640–645.

Steffey, M. A., Griffon, D. J., Risselada, M., Scharf, V. F., Buote, N. J., Zamprogno, H., & Winter, A. L. (2023). Veterinarian burnout demographics and organizational impacts: A narrative review. Frontiers in Veterinary Science, 10, 1–22.

Stein, M., Vincent-Hoeper, S., & Gregersen, S. (2020). Why busy leaders may have exhausted followers: A multilevel perspective on supportive leadership. Leadership & Organization Development Journal, 41(6), 829–845.

Stillman, M., Sullivan, E. E., Prasad, K., et al. (2024). Understanding what leaders can do to facilitate healthcare workers' feeling valued: Improving our knowledge of the strongest burnout mitigator. BMJ Leader.

Sudol, N. T., Guaderrama, N. M., Honsberger, P., Weiss, J., Li, Q., & Whitcomb, E. L. (2021). Prevalence and nature of sexist and racial/ethnic microaggressions against surgeons and anesthesiologists. JAMA Surgery, 156(5), e210265–e210265.

Szczygiel, L. A., Greene, A. K., Cutter, C. M., et al. (2024). Professional experiences and career trajectories of mid- to senior-career women clinician-scientists: A qualitative study. JAMA Network Open, 7(4), e246040–e246040.

Tawfik, D. S., Scheid, A., Profit, J., Shanafelt, T., Trockel, M., Adair, K. C., et al. (2019). Evidence relating health care provider burnout and quality of care: A systematic review and meta-analysis. Annals of Internal Medicine, 171(8), 555–567.

Templeton, K., Bernstein, C. A., & Sukhera, J, et al. (2019). Gender-based differences in burnout: Issues faced by women physicians. NAM Perspectives.

Toker, S., & Biron, M. (2012). Job burnout and depression: Unraveling their temporal relationship and considering the role of physical activity. Journal of Applied Psychology, 97(3), 699–710.

Toker, S., Shirom, A., Shapira, I., Berliner, S., & Melamed, S. (2005). The association between burnout, depression, anxiety, and inflammation biomarkers: C-reactive protein and fibrinogen in men and women. Journal of Occupational Health Psychology, 10(4), 344–362.

Torlak, N. G., Kuzey, C., Sait Dinc, M. & Budur, T. (2021). Links connecting nurses' planned behavior, burnout, job satisfaction, and organizational citizenship behavior. Journal of Workplace Behavioral Health, 36(1): 77–103.

Trinkenreich, B., Santos, F., & Stol, K. J. (2024). Predicting attrition among software professionals: Antecedents and consequences of burnout and engagement. ACM Transactions on Software Engineering and Methodology, 33(8), 1–45.

Trockel, J., Bohman, B., Wang, H., Cooper, W., Welle, D., & Shanafelt, T. D. (2022). Assessment of the relationship between an adverse impact of work on physicians' personal relationships and unsolicited patient complaints. Mayo Clinic Proceedings, 97(9), 1680–1691.

Tulili, T. R., Capiluppi, A., & Rastogi, A. (2023). Burnout in software engineering: A systematic mapping study. Information and Software Technology, 155, 107116.

Turnbach, E., Coates, L., Vanek, F. D., Cotter, E., Pogue, C. A., Clark, R. R. S., Aiken, L. H., & United States Clinician Well-being Study Consortium, Philadelphia, PA. (2024). Emergency nurses' well-being in magnet hospitals and recommendations for improvements in work environments: A multicenter cross-sectional observational study. Journal of Emergency Nursing, 50(1), 153–160.

Van Emmerik, I. H. (2002). Gender differences in the effects of coping assistance on the reduction of burnout in academic staff. Work & Stress, 16(3), 251–263.

Vermeulen, M., & Mustard, C. (2000). Gender differences in job strain, social support at work, and psychological distress. Journal of Occupational Health Psychology, 5(4), 428.

Wallace, J. E., & Lemaire, J. (2009). Physician well-being and quality of patient care: An exploratory study of the missing link. Psychology, Health and Medicine, 14(5), 545–552.

Weber, A., & Jaekel-Reinhard, A. (2000). Burnout syndrome: A disease of modern societies? Occupational Medicine, 50, 512–517.

Welle, D., Trockel, M. T., Hamidi, M. S., Hickson, G. B., Menon, N. K., Shanafelt, T. D., & Cooper, W. O. (2020). Association of occupational distress and sleep-related impairment in physicians with unsolicited patient complaints. Mayo Clinic Proceedings, 95(4), 719–726.

West, C. P., Huschka, M. M., Novotny, P. J., Sloan, J. A., Kolars, J. C., Habermann, T. M., & Shanafelt, T. D. (2006). Association of perceived medical errors with resident distress and empathy: A prospective longitudinal study. Jama, 296(9), 1071–1078.

West, C. P., Tan, A. D., Habermann, T. M., Sloan, J. A., & Shanafelt, T. D. (2009). Association of resident fatigue and distress with perceived medical errors. JAMA, 302(12), 1294–1300.

West, C. P., Dyrbye, L. N., & Shanafelt, T. D. (2018). Physician burnout: contributors, consequences and solutions. Journal of Internal Medicine, 283(6), 516–529.

Wilkinson, H., Whittington, R., Perry, L., & Eames, C. (2017). Examining the relationship between burnout and empathy in healthcare professionals: A systematic review. Burnout Research, 6, 18–29.

Williams, E. S., Rathert, C., & Buttigieg, S. C. (2020). The personal and professional consequences of physician burnout: A systematic review of the literature. Medical Care Research and Review, 77(5), 371–386.

Yang, Y., & Hayes, J. A. (2020). Causes and consequences of burnout among mental health professionals: A practice-oriented review of recent empirical literature. Psychotherapy, 57(3), 426–436.

Zheng, H., Shao, H., & Zhou, Y. (2018). Burnout among Chinese adult reconstructive surgeons: Incidence, risk factors, and relationship with intraoperative irritability. The Journal of Arthroplasty, 33(4), 1253–1257.

Zhou, A. Y., Panagioti, M., Esmail, A., Agius, R., Van Tongeren, M., & Bower, P. (2020). Factors associated with burnout and stress in trainee physicians: A systematic review and meta-analysis. JAMA Network Open, 3(8), e2013761–e2013761.

Zimmermann, C., Strohmaier, S., Herkner, H., Niederkrotenthaler, T., & Schernhammer, E. (2024). Suicide rates among physicians compared with the general population in studies from 20 countries: Gender stratified systematic review and meta-analysis. BMJ, 386, 1–11.

Appendix D

Breaking the Burnout Cycle: Building Organizational Strategies to Address Burnout Sources and Symptoms

Arla Day

This paper was commissioned by National Academies of Sciences, Engineering, and Medicine's Committee on Women in Science, Engineering, and Medicine. Opinions and statements included in the paper are solely those of the individual authors, and are not necessarily adopted, endorsed, or verified as accurate by the committee or the National Academies of Sciences, Engineering, and Medicine.

ABSTRACT

From its "inception" in the 1970s, we have accumulated decades of research outlining the antecedents and outcomes of burnout. The definition of burnout has remained comparatively stable, such that there is a degree of consensus on what burnout is (i.e., a syndrome of feeling emotionally exhausted, feeling detached/cynical toward others, and having a low sense of professional efficacy) (Maslach, 1976). An integral premise of job burnout is that its root causes are due to work-related factors, rather than individual "characteristics." Therefore, when trying to ameliorate job burnout, efforts targeting the job (e.g., job redesign), the leader (e.g., effective leadership training), and the overall organization may be the most effective. Despite the abundance of burnout research, there is a relative paucity of actual intervention studies and best practices for individuals and organizations aimed at reducing the sources of burnout. Ironically, most interventions aim to manage symptoms of burnout rather than eliminate the sources of burnout, such that they target individual workers—despite acknowledging the organization as the source of the burnout, creating a burnout intervention dilemma. The goal of this paper is to review burnout inventions, create a conceptual framework identifying the sources and intervention points for burnout, understand why there is symptom treatment vs. source discrepancy, identify gaps and discrepancies in the current literature, and provide suggestions for novel practices in addressing burnout.

INTRODUCTION

The early works of Freudenberger (1974, 1975) and Maslach (1976), which identified a pattern of worker exhaustion, cynicism/depersonalization of others, and feelings of a lack of accomplishment and professional efficacy, commenced a long and in-depth research and practice journey on burnout. There has been much written about burnout's prevalence (Papazian et al., 2023; Woo et al., 2020), antecedents, and outcomes (Maslach et al., 2001). In stark contrast to this long history and the close to 2 million articles, books, and chapters written on it (Google Scholar, accessed August 17, 2024), our understanding of how we can best address burnout and reduce the sources of burnout is strikingly minimal. That is, by and large, we are lacking substantial knowledge in this area. Nevertheless, there are excellent studies demonstrating the utility of specific interventions, and there has been a recent growth of these intervention studies, as well as in meta-analyses on burnout interventions. These works highlight the areas of consistency in our knowledge, as well as the gaps, and the questions about quality of designs to improve our knowledge. Therefore, this paper incorporates the key literature, focusing on meta-analyses of work-related burnout interventions, identifying types of interventions, their overall efficacy, along with paths forward for research and practice.

More specifically, the purpose of this paper is threefold:

1. To outline current knowledge as well as gaps in knowledge about burnout intervention research, with a focus on the sources of burnout (as a mechanism to look at interventions and required components of intervention programs)
2. To provide a conceptual framework/overview of burnout, integrating the levels of burnout interventions to reduce the sources of burnout (i.e., primary interventions) and address burnout

responses/symptoms by supporting employees who may develop burnout (i.e., secondary interventions) or who currently are burnt out (i.e., tertiary interventions)
3. To understand rationales behind the lack of organizational practices, identify best practices and novel ways to address burnout, and create tips for organizations

WHAT IS BURNOUT: CONCEPTUALIZATION, DEFINITION, AND MEASUREMENT

Although some slight definitional variations exist, in general burnout is conceptualized as a response to prolonged exposure to workplace stressors (Freudenberger, 1974; Maslach, 1976; Maslach and Leiter, 2021). The World Health Organization (2022, p. 1748) classifies burnout as an occupational phenomenon and syndrome resulting from "chronic workplace stress that has not been successfully managed," stipulating that it "refers specifically to phenomena in the occupational context and should not be applied to describe experiences in other areas of life."

The most widely accepted definition of burnout classifies it as an ongoing syndrome characterized by emotional exhaustion (EE); depersonalization (DP) or cynicism (CYN); and a lack of personal accomplishment (PA) or professional efficacy (PE) (see Maslach, 1976; Maslach et al., 1997; Maslach et al., 2001).[1] EE involves feelings of physical and psychological fatigue, a loss of energy to complete tasks, and being unable to replenish one's energy levels. DP/CYN involves negative, cynical, detached feelings and behaviors toward others at work, with a corresponding dismissal of them. Finally, reduced PA/PE involves a diminished feeling of accomplishment, professional competence, and self-efficacy, such that they do not feel like they are contributing or making a "real" difference in their work. Overwhelmingly, the primary measure of this concept of burnout is the Maslach Burnout Inventory (MBI; Maslach et al., 1997), often being called the burnout "gold standard" (Thomas Craig et al., 2021).

However, despite the popularity of the MBI and its three-phase conceptualization, researchers have created alternative, but similar, scales. In general, these measures either use a similar framework as the MBI (e.g., Salmela-Aro et al., 2011), or a more simplified framework, focusing solely on exhaustion-like constructs and outcomes. For example, the Oldenburg

---

[1] See Chen et al. (2012) for other definitions of burnout.

Burnout Inventory, or OLBI, measures two factors of exhaustion and disengagement (Demerouti et al., 2001; Demerouti et al., 2003; Halbesleben and Demerouti, 2005). The Shirom-Melamed Burnout Questionnaire measures physical fatigue and cognitive weariness (Shirom and Melamed, 2006) and tension and listlessness (Lundgren-Nilsson et al., 2012). The Bergen Burnout Inventory, or BBI, measures exhaustion, cynicism, and inadequacy (Matthiesen, 1992; Feldt et al., 2014; Salmela-Aro et al., 2011),[2] and the Karolinska Exhaustion Scale measures aspects based on exhaustion: lack of recovery, cognitive exhaustion, somatic symptoms, and emotional distress. (Saboonchi et al., 2013). Finally, the Copenhagen Burnout Inventory (Kristensen et al., 2005) assesses fatigue/exhaustion. Focusing solely on a fatigue/exhaustion component is deficient in examining burnout because exhaustion is a necessary, but not sufficient, criterion for burnout (Maslach et al., 2001). "Exhaustion is not something that is simply experienced—rather, it prompts actions to distance oneself emotionally and cognitively from one's work" (Maslach et al., 2001, p. 403). Thus, studies typically use the MBI, and caution is advised when reading studies with single-item "measures" of burnout.

Organizing Framework to Study Burnout Interventions

The first step in understanding how to address burnout is to examine its relationships with individual and organizational demands and resources, as well as individual and organizational outcomes. Figure D-1 is a general conceptual framework, encapsulating both burnout outcomes and sources, while categorizing these sources in a meaningful way to aid in developing burnout interventions. Figure D-1 builds on the premise that there are multiple sources of burnout, and thus, incorporating different levels of interventions (primary, secondary, and tertiary), and differentiating when and how to reduce sources of burnout versus address symptoms of burnout, is important. It also recognizes the importance of planning interventions that focus on the individual, group, leader, and organization levels (Nielsen et al., 2013), identifying these burnout sources and how they can influence the burnout response.

---

[2] Matthiesen (1992) is the original author of the BBI, and Salmela-Aro et al. (2011) have a nine-item reduced version of the scale. Although the Matthiesen document is not publicly available, the items from the BBI are in Salmela-Aro et al.

153

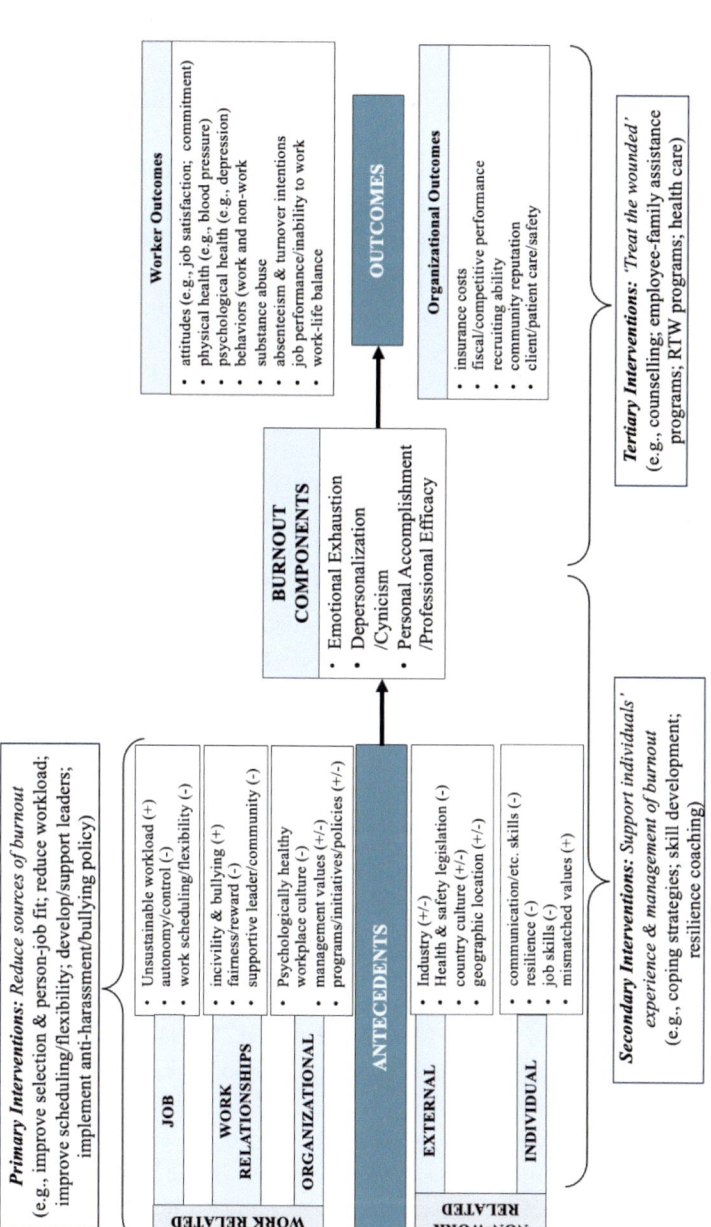

FIGURE D-1 Burnout antecedents and outcomes and corresponding levels of interventions.

Outcomes of Burnout

Multiple works have demonstrated the negative impact burnout can have on individual and organizational outcomes (e.g., Maslach et al., 2001; Swider and Zimmerman, 2010). As shown in Figure D-1, burnout can lead to negative psychological, physical, and behavioral outcomes for individuals. It also can lead to negative outcomes for the organization. Burnout also may have negative outcomes for families, such that burnout can affect burnout and well-being in one's partner (e.g., Bakker, 2009; Thompson et al., 2020; Westman et al., 2001).[3] For example, women's EE (which results from job and emotional demands at work) affected their male partner's level of EE (Demerouti et al., 2005).

Burnout can affect job attitudes (e.g., reduce job satisfaction; Iverson et al., 1998; Madigan and Kim., 2021) and affect overall life satisfaction and well-being (Demerouti et al., 2005). Burnout can increase levels of absenteeism (Iverson et al., 1998) and intentions to quit (Madigan and Kim, 2021). Burnout has been associated with increased use of psychotropic medication (Leiter et al., 2013) and negative physical health (e.g., blood pressure) and psychological health (Salvagioni et al., 2017). In their meta-analysis of burnout and safety, Salyers et al. (2017) found that higher burnout (higher EE and DP, and lower PA) was associated with reduced job performance and increased errors on the job (e.g., reduced patient safety, lower quality of healthcare). In their meta-analysis of burnout and job performance, Corbeanu et al. (2023) found that exhaustion, depersonalization, and inefficacy were associated with lower job performance. These relationships with well-being outcomes have implications for when and how we address burnout via tertiary interventions (see below).

Sources of Burnout

There also is a significant amount of research on the antecedents of burnout (see Leiter and Harvie, 1996; Maslach et al., 2001). Understanding the factors that foster/exacerbate burnout can help us to better understand how to address burnout. Leiter and Maslach (1999) identified six areas of work that contribute to burnout: workload, control, reward, community, fairness, and values, and they measure these factors based on the perceived mismatch between worker and workplace. Although originally developed

---

[3] For the purpose of this paper, individual factors and the work/organizational environment are the primary focal areas.

as antecedents of job stress, Sauter et al.'s (1990) psychosocial risk factors (e.g., workload and work pace, work schedule, roles stressors, career security, interpersonal relationships, and job content) also contribute to the development, and our understanding of, burnout. Figure 1 provides an abridged framework of these working life antecedents and psychosocial risk factors, clustering them into three work categories, and two nonwork categories: (a) job-level factors; (b) group or interpersonal factors, including leadership relationships and effectiveness; (c) organizational-level factors/culture; (d) individual-level characteristics; and (e) external factors.[4] Based on Leiter and Maslach, there is also the understanding that person-job/organization misalignment of the factors within these categories can create burnout.

Job Factors

Job characteristics tend to be viewed as the key predictors of the occurrence of emotional exhaustion (Maslach et al., 2001). Workload (Iverson et al., 1998), long shifts and limited staffing (Dall'Ora et al., 2020), job control (Aronsson et al., 2017), autonomy (Iverson et al., 1998), and lack of schedule flexibility (Dall'Ora et al., 2020) are all associated with increased burnout. Leiter et al. (2013) found that specific job characteristics, such as information flow, skill discretion, decision authority, and predictability, were associated with reduced burnout over an 8-year time span. In their meta-analysis, Aronsson et al. (2017) found an association between workload and EE. Job-specific demands associated with COVID-19 also increased burnout: increased workload and a lack of specialized training regarding COVID-19 was associated with higher levels of burnout in nurses (Galanis et al., 2021). Similarly, healthcare workers who worked prolonged night shifts during the pandemic and were exposed to traumatic events experienced higher levels of burnout (Chirico et al., 2021).

Work Relationships

Negative work relationship factors (including team interactions and supervisor support) are associated with increased burnout (e.g., Iverson et al., 1998; Spector and Nixon, 2023). Conversely, overall workplace support can

---

[4] The focus of this paper is on **work factors**, so while acknowledging there are multiple nonwork factors that could potentially affect burnout, **nonwork factors** are excluded from any in-depth reviews here.

be associated with lower EE (see Aronsson et al.'s meta-analysis, 2017). EE is associated with other mistreatment factors, such as specific supervisor and co-worker support, justice, and reward (Aronsson et al., 2017). Cynicism was associated with job demands, such as a lack of control and support, and personal accomplishment was only associated with reward (Aronsson et al., 2017). Supervisor, coworker, and peer support all tend to be associated with lower burnout (see, e.g., Iverson et al., 1998).

Leadership is an important relationship factor: In their meta-analysis, Harms et al. (2017) found that transformational leadership and leader-member exchange is associated with lower levels of EE and DP, and higher PA, whereas abusive supervision is associated with higher levels of all three components of burnout. In their logistic regression, Dyrbye et al. (2020) found that each 1-point increase in leadership score was associated with a 7 percent decrease in burnout.

The leadership-burnout relationship may be mediated by thriving, such that transformational leadership increases one's levels of thriving, which reduces one's levels of burnout (Hildenbrand et al., 2018). Harms et al.'s (2017) meta-analysis also highlighted an often-ignored part of the relationship: leaders' levels of burnout can influence their own leadership behaviours. That is, leader burnout was associated with lower transformational leadership and higher levels of abusive supervision. Lower levels of transformational leadership and leader-member exchange and higher levels of abusive supervision are associated with higher levels of burnout for their followers.[5] Similarly, workplace bullying is associated with increased burnout: bullying was related to a lack of satisfaction of employees' need for autonomy, and this unmet need was associated with increased burnout (Trépanier et al., 2013).

Organizational Factors

Finally, poor organizational environments and a lack of resources are also associated with increases in burnout (Leiter et al., 2013). Organizational variables have been identified as the primary drivers to burnout (Gómez-Urquiza et al., 2020). Collectively, Kroth et al. (2019) found that general working conditions accounted for 36.2 percent of variance in burnout. In a prospective study on burnout in Finnish workers, working

---

[5] Harms et al. (2017) caution that most of the studies in their meta-analysis used same source data. Thus, followers who had higher levels of burnout may have rated their leaders/supervisors more negatively.

conditions (measured in 1985) were associated with job burnout measured 13 years later in 1998 (Hakanen et al., 2011). There also is some limited evidence that job insecurity (which may reflect stressful or unstable work environments/cultures) is associated with EE and CYN (Aronsson et al., 2017).

Specific organizational practices, and ineffective practices, can negatively affect workers as well. For example, in their systematic review of interventions addressing health information technology stressors, Thomas Craig et al. (2021) argued that "the primary drivers of burnout for physicians have been related to electronic health records (EHRs) and overwhelming inefficiencies in clinical practice" (p. 986; see also Tutty et al., 2019), both of which can create ineffective workflows and reduced patient care. Similarly, Kroth et al. (2019) found that the usage and design of EHRs accounted for small, but significant, increases of variance in burnout. Day et al. (2017) studied workers in a healthcare organization that was going through a large reorganization: Workers' perceptions of the organizational changes and demands they experienced during this reorganization was associated with increased EE and CYN levels, and reduced PE.

Types of work cultures can contribute to burnout: Masculinity contest culture occurs when workplaces (and organizational leaders) promote norms, practices, and values centered on competition and dominance in line with traditional masculinity ideals (Berdahl et al., 2018), and they have been associated with higher levels of burnout (Regina and Allen, 2023). Conversely, a supportive workplace culture that promote worker health and well-being are associated with lower levels of burnout. For example, after controlling for baseline levels of burnout, organizational culture that valued a focus on health was associated with reduced burnout 1 year later (Ybema et al., 2011).

External factors, such as COVID-19, also can increase organizational demands, creating more opportunities for burnout to occur, especially in healthcare workers. Not surprisingly, nurses experiencing increased demands/threats within their workplace had a higher risk of burnout: Having increased threats of COVID-19, working in high-risk environments, working long hours in quarantined spaces, and having insufficient supports (e.g., personal safety equipment, human resources support) were all risk factors for burnout (Galanis et al., 2021).

Individual Risk Factors

Although not the focus of this review, it is worth noting that individual factors can affect the level and experience of burnout. Therefore, we need to take these factors into consideration when assessing burnout and designing and implementing burnout interventions. Simionato and Simpson (2018) found that younger psychotherapists with less work experience tended to have a higher risk for experiencing burnout. Similarly, during the pandemic, younger nurses (Galanis et al., 2021) and trainees and younger healthcare workers with less work experience (Chirico et al., 2021) also tended to be at more risk for burnout. There also is some suggestion that individual characteristics affect how one interprets, reacts to, and benefits from burnout interventions (Bartunek et al., 2006). Therefore, these factors can influence intervention effectiveness.

A MULTI-LEVEL ORGANIZATIONAL BURNOUT STRATEGY

Despite a solid appreciation of the effects of these antecedents on burnout, there has been limited progress in effectively "addressing" job burnout. Understanding these burnout sources (as shown in Figure D-1) highlights the complexity of the task: If burnout can arise from different antecedents and contexts, there probably is no simple, magic bullet to eliminate/manage burnout. Understanding burnout also highlights the substantial philosophical and practical differences in what it means to address burnout; that is, addressing burnout can either mean eliminating the sources of burnout or simply managing the symptoms of burnout.

Thus, as shown in Figure D-1, burnout can be addressed by (a) reducing the source of burnout, (b) changing one's capabilities to handle burnout, and/or (c) reducing the symptoms of burnout (i.e., primary, secondary, and tertiary work interventions, respectively). Primary initiatives are aimed at changing the work environment (i.e., reducing the source of burnout and/or redesigning the workplace to minimize the stressors and/or increase resources to do one's job; Hurrell and Sauter, 2013) and prevent burnout (LaMontagne et al., 2007). Primary interventions involve initiatives such as job redesign, organizational health regulations, and culture initiatives (Hurrell and Sauter, 2013), as well as workload management, increasing flexibility/autonomy to manage workload (e.g., De Simone et al., 2021); leader training (to support their team); and group training (e.g., to improve poor interpersonal relationships; e.g., Leiter et al., 2011, 2012).

Secondary programs target the individual and have the goal of providing support/training to help the employee cope with existing stressors (Maricuțoiu et al., 2016), to prevent the worsening of burnout symptoms (Bes et al., 2023), or to better cope with potential or anticipated daily or ongoing work stressors (e.g., technology breakdowns, client rudeness). These interventions involve individual-based training and support, such as Cognitive Behavioral Therapy (CBT), mindfulness, relaxation training, as well as work-related skills training (job training, communication skills training, etc.). Secondary programs aimed at general stress management and work-life balance (Hurrell and Sauter, 2013) also have been used to address burnout (Lloyd et al., 2013). Finally tertiary interventions address the burnout symptoms (i.e., "healing the wounded"), such that they prevent the progress of symptoms, reduce the extent of the disability, provide accommodations, and help to restore individual functioning (Hurrell and Sauter, 2013). These initiatives may include employee assistance programs, accommodations, and return-to-work programs.

REVIEW OF BURNOUT INTERVENTION META-ANALYSES

To provide an overview of the status of the burnout intervention literature, I reviewed meta-analyses that have been conducted on the different types of interventions addressing job burnout across organizations. I screened out most papers that were not true meta-analyses (e.g., systematic reviews, or "meta-analyses" with only two studies), or that did not look at the efficacy of some type of organizational or individual focused work process or intervention, or that did not have a worker sample. Table D-1 is an overview of these meta-analyses conducted on the efficacy of burnout interventions. I included meta-analyses up to 2024. I then reviewed the literature to search for additional relevant articles from the past few years that had not been included in a meta-analysis.

There was considerable variability in the types of interventions offered across the studies/meta-analyses. Compared with the vast literature on individually focused (primarily self-care) types of interventions, there are relatively few studies of organizational-based burnout interventions (Gregory et al., 2018). That is, despite a need to change the environment to reduce stressors, most interventions focus on making the individual more resilient to the ongoing work demands/stressors (Gregory et al., 2018). For example, of the 33 studies of healthcare workers in Cohen et al.'s (2023) meta-analysis, only 3 involved organizational-focused interventions (the other 30 involved individually focused interventions). Similarly, only 3 of the 39 interventions studies in de Wijn et al.'s (2022) meta-analysis, and 2 of 11 studies in the Bes et al. (2023) meta-analysis, involved organizational-based interventions.

TABLE D-1 Meta-Analysis-Based Studies of Burnout Interventions

1st Author Date Journal	Primary Findings	Studies & Sample Information	Overview of Intervention Types	Other Comments
Ahola et al., 2017 *Burnout Research*	~only 4 individual RCTs using MBI and had similar controls were used in meta-analysis ~there were no significant reductions in EE or CYN (did not include PE)	~14 studies (18 interventions) of European workers ~all had a control group	~14 individual-focused (e.g., CBT; meditative/physical) ~4 joint individual & organizational (meetings with work representatives to look at work changes)	
Beames et al., 2023 *Educational Psychology*	~RCT programs had moderate effects on EE (g = 0.57) ~short-term follow-up intervention effect sizes were moderate for professional burnout (g = 0.82) ~nonsignificant effects on burnout for non-RCTs	~88 studies with a 8763 school teachers (48 RCTs; 40 nRCTs) ~included studies with any type of control group ~only used the EE subscale	~all individual-focused (e.g., CBT; relaxation; mindfulness emotional-skills training) ~mostly in-person, group programs, supported & sometimes resourced by the school; ~70% delivered 1–12 weeks with sessions lasting 1–4 hours	~authors note heterogeneity in design and poor methodological quality (especially in nonrandomized controlled trials [nRCTs])

Author/Year			
Bes et al., 2023 *International Journal of Occupational and Environmental Health*	–small overall effect across **all interventions** in reducing EE (= –.30; and "very low quality of evidence") –larger effect for **combined interventions** (2 studies; – 0.54) than for organizational interventions (–.25; 11 studies) –both participatory interventions (–.34) and workload-reduction interventions (–.44) reduced EE	–11 articles (13 studies - 11 organizational interventions & 2 combined interventions –included articles up to 2022 –10 non-RCT - 3RCT articles	–organization focused - participatory (n = 9), focused on workload (n = 2), or on work schedule (n = 2). (or combined) –job constructing intervention; workload; participatory; team stressor-management; team - interpersonal; skill training + team support	–focused on EE only –despite moderate to large effects, authors noted overall quality of evidence (using GRADE approach), thus they had no practical recommendations
Burton et al., 2017 *Stress & Health*	–could not do meta-analysis of burnout as it was only used in some studies –Fortney et al. (2013) found improvements in EE, DP, & PA	–9 studies - healthcare professionals in USA, Australia, Columbia, Sweden, Spain	–included a range of individual-based mindfulness techniques (e.g., breathing, meditation, yoga, group discussion) –intervention length ranged from 1 day to 10 weeks	–6 studies used pre-post intervention designs; 1 used a quasi-experimental design; 2 used RCTs; 7 included pre- and post-measures
Chakraborty et al., 2023 *The Malaysian Journal of Nursing*	–mobile app-based interventions were associated with reduced burnout in nurses (not a meta-analysis; only 2 studies examined burnout)	–5 RCTs involving nurses during Covid (2019–2023); –only 2 studies included burnout	–individual focused interventions using mobile applications (Unguided Digital Mindfulness Based Self-Help App, mHealth Intervention App, Mobile Intervention App, PsyCovid App, Headspace App, and Mobile Mindfulness App)	–not a true meta-analysis; only 2 studies using burnout

continued

TABLE D-1 Continued

1st Author Date Journal	Primary Findings	Studies & Sample Information	Overview of Intervention Types	Other Comments
Thomas Craig et al., 2021 *Journal of the American Medical Informatics Association*	–**NOTE: Systematic review only***** –68% of the 38 studies reported reductions in burnout (or "proxy" measures, which may not be accurate reflections of burnout) –combined interventions are more effective than are organizational interventions in reducing burnout	–38 studies of physicians reported interventions that aimed to reduce burden/demands of health digital tools	–most common interventions involved ones dealing with process improvements (e.g., workflow improvements; quality improvement; "lean" initiatives; improve info technology processes; reduce workload & work disruptions)	–general workflow changes tended to be more successful than quality improvement & lean interventions
De Simone et al., 2021 *Aging Clinical and Experimental Research*	–pooled interventions were associated with **small** significant reductions in burnout –organization-directed interventions were associated with a **medium** reduction in burnout –physician-directed interventions were associated with a **moderate** reduction in burnout –"physicians could gain important benefits from interventions to reduce burnout, especially from organizational strategies, by viewing burnout rooted in issues related to the working environment and organizational culture" (np)	–20 RCTs with physicians (13 - individual focused; 7 - organizational focused) –NOTE: Systematic Review only	–individual interventions (e.g., mindfulness stress reduction; educational interventions targeting communication skills & self confidence) –organizational interventions (e.g., workload interventions, including rescheduling & reducing workload; meetings to enhance teamwork/leadership, structural changes)	–authors noted that, generally, studies had poor design and methodologies (especially in the nRCTs)

Citation			
de Wijn et al., 2022 *International Journal of Stress Management*	~overall, interventions were associated with improved levels of overall burnout: • person-level interventions (k = 39) had moderate effects • multilevel interventions (k = 3) had moderate effects • organization-interventions (k = 3) had small effects	~nurses; extracted studies from 2007 to 2020 (as part of a larger well-being meta-analysis)	~person- and organization-directed, and multilevel interventions
Dreison et al., 2018 *Journal of Occupational Health Psychology*	~overall, interventions had a small but positive reductions in burnout • person-directed interventions were more effective than organization-directed interventions at reducing EE • job training/education was the most effective organizational intervention subtype • some variability in effects based on study design and time of measurement • study quality indicators, intervention intensity, and publication status were not significant moderators	~27 published or unpublished studies (1980–2015) of mental-health providers, using either RCT or uncontrolled designs ~from US; Great Britain, Australia, Sweden, Netherlands ~all but 1 study used MBI	~individual- & organizational-focused interventions ~most interventions were organization-directed (70.4%), with job training/ education being the most commonly reported subtype ~intervention length varied a lot (3 to 314 hours; M = 32.9 hours) ~average # of sessions = 6.8 ~70.4% followed a treatment manual; only two studies measured treatment fidelity	~positive effects of burnout interventions can be maintained over time ~results are weaker than for general stress/strain studies, suggesting that it may be more difficult to address burnout

163

continued

TABLE D-1 Continued

1st Author Date Journal	Primary Findings	Studies & Sample Information	Overview of Intervention Types	Other Comments
Estevez-Cores, 2021 Journal of Occupational Health Psychology	–overall, individual-focused burnout interventions were associated with reduced EE and DP, but not improved PA –cognitive interventions were associated with reduced EE and DP –relaxation interventions were associated with reduced EE & DP, and improved PA	–part of a larger study on occupational health interventions –k = 8–24 studies - EE –k = 5–14 studies - PA	–individual-focused interventions: cognitive; relaxation; multimodal	–multimodal interventions did not have significant effects on burnout levels
Fendel et al., 2021 Academic Medicine	–mindfulness-based interventions were associated with a small, but significant, reduction in burnout	–25 studies with 925 physicians	–all were mindfulness-based interventions	–included both RCTs and nonrandomized trials, including controlled and noncontrolled before-after studies
Haslam et al., 2024 American Journal of Medicine	–burnout interventions led to statistically significant, but "clinically meaningless" reductions in emotional exhaustion and depersonalization (and not significant for professional efficacy)	–38 studies of physicians –randomized trials only	–coaching/counseling (k = 2) –discussion group (k = 31) –drug (cannabinol) (k = 1) –education on stress reduction/coping strategies (k = 1) –mindfulness/meditation/yoga (k = 1) –schedule changes (k = 1)	–effects primarily "driven by coaching interventions"

Study	Findings	Sample	Intervention types	Quality
Iancu et al., 2018 *Educational Psychology Review*	–overall effects across studies were significant for EE & CYN, not for DP –In terms of **types of interventions**: CBT & mindfulness reduced EE, & mindfulness & support reduced PA –length of program ranged from 1 day to 1 school year)	~23 controlled trials (19 journal articles and 4 unpublished dissertation of **teachers**) –studies from Canada; Congo; China; Germany; Netherlands; New Zealand; South Africa; South Korea; US	~6 types of individual interventions: 1-CBT (rational emotive; goal-setting, etc.); 2-mindfulness/meditation; 3-professional development (developing student interaction & classroom management skills); 4-psychoeducational (burnout/stress/mental health lectures); 5-social support (peers/teams); & 6-socio-emotional skills	–more than 2/3 of studies had optimal quality –intervention effectiveness was unrelated to its risk of bias –small traces of publication bias
Lee & Cha, 2023 *Scientific Reports*	–interventions reduced EE and DP, but they did not improve low PA	~24 studies (11 in meta-analysis) from 2011 to 2020; clinical nurses (RCT 7 quasi-experimental) - 2011–2020; Asia; India; Turkey; UK; US	–face-to-face mindfulness & group intervention was the most common intervention approach; –stress management, coping training, & refresher session; team-based support groups; mindfulness; cognitive coping strategies; problem-solving methods	

continued

TABLE D-1 Continued

1st Author Date Journal	Primary Findings	Studies & Sample Information	Overview of Intervention Types	Other Comments
Lee et al., 2016 *Applied Nursing Research*	–participants were measured immediately after the intervention and 6 months, 1 year, 2 years, 2.5 years, and 4 years thereafter. –coping strategies decreased burnout in most of the 7 studies, and effects were relatively maintained (unchanged or increased) for 1 year for EE and DP and 6 months for PA	–N = 1521 nurses across 7 studies selected from 1979 to 2014 (n = 872-treatment group; 649-control) –English & Chinese language	–coping strategies –programs ranged up to 8 weeks	–all had control group and only used MBI-HSS
Li et al., 2023 *Behavioral Sciences*	–CBI had strong effects on EE –mindfulness had the 2nd strongest effects –professional training had significant effects –emotional-based effects were inconclusive –only CBI was significant when considering effects on EE (other interventions had no effects)	–k = 29 studies of teachers from: Canada (2); China (3); Germany (3); Iran (2), Ireland (1); Israel (2); Italy (2); Nigeria (5); South Africa (1); Spain (1); the Netherlands (1), UK (1); US (4), from 2003–2022	–CBI (cognitive training/ strategic behavioural practices to manage stress) –mindfulness (awareness and acceptance without judgment; relaxation; yoga) –teaching (training, classroom management training, training for communicating with students and colleagues, and self psychological adjustment training) –emotional (physical energy exercises; emotional freedom)	–most used MBI

Study	Findings	Details	Notes
Ma et al., 2023 *Journal of Clinical Nursing*	~only 3 burnout studies (no quantitative analyses) ~each study showed some reductions in EE reductions in EE only 1 and 7 months after program (Edmonds, 2012); reductions in EE only immediately after training (Onan et al., 2013)	~3 intervention studies (as part of a larger prevalence meta-analysis) of 149 oncology nurses	~1-day group workshop on trauma/compassion fatigue; stress reduction/relaxation/ yoga-Edmonds ~coping with stress training ~psychological empowerment program/psychodrama (coping with stress, cognitive distortion; relaxation; problem-solving, empathy, dispute resolution)	~only 3 studies included (Edmonds, 2012; Onan, 2013; Özbas, 2016)
Maricuțoiu et al., 2016 *Journal of Occupational and Organizational Psychology*	~significant overall effects of interventions on general BO scales (only used 13 of the 47 studies) ~EE (34 studies)- significant reduction (d = .172); ns for DP & PA ~significant for EE across all times (except 1–3 month measurements); ~significant effects for relaxation & job skills training on EE, and for interpersonal soft skills training on PA	~47 studies (all with control group) general workers, including physicians, nurses, residents; social workers; students; managers; and "mixed" occupations in 8 studies	~CBT; meditation/ relaxation; interpersonal skills development; knowledge/ work skills development	~37 used MBI; others used OLBDI; PBQ; IDB

continued

167

TABLE D-1 Continued

1st Author Date Journal	Primary Findings	Studies & Sample Information	Overview of Intervention Types	Other Comments
Ochentel et al., 2018 *Journal of Sports Science & Medicine*	~does not support "widespread assumption that exercise therapy [is a] successful means to alleviate burnout symptoms" (p. 475)	~4 studies; not explicitly a "work" study, but all were employed (except 1 study)	~all dealing with physical exercise programs: fitness/exercise/cardio (1 study was Qigong & mindfulness) - running, cycling, water exercise; aerobics	
Oliveira et al., 2021 *Educational Psychology Review*	~medium effect size of social/emotional learning on EE and PA (but no significant effects for DP)	~13 studies of 994 teachers	~social and emotional learning (SEL) ~yoga and mindfulness intervention	
Panagioti et al., 2017 *JAMA Internal Medicine*	~small significant reductions in burnout ~moderate reductions for organization interventions ~overall organization-directed interventions (SMD = −0.45) had larger effects on burnout than did individual/physician-directed interventions (SMD = −0.18)	~19 studies with 1550 physicians (primary, secondary, or intensive care setting including residents and fellows; other healthcare professionals may have been a small part of some samples)	~physician-focused interventions (e.g., CBT; mindfulness/stress reduction techniques; educational communication skills programs); ~organization-focused interventions (e.g., increase resources; change working environment/workload/ scheduling tasks; decrease stress; improve organizational/ team operation)	

Perski et al., 2017 *Scandinavian Journal of Psychology*	~no effect of tertiary interventions on levels of burnout ~that is, interventions improved time to RTW, but did not improve levels of burnout	~3 studies examined burnout (as part of a larger meta-analysis); Blonk et al., 2006; de Vente, 2008; Stenlund, 2009	~tertiary psychosocial interventions for stress-related mental disorders or "clinical burnout" ~e.g., coping; health education; social skills training, etc. ~either individual or group	~findings may suggest employees are returning to work, but are still burned out
Salvado et al., 2021 *Healthcare*	~mindfulness-based interventions significantly reduced EE and DP, and they significantly increased PA	~10 studies in systematic review; only 4 were RCTS, and only 6 were included in meta-analysis of 417 primary healthcare professionals (78.5% = physicians, 20.1% = nurses, & 1.4% others – e.g., social workers/psychologists)	~e.g., yoga; breath awareness; stress coping; cognitive therapy; self-care; managing conflict; mindfulness meditation; mindful communications; body scan; acceptance; self-compassion; most involved 8 weeks of training (one shorter intervention involved 14 hours)	~authors rated the studies as having a high risk of bias, and thus, rated the studies as having a lower quality of evidence ~used MBI only

continued

TABLE D-1 Continued

1st Author Date Journal	Primary Findings	Studies & Sample Information	Overview of Intervention Types	Other Comments
Soriano-Sánchez and Jimenez-Vazquez, 2023 *Revista Acciones Médicas*	~the interventions reduced EE in nurses	~13 studies of nurses (n = 563-post-test) in Colombia; Germany; Japan; Norway; Portugal; UK; US	~a variety of interventions: • change the work environment • increase personal resources • reduce workload • professional development • increase peer support	~used mindfulness practice; yoga stress management programs
Suleiman-Martos et al., 2020 *Journal of Advanced Nursing*	~only 2 studies included; only examined intervention vs. control group at post intervention, which missed the higher EE scores for the intervention- see comments (no independent info available on the Norouzinia et al., 2017 study; as such, it is not included in references)	~17 studies of nurses (only 2 in meta-analysis) from Australia; Brazil; Canada; Iran; Ireland; Japan; Portugal; US ~8 RCT; 9 quasi-experiment ~mainly women	~individual practices, such as: • mindfulness training • coping strategies in MSBR • aromatherapy • communication skills • breathing exercises • yoga/stretching • meditation/mindfulness • cognitive training therapy	~review of the Mackenzie et al., 2006: ~significant interaction, such that EE decreased (pre- to post) compared to control group; significant interaction for DP (increased for control; stayed the same for intervention)

Wang et al., 2023 *Frontiers in Psychiatry*	–the training was effective in reducing EE, DP, and improving PA –there was a delayed benefits for burnout (only 2 studies with longer follow-ups, but not longer-term effects)	–15 studies of 1,165 nurses from: China; Iran; Japan; Portugal; Turkey; US	–randomized; used mindfulness interventions
West et al., 2016 *The Lancet*	–levels of EE and DP significantly decreased after the intervention	–37 studies of 2914 physicians across disciplines (e.g., oncology; OBGYN; surgical; neurology; family; internal medicine; palliative) –15 RCTs & 37 observational studies)	–17 studies had structural interventions, (e.g., "USA duty hour requirements" & practice delivery changes) –20 had individual-focused interventions (e.g., facilitated & non-facilitated small group sessions; mindfulness/ stress management/selfcare; training; communication skills training) –4 cohort studies had funding/coverage for physicians to participate during the workday	–suggest combining individual and organizational interventions to better address physician burnout –all but 3 studies use the MBI

continued

TABLE D-1 Continued

1st Author Date Journal	Primary Findings	Studies & Sample Information	Overview of Intervention Types	Other Comments
Yildirm et al., 2023 *Japan Journal of Nursing Science*	~burnout interventions had a small effect on EE and DP, and a moderate effect on PA	~19 studies of 1,139 nurses (13 included in the meta-analysis) between 1979 & 2022 ~all RCTS with pre-post-tests; quasi-experimental	~included both person and organization interventions ~person-directed = coping, social support, relaxation training); ~organization-directed = work process changes, such as task restructuring; supervision) ~combined interventions (both individual & organizational)	

APPENDIX D

Not surprising, there is some variability in the efficacy across different programs/interventions and across the three components of burnout.[6] There are many variables that may affect effectiveness of burnout interventions in terms of the content of the initiative, and its primary target or level of intervention (see more on the methodological review of burnout intervention studies in the appendix). Overall, most of these articles (the vast majority of which were published) demonstrated that the interventions offer some reduction in burnout. However, although disappointing, it also may not be surprising that many meta-analyses and systematic reviews also concluded that there was considerable variability across the content, focus, and quality of interventions, such that results are either "inconclusive" or must be viewed with caution (e.g., Ahola et al., 2017; De Simone et al., 2021; Thomas Craig et al., 2021).

To better understand the details of the interventions used in these meta-analyses, Table D-2 highlights examples of individual and organizational interventions. Most of the current burnout intervention literature has typically used an "individual vs. organization-intervention" dichotomy. Individual interventions include programs aimed to support coping skills, resilience, and/or job skills, including communication and interpersonal skills. Organization-directed interventions involve changes to the job or work-environment, such as increasing work flexibility, reducing workload, providing additional resources, or more in-depth job and organizational redesign (De Simone et al., 2021). These interventions are further differentiated by the types of interventions within these two categories: Within individual interventions, most interventions in the meta-analyses involved cognitive/emotional support training, with some focusing on skills training, and a few on physical exercise (although many of the exercise interventions were part of the cognitive, emotional support training. Organizational interventions were divided into interpersonal interventions (e.g., group, leadership, interpersonal skills) and participatory job redesign and organizational change (e.g., job/work redesign, participatory action interventions, and organizational change).

Individual-Focused Interventions

Ironically, even though burnout is classified as a reaction to deficient or difficult workplace environments, most burnout interventions tend to

---

[6] Many studies did not include CYN/DP and PE/PA, and as such many of the meta-analyses did not have sufficient studies to look at the effects of these two components of burnout.

TABLE D-2 Examples of Individual and Organizational Interventions to Address Burnout

Types of Interventions	Level[a]	Example Studies	Example Programs/Intervention Components[b]
INDIVIDUAL			
Cognitive/Relaxation/Emotional			
• Cognitive Behavioral Therapy (CBT) & Acceptance & Commitment Therapy (ACT)	2°	Lloyd et al. (2013)	• CBT is a popular burnout tool • ACT is known as a second wave CBT (but less studied) • Three 3-hour group ACT training sessions (2 occurred on consecutive weeks; the 3rd occurred 2 months later) • Goals – 1-increase present moment awareness; reduce "unhelpful avoidance" of thoughts/emotions; 2-use acceptance/mindfulness to deal with problematic thoughts/feelings, and create values-based actions • There was a significant decrease in EE from T2 to T4 in the ACT group, and no change in DP in the ACT group (whereas the control group had a significant increase in DP)
• Mindfulness/ Meditation/ Relaxation/ Breathing	2°	Li et al. (2023) -meta-	• Mindfulness is one of the most widely studied techniques for stress and burnout • This intervention involved body scanning (being aware of your physical self; scanning body for tension, pain, etc.), awareness of thoughts and emotions; breathing exercises; walking meditation, sitting meditation; coping with stress; group-based training sessions, & using audio recordings of sessions for individual practice at home
Physical			
• Physical activity (exercise & movement-based therapy)	2°	Ochentel et al. (2018)	• Included aerobics, swimming, walking, running – group & alone, rowing; treadmill/indoor cycling, etc. • 3 of the 4 studies reviewed found significant effects of physical activity on burnout • Overall, however, there was no evidence for effects of physical programs on burnout in the metanalysis

TABLE D-2 Continued

Types of Interventions	Level[a]	Example Studies	Example Programs/Intervention Components[b]
• Yoga (& mindfulness)	2°	Di Mario et al. (2023)	• Qualitative review of 12 systematic reviews and meta-analyses of yoga and mindfulness-based interventions • Overall positive effects for both on reduction of burnout
Skill Training			
• Job skills development	1°	Cohen and Gagin (2005)	• 2 group-intervention skills training groups: 1-more experienced social workers and general hospital social-work skills for less experienced employees; burnout was reduced in both groups
• Emotional skills training	1°	Schoeps et al. (2019)	• 3-wave training study with groups of teachers'; training consisted of five 2-hour group sessions on efficacy in emotional regulation (seen as a required job-skill, rather than reducing burnout emotional symptoms) • Teachers experienced a reduction in burnout at T2, which was partially maintained at T3
• Coaching	1°	Dyrbye et al. (2019)	• 3.5 hours of custom coaching on topics such as: work-life integration; building work support/community; addressing workload & work efficiency; optimizing meaning of work; developing leadership skills; self-care, non-work relationships; pursuing hobbies; optimizing meaning in work (as requested by participant) • Reduced EE and DP
Accommodation/Return to Work			
• Return to work	3°	Ahola et al. (2017)	• Generally, "Few interventions to support recovery from burnout and subsequent return to work have been conducted and evaluated in a coherent way"

continued

TABLE D-2 Continued

Types of Interventions	Level[a]	Example Studies	Example Programs/Intervention Components[b]
• Return to work	3°	Blonk et al. (2006)	• Compared a CBT vs. a combined program for self-employed who had applied for sickness benefits • Combined program = 5-6 1-hour CBT sessions 2x/week on CBT & work-based topics (stress & time management; work processes such as reducing workload, conflict management; delegation; etc.) • Combined program had significant effects on RTW • However, EE and DP decreased for all groups (including control; no significant interaction effects)
• Coping strategies for workers referred for burnout rehabilitation	3°	Hätinen et al. (2013)	• 1-year rehab intervention with 6-month follow-up • 2 rehab interventions (each lasting 5 and 12 days) & had 4 assessment times • Intervention helped EE recovery only • Avoidance coping was associated with nonrecovery (i.e., stable or increased serious burnout) • "More precise targeting and tailoring of burnout rehabilitation is clearly needed"

ORGANIZATIONAL

Interpersonal/Group

• Team action planning (with peer support component)	1°	Le Blanc et al. (2007)	• Healthcare teams engaged in activities to address the issues/challenges affecting the team • They set goals for the team, developed and enacted actions plans • They designated roles for team members to check in on other team member's well-being • Program associated with decreased EE & PA

TABLE D-2 Continued

Types of Interventions	Level[a]	Example Studies	Example Programs/Intervention Components[b]
• Participatory peer support team	1°	Peterson et al. (2008)	• Labeled as a combined (but had a large interpersonal component) • 2-hour weekly team sessions for 10 weeks; composed of individual (relaxation) component, and interpersonal/group discussions • Program associated with decreased EE between intervention and control group from T1 to T4
Leadership Training			
• Leader support/ally	1°	(few in-depth programs)	• Generally target leaders as mentors/allies to help support direct reports; training varies
• Empathic leadership & self-care	1°	Gilin et al. (2023)	• Trained leaders on developing empathy and self-care behaviours through workshops and an app • Program had no significant reduction in burnout levels
(Participatory) Job Redesign & Organizational Change			
• Workload (management/reduction)	1°	Gregory et al. (2018)	• Redesign healthcare group to increase resources, expand accountability for treatment and processing, and reduce team members' burnout • Gregory et al. (2018) conducted an intervention study (consisting of an organizational work-process change designed reduce physician workload) in 8 healthcare clinics (4 treatment; 4 control clinics). The intervention was successful in significantly reducing workload, corresponding with a significant reduction in levels of emotional exhaustion for physicians in the "intervention" clinics
• Workload/work schedule	1°	Best et al. (2023)	• In their meta-analysis, Bes et al. concluded that, in general, interventions aimed at addressing work schedules were not effective

continued

TABLE D-2 Continued

Types of Interventions	Level[a]	Example Studies	Example Programs/Intervention Components[b]
• Stressor/ workload reduction		van Weert et al. (2005)	• However, some studies have used participatory work redesigns successfully by targeting specific issues that can affect workload: ○ Van Weert et al. implemented "Snoezelen" training for healthcare workers in psychogeriatric care (i.e., multisensory stimulation that actively stimulates the resident's senses—hearing, touch, vision; smell) to "reduce maladaptive behaviors and increase positive behaviors" (p.408), which may reduce caregivers' demands/stress ○ Program reduced EE for intervention group
• Job crafting	1°- & 2°-	Hakanen et al. (2017)	• Job crafting = workers increase the structural & social resources & the challenging demands in the job/work (as measured by Tims et al., 2014, job-crafting scale) • Job-crafting activities "buffered" the negative effects of job demands on burnout • Note: This study (and much job-crafting literature) is less intervention research, and more cross-sectional measuring what job-crafting activities workers engage in to increase structural & social resources & challenging demands (as measured by Tims et al., 2014, job-crafting scale) • However, organizations may create initiatives to encourage job crafting (perhaps through participatory organizational interventions)
• Workplace quality improvement	1°	Dyrbye et al. (2020)	• Medical residents create a Wellness Action Team to begin a workplace quality improvement project over the course of 1 year • Both work and client burnout decreased from pre- to post-intervention

TABLE D-2 Continued

Types of Interventions	Level[a]	Example Studies	Example Programs/Intervention Components[b]
• Participatory organizational interventions (individual and collective participation)	1°	Nielsen et al. (2021) Reduced burnout	• Interventions aimed at improving work conditions and worker well-being by changing the way work is designed, organized, and managed • Used 5-step process participatory organization steps: ○ start-up, screening, action planning, implementation and evaluation (Nielsen & Noblet, 2018) • Helped Danish postal workers identify demands/resources and implement action plans via individual and collective participation processes • Both individual and collective participation were associated with reduced burnout post-intervention (but individual participation became nonsignificant after controlling for the collective participatory process)
• Participatory action research (team civility training)	1°	Leiter et al. (2011, 2012)	• CREW (Civility, Respect, & Engagement at Work) used a variety of hospital unit-led initiatives to improve team collegiality: identify sources of incivility; identify and implement team agreed-upon actions • Improved civility and reduced burnout
• Workplace reorganization and shifted organizational values		Dunn et al. (2007)	• 5-year work reorganization, aimed at increasing control, increase efficiency, and meaning of work for physicians. Elevated physician well-being as a core organizational outcome; encouraged physicians to identify and help improve aspects of their work that affected their well-being/burnout

continued

TABLE D-2 Continued

Types of Interventions	Level[a]	Example Studies	Example Programs/Intervention Components[b]
• Organizational change • Lean-based workflow redesigns		Hung et al. (2018)	• Program involved removing waste and streamlining workflow; implemented by management; redesign of care teams roles and their workflow; included daily "huddle" of care team • Physicians had higher levels of PA, and nonphysicians had lower levels of DP • However, both physicians and nonphysicians also had **higher** levels of EE • The study emphasizes the importance of participatory processes, and the risk of increasing burnout by increasing workload
• Organizational change (role/accountabilities)		Reid et al. (2010)	• Enacted changes to physician roles and accountabilities, which reduced levels of EE and DP (not PE)
COMBINED/MULTI-FOCUSED			
(not a specific 'type' of intervention per se, but interventions that explicitly combine individual and organizational interventions)			
• Individual/Organizational	1°/2°	Ansley et al. (2021)	• 4-week, online program involving background on educator stress; basic self-care; mindfulness; relaxation response activation & cognitive restructuring; routines and relationships at work; de-escalation; & maintaining progress • Described as an individual "stress reduction" program, but also had elements of job crafting and interpersonal skills (but it was not explicitly labeling it as a combined program) • Participation in program was associated with decreases in EE & DP, and increases in PA

[a]Most studies did not specifically identify the level of intervention (primary, secondary, tertiary). Therefore, the level was inferred based on the description and goals of the interventions.
[b]These interventions are examples of programs within each of the intervention category that may provide insight for readers (and not necessarily the best of the category, but representative of programs within each specific category).

be individual focused (see Ahola et al., 2017; Awa et al., 2010; Maricuțoiu et al., 2016; Panagioti et al., 2017; West et al., 2016, for overviews), with the most common being CBT, mindfulness, and relaxation training. These types of individual training have a stress management focus and tend to adopt cognitive-behavioral related interventions or mindfulness "stress reduction" strategies, including counseling and relaxation techniques (see, Awa et al., 2010; Maricuțoiu et al., 2016). Relaxation training reduced EE across six studies in Maricuțoiu et al.'s (2016) meta-analysis.

Another interesting line of individual interventions involves skills-based individual training, including specific job skills training and development in terms of "soft" interpersonal and communication skills. Maricuțoiu et al.'s (2016) meta-analysis provided evidence to demonstrate the effectiveness of these types of programs overall. Typically, the interventions involved some form of group workshop or individual coaching sessions (or a combination of both).

Although examined to a much lesser degree, other types of job skills training may reduce burnout if the source of burnout is a lack of knowledge or skills (e.g., which may result in increased workload, poor productivity, errors, or safety incidents). Within the individual interventions, there are "skills development" both in terms of soft and job-specific skills. For example, role-related hard skills (i.e., job/skill training) reduced EE across the five studies in Maricuțoiu et al.'s (2016) meta-analysis. Training aimed at general hospital job skills for less experienced social workers significantly reduced burnout (Cohen and Gagin, 2005). These types of interventions may be considered as primary interventions, as they are aimed at reducing the source of the burnout (improved job skills, improved safety, etc.).

Interpersonal-Focused Interventions

Although burnout was initially conceptualized with service-industry workers having to deal with challenging interpersonal interactions (suggesting that burnout interventions should help improve these social interactions), few studies have examined interpersonal-based interventions[7] directly, although there are some that look at training interpersonal skills (e.g., communication skills training) at an individual level. Interpersonal

---

[7] Interpersonal interventions may be subsumed under organization-focused interventions. However, I use Nielsen et al.'s (2018) IGLO (individual, group, leader, and organization) categorization to create greater differentiation of the causes and potential targets of the intervention, which can help both researchers and practitioners study burnout and redesign workplaces.

soft skills increased PA across four studies in Maricuțoiu et al.'s (2016) meta-analysis.

In a participative, interpersonal-focused study reducing incivility and burnout (i.e., primary intervention), Leiter et al.'s (2011, 2012) group-based CREW (Civility, Respect, and Engagement at Work) intervention used an incivility intervention (that aimed to improve the social relationships and levels of civility in healthcare units). In general, incivility in the intervention units was reduced over the program, and it was unchanged in the control units. Through these reductions, the nurses also experienced decreased levels of job burnout in the intervention group (unchanged/increased in the control group), providing some support for the efficacy of tailored, interpersonal-focused interventions.

Leadership training also may be considered a type of primary intervention aimed at improving interpersonal relationships in organizations. Dyrbye et al. (2019) conducted coaching interventions via trained leader coaches for physicians on diverse topics such as building work support/community; addressing workload and work efficiency; optimizing meaning of work; developing leadership skills; and engaging in self-care. Compared with the control group, physicians in the intervention group had significantly greater reductions in EE scores from baseline to post-intervention. Moreover, they examined the proportion of physicians reporting high EE: After 5 months, the percentage of physicians from the intervention group reporting high burnout reduced by 19.5 percent (compared with a 9.8 percent increase in the control group). However, there were no statistically significant reductions in DP scores.

Finally, Le Blanc et al. (2007) implemented a team-based, participatory burnout intervention for healthcare providers (i.e., physicians, nurses, radiotherapy assistants) from 29 oncology wards in the Netherlands to improve team support (and to increase control and participation). The healthcare providers engaged in various activities (e.g., set team goals, identified issues, and developed actions plans; designated members to check in on team member's well-being). The team intervention was successful in reducing both EE and DP. Compared with healthcare providers in the control teams/wards, healthcare providers in the intervention wards experienced lower EE and DP at Time 2 and lower EE at Time 3.

Organizational-Focused Interventions

Organizational interventions subsume many very different programs, typically defined by targeting some aspect(s) of the workplace (e.g., changing work environment) to reduce sources of burnout (e.g., workload; poor scheduling; poor interpersonal relationships) and increase resources to do one's job (e.g., Soriano-Sànchez and Jimenez-Vazquez, 2023). The meta-analyses provided some support for organizational initiatives, although conclusions are not definitive about the efficacy of these programs. Given the extreme variability in the types of organizational interventions, it is not surprising that there would be a corresponding variability in their effectiveness.

Many of the organizational interventions have worker input into the design: For example, participative action research involves empowering employees to identify workplace stressors and develop and initiate solutions (de Wijn and van der Doef, 2022; Nielsen et al., 2021). Participatory action research may be effective as it "offers the opportunity for joint creation of meaning [such as] . . . shared mental models of what changes need to be made to the way work is organised, designed and managed, joint decision making and action to make such changes" (Nielsen et al., 2021, p. 391). Organizational interventions can include "lean principles" (optimizing workflow to reduce waste of resources; Hung et al., 2018) and increased participative management style to improve worker well-being (Van Bogaert et al., 2017).

Job crafting (i.e., changing one's job role and/or interpersonal relationships, or increasing resources and decreasing demands; Tims and Bakker, 2010) may be viewed as an individual-, interpersonal-, or organizational-level initiative, depending on the exact focus and design. Several studies look at the effect of job-crafting interventions (empowering workers to make changes in their jobs and work environment) on burnout (e.g., emotional exhaustion; Gordon et al., 2018), improving social relations to reduce burnout (Yang et al., 2023), and the selection-optimization-compensation model as a process to job crafting (e.g., Müller et al., 2016).

Group Health implemented organizational changes to improve access, physician productivity, and financial performance of the organization. Although the program was successful in achieving access and productivity, it also increased physician burnout. In response to this increased burnout, Reid et al. (2010) examined the efficacy of a 2-year, quasi-experimental (before and after treatment, with a control group) program. This participative program involved workshops with all clinic staff (i.e., frontline physicians, managers, staff), patients, and researchers to identify "the redesign components that care teams refined and implemented during the first year" (p. 836). They then implemented best practices to address these issues (e.g., reduced patient load, increase patient appointment times; daily team meeting/huddles). The "underlying premise is that care teams, led by primary-care physicians, retain accountability for delivering primary care to patients in their practices" (p. 836). Compared with the control group, the intervention group had significantly lower levels of EE and DP 24 months after the beginning of the program; however, there was no significant difference in PA scores.

Dunn et al. (2007) examined the effects of a 5-year organization intervention/change at a primary healthcare group, Legacy Health Clinic. Legacy Health expanded their key organizational outcomes to include physician well-being, such that they "prioritized physician well-being equal to care quality and financial viability" (p. 1545) and created initiatives to support this focus. Over the 5-year period, the changes to the work process resulted in significant decreases in levels of physician exhaustion, as well as reduced turnover (Dunn et al., 2007).

Combined Interventions

There is some evidence that interventions that combine individual and organizational focused initiatives may be effective in reducing burnout (Awa et al., 2010; Bes et al., 2023; Thomas Craig et al., 2021); however, overall, there is little evidence that they are more effective than individual/organizational alone. For example, some research suggests that multimodal programs are not successful (e.g., Estevez Cores et al., 2021). In their meta-analyses, De Simone et al. (2021) found that combined interventions were effective in reducing burnout, but organizational programs tended to have larger reductions in burnout.

Although somewhat speculative, there are a few potential reasons why combined interventions may be effective, including the following: (1) multiple issues are being addressed simultaneously (e.g., reducing work/organizational demands, improving group functioning and relationships, improving individual skills and coping), thus addressing the complexity of burnout antecedents; (2) an organization's engagement in creating combined initiatives may reflect their commitment to improving worker well-being, thus creating additional (and potentially unmeasured) supports for employees; and (3) having multiple aspects of the program may increase the overall "dosage" of the intervention. That is, participants may be more involved and spend more time addressing burnout from various standpoints, thus resulting in a higher treatment/dosage.

SUMMARY OF BURNOUT INTERVENTIONS

The review of burnout meta-analyses is far from conclusive, but it provided evidence for both individual and organizational-based initiatives, typically with individual-focused ones having some stronger results. However, some meta-analyses have found that having combined individual-organization initiatives are the most effective (e.g., Bes et al., 2023). Dreison et al. (2018) also noted a need for more studies evaluating this combined intervention approach and organizational interventions, beyond simply job training/education. That is, not all (organizational) interventions are equal, either in the quality of the intervention process or in its content. Moreover, the number of studies focusing on individual interventions far outnumbers the ones on organizational interventions (e.g., Bes et al., 2023; de Wijn and van der Doef, 2022).

Dreison et al. (2018) has called for more research looking at multiple ways of addressing burnout. This multifaceted approach also has the benefit of addressing the burnout intervention dilemma, such that focusing on multiple aspects of the sources of burnout could improve both the workplace and individual functioning. Only when we can create this holistic focus can we truly address job burnout and reduce the sources of burnout.

Therefore, from the evidence across these meta-analyses and interventions studies, it is obvious that there may be no "one" correct answer: That is, program efficacy may depend on the specific details of the intervention and organizational context, as well as the sample characteristics and the sources of the burnout. In general, it may be folly to think that burnout is always explained solely by a single factor. Instead, we must appreciate the complex interplay of individual, group, leader, and organizational antecedents that create environmental demands, as well as individual responses to these demands, that can lead to burnout. Therefore, a key aspect in addressing burnout is understanding burnout in the specific context. For example, Leiter et al. (2011) conducted an intervention to address a specific problem of incivility and poor collegial relationships in hospital workgroups, which was leading to burnout and other negative organizational outcomes. It also included supportive team activities, and a team facilitator. By using a participatory method to help teams identify their specific sources of burnout, the program allowed activities to be tailored to reduce incivility and thus reduce burnout. These types of tailored intervention, which focus on the source of the burnout, allowing participatory input into the design and solutions, and allowing for support for individuals, may be integral in making significant progress in burnout intervention research and practice.

DISCUSSION

The field [of burnout interventions] has made limited progress in ameliorating mental health provider burnout. Based on our findings, we suggest that researchers implement a wider breadth of interventions that are tailored to address unique organizational and staff needs and that incorporate longer follow-up periods.

– Dreison et al., 2018, p.18

This current review supports Dreison et al.'s conclusions about the state of the burnout intervention research. Despite the abundance of studies on burnout in general, the relative number of high-quality organizational-based intervention studies is low. Moreover, there are inconsistencies in findings across the studies, and many of them are plagued by bias and methodological issues. These problems are not necessarily surprising given the challenges involved in conducting high-quality organizational interventions aimed at changing the work environment to support workers. However, these studies, along with their quality and conceptual issues, can provide insights and (some cautious) suggestions for future research and organizational practice in addressing burnout and supporting worker health.

First, it is valuable to understand the rationale as to why there is this disconnect between having organizational sources of burnout and proposing individual solutions for burnout. That is, to address burnout we need an understanding of the possible reasons for the lack of validated interventions. Several reasons are suggested by the literature: (1) a lack of awareness about the problem and solutions; (2) a lack of organizational culpability; (3) organizational inertia (and lack of expertise); (4); burned-out leaders; and (5) practical issues (cost; access; productivity pressures).

Lack of Awareness/Knowledge

Leaders may not fully understand the sources of burnout and may view individual-based, resilience-building as a legitimate fix rather than a mere band-aid step in covering deeper organizational-based issues. Indeed, research shows that individual-focused interventions can help. Thus, the awareness and impetus for organizational change is decreased. Therefore, continued communication about the sources of burnout, along with ways organizations can address it, is critical.

Blame and Culpability

Even with general awareness of the causes of burnout, the organization must explicitly accept culpability that the workplace is a key source of the burnout. It is much easier (and cheaper, see below) to place the 'blame' on the employees. By framing burnout as an individual worker problem, organizations that prioritize productivity and efficiency (even at the expense of worker well-being) do not have to examine deeper, systemic issues like toxic work cultures, unrealistic expectations, or inadequate support structures and change fundamental business practices.

By blaming employees, organizations: (a) do not have to acknowledge their own responsibility in the role of burnout; (b) do not engage in organizational change mechanisms; and (c) do not have to design and implement (potentially seemingly costly and time-consuming) organizational change strategies. Basically, they can continue with business as usual, with the employee—not the employer—paying the cost. In essence, pushing employees may benefit the organization, or at least do so in the short-term (Walker, 2025). Getting organizations to accept responsibility is the most difficult rationales to overcome. Finding a champion at senior management levels may be an effective way forward.

Organizational Inertia

Even if there is an awareness and acceptance of the role the organization plays in burnout, organizational inertia is a powerful force to overcome. Organizational change is a challenging process, and the status quo can be affirming and safe. When there is a focus on short-term, rather than long-term, goals, leaders may argue that it makes procedural and fiscal sense to fix people rather than the organization. Therefore, there must be a concerted effort, preferably with a champion and upper management support, to identify and implement the required change. Importantly, part of the inertia may be related to a lack of expertise to identify and implement organizational strategies to engage in change. Having access to people knowledgeable in validation techniques (e.g., internal consultants; I/O psychology consultants; graduate students/faculty; etc.) could help them to identify, develop, and validate key strategies for the workplace. There are other reasons for this inertia including a perceived lack of organizational resources.

Burned Out Leaders

One of these organizational resources is the required personnel to create change. The role of creating change rests largely on leaders. Ironically, because leaders are operating in the same environment, there is a good chance they are overwhelmed and burned out as well. This depletion of energy and focus detracts from their ability to create effective organizational change. This becomes a Catch-22, such that we need energized and effective leadership to create organizational change to reduce burnout, but the leaders are too burned out to create the change that would ultimately reduce their burnout. That is, reducing burnout requires effective leadership, but burnout itself prevents leaders from being effective.

Practical Change Issues

As noted above, inertia can arise from the practical issues, such as a lack of access to experts, effective leadership, and fiscal resources, or a conflicting long-term organizational vision. Structural changes to reduce the sources of burnout—such as reducing workloads, increasing staffing, or modifying job expectations—can be expensive and require long-term investment. Conversely, training employees in mindfulness, stress management, or resilience is relatively cheaper and quicker to implement than overhauling work policies. Moreover, there are psychological constraints to overcome: Change is scary and perceived to be expensive and time-consuming, such that smaller and equally efficient changes are often overlooked. However, small and cheap changes can be effective: We often challenge organizations to think of how small and cheap changes can be effective. For example, mistreatment is a key source of burnout, but treating employees with respect is free.

Collectively, these rationales for not pursuing organizational interventions to reduce the sources of burnout can negate attempts to address the burnout problem. Understanding, and overcoming, these rationales can help ensure the success of existing organizational interventions as well as create new approaches to this old problem.

Novel Approaches to Addressing Burnout

Part of the original purpose of this paper was to identify unique, innovative initiatives to address burnout. However, once immersed in the literature, and having identified some of the key sources, it becomes apparent that the search for unique "cures" to burnout is unrealistic. Expecting one single, definitive cure for burnout, given that it is influenced by a wide array of individual and organizational factors, is not feasible.

Moreover, searching for novel ways to address burnout may once again divert attention away from the underlying tenets of burnout in targeting primary initiatives aimed at reducing sources of burnout. However, this review identified effective interventions and processes, and in identifying some of the gaps, it has provided some novel ways at looking at burnout interventions. Therefore, in looking at unique ways of addressing burnout, we must (1) accurately assess both the sources of burnout and the extent to which workers are burned out; (2) envision burnout interventions as holistic, participatory processes/strategies, rather than individual programs (e.g., BUILDs process model, as described later in this section); which leads to (3) tailoring burnout interventions at the organizational, group, and individual levels by (a) identifying the specific sources of job burnout, and creating primary interventions to address these sources, (b) offering secondary interventions to help workers deal with ways of managing these stressors, (c) maintaining tertiary supports, which helps us to (d) create multifocal, combined interventions; and (4) understand and measure the exposure/strength/dosage of programs.

Addressing Burnout and Its Sources

We need to clarify the language for understanding and measuring sources of burnout versus assessing symptoms of burnout. Although there is relative consistency in the meta-analyses in how to assess burnout EE, CYN/DP, and PA/PE symptoms (most studies used the MBI), there is little mention of validly identifying and measuring the sources of burnout, even though many valid measures are available (e.g., leadership, bullying). More work must focus on understanding/measuring these sources with respect to burnout.

Moreover, in some research, burnout was conflated with stress, strain, and/or general fatigue. We must maintain the distinction between burnout (as a three-phase syndrome in response to poor organizational environments) and more general strain response (physical, psychological, and behavioural outcomes to stressors). Some studies only use EE, ignoring the DP/CYN and PA/PE components, providing an incomplete (and potentially misleading) indicator of the entirety of burnout. Finally, some studies used a one-item self-report scale as to how much people feel they are burned out, which not only fails to assess the three components of the burnout construct but also relies heavily on individual interpretation of what burnout is supposed to be.

'BUILD'ing Participatory Organizational Burnout Strategies

A primary focus on novel content of interventions distracts from an overall organizational burnout process/strategy. That is, as demonstrated by participatory organizational intervention process steps (e.g., Nielsen et al., 2021), a process/strategy provides a template for organizational leaders and employees to develop action plans to address their specific demands (using their specific resources) to help maintain and improve employee functioning.

Therefore, regardless of the interventions used, organizations must have a process to accurately assess their status quo, in terms of their employees' levels of burnout, and the specific sources of burnout (as well as intervention effectiveness). Because the organizational sources of burnout are varied, organizations need to design interventions around the specific sources within their organization and have specific supports in place. Also, having a means to gather input and feedback from employees is integral to the intervention process. What works for one individual or environment may not work in the another. Using process models, such as the BUILDs model (Day, 2019) can help identify steps in addressing burnout at all levels. It involves getting buy-in from stakeholders, in terms of understanding the importance of measurement and burnout initiatives. Understanding and assessing the organizations' status quo, in terms of their employees' levels of burnout, and understanding that the specific sources of burnout are key steps in resolving burnout. Once the sources are identified, identifying and implementing key, targeted interventions are critical. Finally, organizations must support ongoing learning, getting feedback on program efficacy, and developing sustainability in organizational learning to support work well-being via continuous improvement and development processes. These types of processes help create meaningful, tailored initiatives to reduce sources of burnout, support employees, and manage employees' experience of burnout.

Tailoring Primary, Secondary, and Tertiary Interventions

Using a participatory process model also can help the overall organization understand the sources and outcomes of burnout to help tailor the program to the organizational context and to the individual. That is, different facets of the workplace can impact worker burnout, such that "one size" of burnout intervention does not "fit all" instances of burnout. Abildgaard et al. (2019) lobbied for participatory organizational interventions, because they create "multiple intervention mechanisms interacting with the specific organizational contexts" (p. 1339).

Moreover, success of initiatives may vary across workers because the workers and leaders involved in organizational interventions may perceive the same intervention very differently (Bartunek et al., 2006). Therefore, more work is necessary to understand variations in perceptions of interventions, as well as intervention efficacy, based on key work (e.g., organizational level; industry) and individual characteristics (e.g., gender; race/ethnicity). However, if organizations take a truly individual-focused, tailored approach to addressing burnout, these individual differences transcend these group categorical data.

A participatory process also may help resolve the individual versus organizational debate; that is, as noted throughout this review, burnout is defined as a reaction to poor work environment and chronic workplace issues. As such, Maslach and Leiter (1997) have argued a need for organizational interventions to reduce these sources of burnout, and not simply ask workers to rethink how they respond to them. However, most interventions focus on secondary interventions (e.g., helping individuals develop coping mechanisms) rather than on primary interventions (i.e., changing the source of the burnout).

This situation may not be surprising given the challenges involved in conducting high-quality organizational interventions aimed at changing the work environment to support workers. Organizational interventions are complex, time-consuming, expensive, and hard to design (Gregory et al., 2018), and it is cheaper and easier to focus on supporting individuals rather than changing systems. That is, it is far easier to ask employees to develop stronger demand/stressor-management techniques (CBT, mindfulness) and "be less burned out" than to identify and reduce the sources of burnout (e.g., reduce workload, improve leadership, reduce patient/client/coworker incivility). However, it creates the key dilemma in addressing burnout by using secondary interventions to manage demands that could be reduced through primary prevention interventions.

In Valcour's (2016) Harvard Business Review article on practical advice to reduce burnout, the three tips she provides to clients all focus on individual care factors: (1) prioritize self care, (2) shift your perspective, and (3) reduce exposure to job stressors. However, she provides the very important caveat up front that "situational factors are the biggest contributors to burnout, so changes at the job, team, or organizational level are often required to address all the underlying issues. However, there are steps you can take on your own once you're aware of the symptoms and of what might be causing them." That is, we need to first improve the cause of job burnout (i.e., the workplace environment), and while that is happening, we can support and develop how employees are able to handle the fallout from job stressors and the resultant burnout.

Similarly, in their study of physician burnout, Gregory et al. (2018) noted that although these types of individually focused self-care programs "have shown a positive effect on reducing burnout, this intervention approach is inconsistent with the underlying theoretical framework for burnout" (p. 341). Therefore, they concluded that even though improving physician resilience "may be an important skill to develop . . . organizationally focused interventions that improve the practice of medicine within organizations is the optimal way to reduce physician burnout" (p. 342; emphasis added).

Primary Interventions: Understanding and Reducing Burnout Sources. As a relatively simple, yet integral, start for both researchers and practitioners, instead of talking about addressing or even reducing burnout (which implies more of a secondary/tertiary management of individual-focused conditions), we must start talking about reducing the sources of burnout (i.e., primary prevention). This simple change of phrase reflects a greater underlying difference in perspectives: Job burnout is, and should continue to be, defined as a syndrome resulting from exposure to work demands, many of which are manageable. As such, we need to stop thinking about burnout as an individual problem and go back to making it an organizational problem.

One understudied method for reducing burnout pertains to the area of recruitment, selection, and training, even though research has demonstrated the key aspect of having a "match" between the individual and the job. Leiter and Maslach's (1999) work on the perceived congruency between the individual and key aspects of his or her organizational environment help us understand how burnout can arise from a mismatch between individual and organization. They proposed that the greater the perceived misalignment between the individual and their job, the higher the likelihood of burnout; conversely, the greater the perceived alignment, the higher the likelihood of feeling more engaged with work. That is, the "degree of perceived congruency between the individual and key aspects of [one's] organizational environment" can influence one's level of burnout (Maslach and Leiter, 2008, p. 501).

Nurses' perceived fit tends to be related to EE, and it also can moderate the relationship between empowerment and EE (e.g., Laschinger et al., 2006). This area has important implications for ways to reduce the sources of burnout: That is, if a person-job/work fit is key to well-being on the job, effective selection methods that assess this fit are essential. However, we see very little work incorporating human resource activities (e.g., recruitment, selection, training) in preventing burnout. A caveat is warranted here: This fit does not denote hiring people who are better able to handle unreasonable organizational demands. For example, organizations still must eliminate sources of supervisor, client, and colleague mistreatment burnout in the workplace. Congruency is meant to ensure that there is alignment in what is legitimately required by the job and key competencies of the incumbent.

Secondary Interventions. Despite a push toward organizational interventions, individual interventions have been shown to be very effective. They often help reduce strain outcomes and burnout, which makes sense. If you are not in control of the stressor and no one else is doing anything to reduce it, there are several possible outcomes: you can leave the organization, "deal with it" (effectively or ineffectively), and/or get sick. Therefore, being better able to deal with it can help you to function and feel better. However, should we be asking workers to develop better coping and recovery techniques to deal with the sources of burnout, such as bullying, overload, and lack of support and autonomy? Or should we strive to improve the work environment to minimize these demands? That is, although secondary approaches show promise in reducing strain and burnout (and although there are some innovative methodologies being offered on apps that can increase the visibility and accessibility of burnout programs), we still must use it as a secondary step, after we have reduced the sources.

Tertiary Interventions. Although advocating for primary and secondary interventions, tertiary interventions are still required. That is, despite best efforts, some people may still experience mild to severe burnout. Therefore, Maslach and Leiter (2008) argued that it can be valuable to look at burnout in a different, more pragmatic way by examining early indicators of burnout in workers:

> If such early indicators were indeed valid predictors of future problems with burnout, then they could be used to identify "high risk" people who could be targeted for early, preventive interventions. This approach is a purely pragmatic one, which simply focuses on

people's experiences at particular points in time rather than making other assumptions or including other variables. The basic premise is that if an individual is experiencing some early signs of burnout, then that information is sufficient for consideration of actions to prevent burnout and build engagement (p. 498).

This perspective does not blame the individual, but it considers the workers' current state (from the interaction between self and work environment) and strives to prevent severe burnout by understanding and addressing these warning signs.

Holistic Multifocused Interventions

Given the value of all three levels of interventions, a systematic way to incorporate all levels, creating a holistic multifocused burnout strategy, is warranted. That is, the intent is to focus on reducing the negative aspects of the organizational environment that are creating burnout, while still supporting individual workers in how they handle work challenges. In Schein's (1990) model of organization culture, he highlights the difference between artifacts (surface indicators of culture) and underlying values and basic assumptions of the organization. Innovative techniques or initiatives (i.e., surface-level artifacts) can be insufficient in reducing burnout if the organizational culture does not reflect an authentic, underlying value of its workers (e.g., views workers as disposable resources rather than a valuable commodity).

For example, in Dunn et al.'s (2007) organizational intervention across several healthcare facilities, management made physician well-being a priority on par with the facilities' financial outcomes; that is, well-being was as important as profits. This action was rooted in changed underlying values, going beyond being a simply surface-level artifact to being a key driver in how they viewed physician health, the decisions they made, and additional actions they took to support physicians.

A caveat regarding using primary interventions (e.g., organizational change) is that, ironically, organizational change—even change for the better—can be challenging and contribute to worker stress (Day et al., 2017). That is, change to improve the workplace (e.g., Reid et al., 2010) and organizational interventions designed to reduce burnout (Van Bogaert et al., 2017) can have the unintended effects of increasing burnout.

However, Day et al. (2017) also found that control and support can buffer the negative effects of perceived change-related stressors on employees' burnout. Therefore, including participatory components may improve autonomy and increase supports while reducing change-related stressors. Similarly, using combined interventions—using both primary and secondary interventions—may help reduce individual strain/burnout during the longer-term change process. For example, when implementing organizational interventions aimed at reducing the sources of burnout, include participatory processes to ensure the change is tailored to the situation and individuals and incorporate ways of supporting employees and leaders through the change. A reduction in leaders' stress can reduce followers' level of burnout as well (Harms et al., 2017).

Strength and Quality of Interventions

A final consideration in developing burnout interventions is the strength (or "dosage"/exposure) of the intervention. Participants in the same intervention may have different dosages or exposure to the intervention, in the number of sessions attended, level of engagement, time spent on practicing new skills, and so forth. It is not always practical (or desired) to standardize the dosage across participants, but measuring dosage, or proxies of dosage, wherever possible is helpful. For example, as part of the CREW intervention (aimed at reducing incivility and burnout), hospital units tailored activities to meet their specific needs. This tailored and participatory nature of CREW added to its efficacy, but it also created ambiguity as to the dosage that each unit was receiving. In response, Leiter et al. (2011) examined the strength of intervention, finding there were no differences in burnout based on the different programs across the eight units. Conversely, de Wijn and van der Doef (2022) found a significant effect of exposure to intervention, such that studies in which nurses participated in most of the intervention sessions had higher effect sizes than did studies in which the sample had a lower participation/exposure. Therefore, some type of measure of intervention strength, exposure, or dosage should be included in burnout intervention studies.

Another way to think of dosage is in terms of organizational resources put toward the initiatives. Van Bogaert et al. (2017) concluded that "it is not surprising that the sites that have invested the most, in terms of financial human resources and facilitation have yielded the most improvements" (p. 34). Therefore, incorporating ways of increasing organizational, leader, and group efforts into the interventions, and integrating them into the operations of the organization, may create more beneficial outcomes.

A template for a holistic workplace burnout strategy for burnout based on all the above areas is presented in Figure D-2. It highlights some

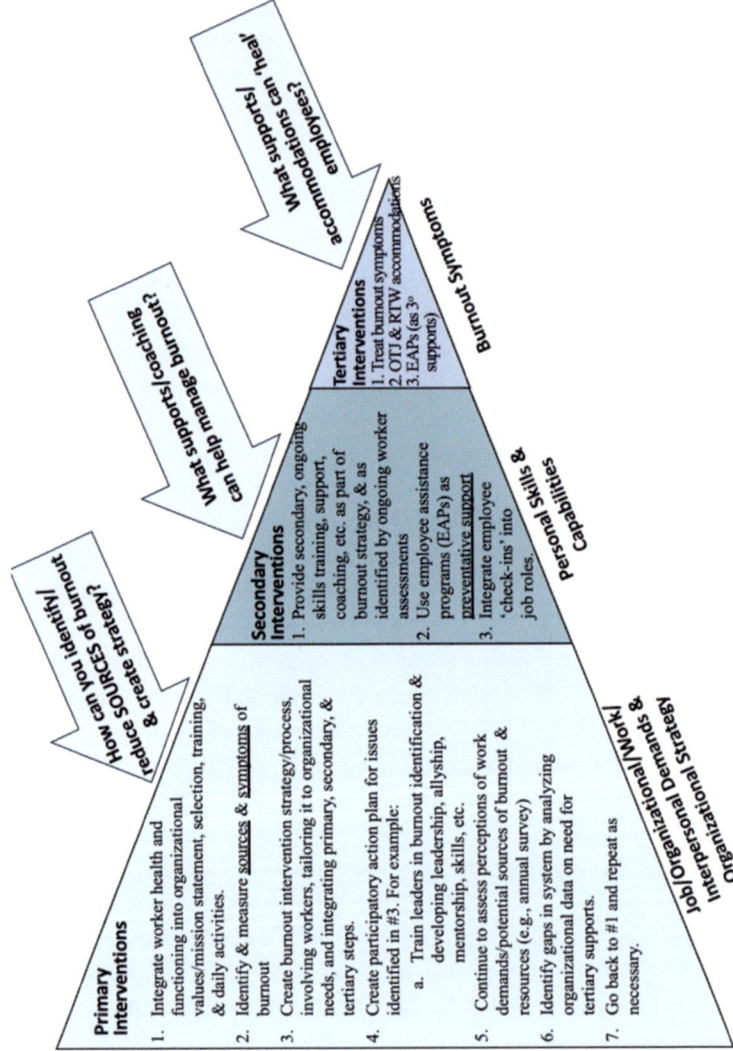

FIGURE D-2 Template for a holistic perspective in addressing burnout, with example initiatives.

potential examples of primary, secondary, and tertiary initiatives that an organization can undertake to concurrently address organizational change and employee functioning. In line with most intervention frameworks, it outlines an initial (and predominant) use of primary interventions, followed by the use of secondary interventions. Ideally, tertiary interventions are seen, and used, as the last step in situations where primary and secondary interventions were not sufficient to reduce sources of burnout and help develop supports/resources for workers. Although (hopefully) used to a lesser extent, their important role in addressing the fallout from burnout is still essential.

CONCLUDING COMMENTS

There have been considerable steps made in understanding the causes of burnout, and substantial increases in recent years in secondary-level individual-focused interventions to address burnout via individual coping skills. However, it has been well documented that despite a general agreement that burnout arises from organizational causes, there are few validated organizational interventions. Moreover, these types of interventions also have greater variability around their content (e.g., interpersonal group initiatives, leadership development, work process changes) and goals (e.g., create manageable workloads, create better work relationships), which make it challenging to make solid conclusions about their effectiveness.

Understanding and directly addressing this disconnect between having organizational sources of burnout and proposing individual solutions for burnout can improve usage of organizational initiatives to reduce the causes of burnout. Organizations can improve awareness about the problem and identifying organizational solutions. They should ensure accountability for their own actions. They need to understand the underlying causes of organizational inertia (including a lack of expertise). Ironically, they must ensure their leaders are healthy and not burned-out to be able to support employees and create organizational change. Finally, they must provide resources to address the root causes of burnout, and still not catastrophize the problem so that it becomes seemingly insurmountable.

Interestingly, some of the key insights from the meta-analyses arise not from the data per se, but from the assumptions made in the studies, and some of the biases and violations of the assumptions. For example, (1) we need to be clear about what we mean my burnout: burnout, stress, and strain are all important worker outcomes and are related to each other, but it is meaningful to keep them distinct. Moreover, we need to look at the full construct of burnout beyond emotional exhaustion (including depersonalization/cynicism and personal accomplishment/professional efficacy). (2) If we accept that the etiology of burnout is multifactorial, we also need to accept that there is no one overall panacea to prevent and reduce burnout. The use of individual-focused programs alone is antithetical to the definition of burnout, and it ignores the work sources of burnout. Thus, although mindfulness may help us get through multiple work (and nonwork) events across our lifetime, it is not the cure for those events. Targeting the actual events (reduce workplace bullying, improve client interactions) is much more effective that looking at ways to handle our reactions. That is, we must stop having a sole focus on managing worker symptoms and start reducing specific workplace sources of burnout. (3) Trying to find novel ways to reduce burnout may impede our ability to reduce both sources and symptoms of burnout. We may prefer novel and quick-fix solutions, yet the tried-and-true (and perhaps more long-term and challenging) option is still more effective. That is, if the causes of burnout are systemic within the organization, reducing burnout requires long-term changes to organizational culture to reduce the root causes of burnout. Therefore, (4) organizations can achieve these goals by creating an overall introspective burnout strategy, which focuses on the root organizational causes of burnout and which values worker well-being and functioning.

REFERENCES

*indicates a meta-analysis of burnout interventions

Abildgaard, J. S., Nielsen, K., Wåhlin-Jacobsen, C. D., Maltesen, T., Christensen, K. B., & Holtermann, A. (2019). "Same, but different": A mixed-methods realist evaluation of a cluster-randomized controlled participatory organizational intervention. Human Relations, 73(10), 1339–1365.

*Ahola, K., Toppinen-Tanner, S., & Seppänen, J. (2017). Interventions to alleviate burnout symptoms and to support return to work among employees with burnout: Systematic review and meta-analysis. Burnout Research, 4, 1–11.

Ansley, B. M., Houchins, D. E., Varjas, K., Roach, A., Patterson, D., & Hendrick, R. (2021). The impact of an online stress intervention on burnout and teacher efficacy. Teaching and Teacher Education, 98, 103251.

Aronsson, G., Theorell, T., Grape, T., Hammarström, A., Hogstedt, C., Marteinsdottir, I., Skoog, I., Träskman-Bendz, L., & Hall, C. (2017). A systematic review including meta-analysis of work environment and burnout symptoms. BMC Public Health, 17, 1–13.

Awa, W. L., Plaumann, M., & Walter, U. (2010). Burnout prevention: A review of intervention programs. Patient Education and Counseling, 78(2), 184–190.

Bakker, A.B. (2009). The crossover of burnout and its relation to partner health. Stress and Health, 25(4), 343–353.

Bartunek, J. M., Rousseau, D. M., Rudolph, J. W., & DePalma, J. A. (2006). On the receiving end: Sensemaking, emotion, and assessments of an organizational change initiated by others. The Journal of Applied Behavioral Science, 42(2), 182–206.

*Beames, J. R., Spanos, S., Roberts, A., McGillivray, L., Li, S., Newby, J. M., Bridianne, O., & Werner-Seidler, A. (2023). Intervention programs targeting the mental health, professional burnout, and/or wellbeing of school teachers: A systematic review and meta-analyses. Educational Psychology Review, 35(1), 26.

Berdahl, J. L., Cooper, M., Glick, P., Livingston, R. W., & Williams, J. C. (2018). Work as a masculinity contest. Journal of Social Issues, 74(3), 422–448.

*Bes, I., Shoman, Y., Al-Gobari, M., Rousson, V., & Guseva Canu, I. (2023). Organizational interventions and occupational burnout: A meta-analysis with focus on exhaustion. International Archives of Occupational and Environmental Health, 96(9), 1211–1223.

Blonk, R. W., Brenninkmeijer, V., Lagerveld, S. E., & Houtman, I. L. (2006). Return to work: A comparison of two cognitive behavioural interventions in cases of work-related psychological complaints among the self-employed. Work & Stress, 20(2), 129–144.

*Burton, A., Burgess, C., Dean, S., Koutsopoulou, G. Z., Hugh-Jones, S. (2017). How effective are mindfulness-based interventions for reducing stress among healthcare professionals? A systematic review and meta-analysis. Stress & Health, 33(1), 3–13.

*Chakraborty, B., Trivedi, K., Kiran, K. A., Chatterjee, P., Kujur, M., & Sarkar, B. (2023). Impact of using mobile applications on the psychological wellbeing of Nurses to reduce job stress and burnout: Systematic review and meta-analysis. The Malaysian Journal of Nursing, 15(2), 143–153.

Chen, H., Wu, P., and Wei, W. (2012). New perspective on job burnout: Exploring the root cause beyond general antecedents analysis. Psychological Reports, 110(3), 801–819.

Chirico, F., Afolabi, A. A., Ilesanmi, O. S., Nucera, G., Ferrari, G., Sacco, A., Szarpak L., Crescenzo P., Magnavita, N., & Leiter, M. (2021). Prevalence, risk factors and prevention of burnout syndrome among healthcare workers: An umbrella review of systematic reviews and meta-analyses. Journal of Health and Social Sciences, 6(4), 465–491.

Cohen, M., & Gagin, R. (2005). Can skill-development training alleviate burnout in hospital social workers? Social Work in Health Care, 40(4), 83–97.

Cohen, C., Pignata, S., Bezak, E., Tie, M., & Childs, J. (2023). Workplace interventions to improve well-being and reduce burnout for nurses, physicians and allied healthcare professionals: A systematic review. BMJ Open, 13(6), e071203.

Corbeanu, A., Iliescu, D., Ion, A., & Spînu, R. (2023). The link between burnout and job performance: A meta-analysis. European Journal of Work and Organizational Psychology, 32(4), 599–616.

Dall'Ora, C., Ball, J., Reinius, M., & Griffiths, P. (2020). Burnout in nursing: A theoretical review. Human Resources Health, 18(1), 41.

Day, A. (2019). Setting the agenda for evidence-based and sustainable psychologically healthy workplaces. In R. J. Burke & A. M. Richardson (Eds.). Creating Psychologically Healthy Workplaces (pp. 65–90). Edward Elgar Publishing.

Day, A., Crown, S. N., & Ivany, M. (2017). Organisational change and employee burnout: The moderating effects of support and job control. Safety Science, 100, 4–12.

*De Simone, S., Vargas, M., & Servillo, G. (2021). Organizational strategies to reduce physician burnout: A systematic review and meta-analysis. Aging Clinical and Experimental Research, 33, 883–894.

*de Wijn, A. N., & van der Doef, M. P. (2022). A meta-analysis on the effectiveness of stress management interventions for nurses: Capturing 14 years of research. International Journal of Stress Management, 29(2), 113–129. doi:10.1037/str0000169.

Demerouti, E., Bakker, A. B., Nachreiner, F., Schaufeli, W. B. (2001). The job demands resources model of burnout. Journal of Applied Psychology 86(3), 499–512.

Demerouti, E., Bakker, A. B., Vardakou, I., & Kantas, A. (2003). The convergent validity of two burnout instruments: A multitrait-multimethod analysis. European Journal of Psychological Assessment, 19(1), 296–307.

Demerouti, E., Bakker, A. B., & Schaufeli, W. B. (2005). Spillover and crossover of exhaustion and life satisfaction among dual-earner parents. Journal of Vocational Behavior, 67(2), 266–289.

Di Mario S, Cocchiara R. A., & La Torre, G. 2023. The Use of Yoga and Mindfulness-based Interventions to Reduce Stress and Burnout in Healthcare Workers: An Umbrella Review. Alternative Therapies in Health and Medicine. 29(1):29–35.

*Dreison, K. C., Luther, L., Bonfils, K. A., Sliter, M. T., McGrew, J. H., & Salyers, M. P. (2018). Job burnout in mental health providers: A meta-analysis of 35 years of intervention research. Journal of Occupational Health Psychology, 23(1), 18.

Dunn, P. M., Arnetz, B. B., Christensen, J. F., & Homer, L. (2007). Meeting the imperative to improve physician well-being: Assessment of an innovative program. Journal of General Internal Medicine, 22, 1544–1552.

Dyrbye, L. N., Major-Elechi, B., Hays, J. T., Fraser, C. H., Buskirk, S. J., & West, C. P. (2020). Relationship between organizational leadership and health care employee burnout and satisfaction. Mayo Clinic Proceedings, 95(4), 698–708).

Dyrbye, L. N., Shanafelt, T. D., Gill, P. R., Satele, D. V., & West, C. P. (2019). Effect of a professional coaching intervention on the well-being and distress of physicians: A pilot randomized clinical trial. JAMA Internal Medicine, 179(10), 1406–1414. https://jamanetwork.com/journals/jamainternalmedicine/article-abstract/2740206.

Estevez Cores, S., Sayed, A. A., Tracy, D. K., & Kempton, M. J. (2021). Individual-focused occupational health interventions: A meta-analysis of randomized controlled trials. Journal of Occupational Health Psychology, 26(3), 189.

Feldt, T., Rantanen, J., Metsäpelto, R. L., Pulkkinen, L., & Kokko, K. (2014). The 9-item Bergen Burnout Inventory: Factorial validity across organizations and measurements of longitudinal data. Burnout Research, 1(2), 63–68.

*Fendel, J. C., Bürkle, J. J., & Göritz, A. S. (2021). Mindfulness-based interventions to reduce burnout and stress in physicians: A systematic review and meta-analysis. Academic Medicine, 96(5), 751–764.

Freudenberger, H. J. (1974). Staff burn-out. Journal of Social Issues, 30(1), 159–165.

Freudenberger, H. J. (1975). The staff burn-out syndrome in alternative institutions. Psychotherapy: Theory, Research & Practice, 12(1), 73–82. https://doi-org.library.smu.ca/10.1037/h0086411.

Galanis, P., Vraka, I., Fragkou, D., Bilali, A., & Kaitelidou, D. (2021). Nurses' burnout and associated risk factors during the COVID-19 pandemic: A systematic review and meta-analysis. Journal of Advanced Nursing, 77(8), 3286–3302.

Gómez-Urquiza, J. L., Albendín-García, L., Velando-Soriano, A., Ortega-Campos, E., Ramírez-Baena, L., Membrive-Jiménez, M. J., & Suleiman-Martos, N. (2020). Burnout in palliative care nurses, prevalence and risk factors: A systematic review with meta-analysis. International Journal of Environmental Research and Public Health, 17(20), 7672.

Gordon, H. J., Demerouti, E., Le Blanc, P. M., Bakker, A. B., Bipp, T., & Verhagen, M. A. (2018). Individual job redesign: Job crafting interventions in healthcare. Journal of Vocational Behavior, 104, 98–114.

Gregory, S. T., Menser, T., & Gregory, B. T. (2018). An organizational intervention to reduce physician burnout. Journal of Healthcare Management, 63(5), 338–352.

Hakanen, J. J., Bakker, A. B., & Jokisaari, M. (2011). A 35-year follow-up study on burnout among Finnish employees. Journal of Occupational Health Psychology, 16(3), 345.

Hakanen, J. J., Seppälä, P., & Peeters, M. C. (2017). High job demands, still engaged and not burned out? The role of job crafting. International Journal of Behavioral Medicine, 24, 619–627.

Halbesleben, J. R., & Demerouti, E. (2005). The construct validity of an alternative measure of burnout: Investigating the English translation of the Oldenburg Burnout Inventory. Work & Stress, 19(3), 208–220.

Harms, P. D., Credé, M., Tynan, M., Leon, M., & Jeung, W. (2017). Leadership and stress: A meta-analytic review. The Leadership Quarterly, 28(1), 178–194.

*Haslam, A., Tuia, J., Miller, S. L., & Prasad, V. (2024). Systematic review and meta-analysis of randomized trials testing interventions to reduce physician burnout. The American Journal of Medicine, 137(3), 249–257.

Hätinen, M., Mäkikangas, A., Kinnunen, U., & Pekkonen, M. (2013). Recovery from burnout during a one-year rehabilitation intervention with six-month follow-up: Associations with coping strategies. International Journal of Stress Management, 20(4), 364.

Hildenbrand, K., Sacramento, C. A., & Binnewies, C. (2018). Transformational leadership and burnout: The role of thriving and followers' openness to experience. Journal of Occupational Health Psychology, 23(1), 31.

Hung, D. Y., Harrison, M. I., Truong, Q., & Du, X. (2018). Experiences of primary care physicians and staff following lean workflow redesign. BMC Health Services Research, 18, 1–8.

Hurrell, J. J., Jr., & Sauter, S. L. (2013). Job stress prevention. In A. M. Rossi, J. A. Meurs, P. L. Perrewé (Eds.). Improving Employee Health and Well Being (p. 187). Charlotte, NC, Information Age Publishing.

*Iancu, A. E., Rusu, A., Măroiu, C., Păcurar, R., & Maricuţoiu, L. P. (2018). The effectiveness of interventions aimed at reducing teacher burnout: A meta-analysis. Educational Psychology Review, 30, 373–396.

Iverson, R. D., Olekalns, M., & Erwin, P. J. (1998). Affectivity, organizational stressors, and absenteeism: A causal model of burnout and its consequences. Journal of Vocational Behavior, 52(1), 1–23.

Kristensen, T. S., Borritz, M., Villadsen, E., & Christensen, K. B. (2005). The Copenhagen Burnout Inventory: A new tool for the assessment of burnout. Work & Stress, 19(3), 192–207.

Kroth, P. J., Morioka-Douglas, N., Veres, S., Babbott, S., Poplau, S., Qeadan, F., Parshall, C., Corrigan, K., & Linzer, M. (2019). Association of electronic health record design and use factors with clinician stress and burnout. JAMA Network Open, 2(8), e199609.

Lamontagne, A. D., Keegel, T., Louie, A. M., Ostry, A., & Landsbergis, P. A. (2007). A systematic review of the job-stress intervention evaluation literature, 1990–2005. International Journal of Occupational and Environmental Health, 13(3), 268–280.

Laschinger, H. K. S., Wong, C. A., & Greco, P. (2006). The impact of staff nurse empowerment on person-job fit and work engagement/burnout. Nursing Administration Quarterly, 30(4), 358–367.

Le Blanc, P. M., Hox, J. J., Schaufeli, W. B., Taris, T. W., & Peeters, M. C. (2007). Take care! The evaluation of a team-based burnout intervention program for oncology care providers. Journal of Applied Psychology, 92(1), 213.

*Lee, H. F., Kuo, C. C., Chien, T. W., & Wang, Y. R. (2016). A meta-analysis of the effects of coping strategies on reducing nurse burnout. Applied Nursing Research, 31, 100–110.

*Lee, M., & Cha, C. (2023). Interventions to reduce burnout among clinical nurses: Systematic review and meta-analysis. Scientific Reports, 13(1), 10971.

Leiter, M. P., Day, A., Oore, D. G., & Spence Laschinger, H. K. (2012). Getting better and staying better: Assessing civility, incivility, distress, and job attitudes one year after a civility intervention. Journal of Occupational Health Psychology, 17(4), 425.

Leiter, M. P., Hakanen, J. J., Ahola, K., Toppinen-Tanner, S., Koskinen, A., & Väänänen, A. (2013). Organizational predictors and health consequences of changes in burnout: A 12-year cohort study. Journal of Organizational Behavior, 34(7), 959–973.

Leiter, M. P., & Harvie, P. L. (1996). Burnout among mental health workers: A review and a research agenda. International Journal of Social Psychiatry, 42(2), 90–101.

Leiter, M. P., Laschinger, H. K. S., Day, A., & Oore, D. G. (2011). The impact of civility interventions on employee social behavior, distress, and attitudes. Journal of Applied Psychology, 96(6), 1258.

Leiter, M. P., & Maslach, C. (1999). Six areas of worklife: A model of the organizational context of burnout. Journal of Health and Human Services Administration, 472–489.

*Li, J., Xue, E., & He, Y. (2023). Investigating the effect of cognitive–behavioral, mindful-based, emotional-based intervention and professional training on teachers' job burnout: A meta-analysis. Behavioral Sciences, 13(10), 803.

Lloyd, J., Bond, F. W., & Flaxman, P. (2013). Identifying psychological mechanisms underpinning a cognitive behavioural therapy intervention for emotional burnout. Work & Stress, 27(2), 181–199.

Lundgren-Nilsson, Å., Jonsdottir, I. H., Pallant, J., & Ahlborg, G. (2012). Internal construct validity of the Shirom-Melamed burnout questionnaire (SMBQ). BMC Public Health, 12, 1–8.

*Ma, Y., Xie, T., Zhang, J., & Yang, H. (2023). The prevalence, related factors and interventions of oncology nurses' burnout in different continents: A systematic review and meta-analysis. Journal of Clinical Nursing, 32(19-20), 7050–7061.

Mackenzie, C. S., Poulin, P. A., & Seidman-Carlson, R. (2006). A brief mindfulness-based stress reduction intervention for nurses and nurse aides. Applied Nursing Research, 19(2), 105–109.

Madigan, D. J., & Kim, L. E. (2021). Towards an understanding of teacher attrition: A meta-analysis of burnout, job satisfaction, and teachers' intentions to quit. Teaching and Teacher Education, 105, 103425.

*Maricuțoiu, L. P., Sava, F. A., & Butta, O. (2016). The effectiveness of controlled interventions on employees' burnout: A meta-analysis. Journal of Occupational and Organizational Psychology, 89(1), 1–27.

Maslach, C. (2003). Job burnout: New directions in research and intervention. Current Directions in Psychological Science, 12(5), 189–192.

Maslach, C., Jackson, S. E., & Leiter, M. P. (1997). Maslach Burnout Inventory. Scarecrow Education.

Maslach, C. & Leiter, M.P. (1997). The Truth About Burnout: How Organizations Cause Personal Stress and What to Do About It. CA, John Wiley & Sons.

Maslach, C., & Leiter, M. P. (2008). Early predictors of job burnout and engagement. Journal of Applied. Psychology, 93, 498–512. doi: 10.1037/0021-9010.93.3.498.

Maslach, C., & Leiter, M. P. (2021). How to measure burnout accurately and ethically. Harvard Business Review, 7.

Maslach, C., Schaufeli, W. B., & Leiter, M. P. (2001). Job burnout. Annual Review of Psychology, 52(1), 397–422.

Matthiesen, S. (1992). The Bergen Burnout Indicator. Bergen: University of Bergen Press.

Müller, A., Heiden, B., Herbig, B., Poppe, F., & Angerer, P. (2016). Improving well-being at work: A randomized controlled intervention based on selection, optimization, and compensation. Journal of Occupational Health Psychology, 21(2), 169.

Nielsen, K., Antino, M., Rodríguez-Muñoz, A., & Sanz-Vergel, A. (2021). Is it me or us? The impact of individual and collective participation on work engagement and burnout in a cluster-randomized organisational intervention. Work & Stress, 35(4), 374–397.

Nielsen, K., Stage, M., Abildgaard, J. S., & Brauer, C. V. (2013). Participatory intervention from an organizational perspective: Employees as active agents in creating a healthy work environment. Salutogenic Organizations and Change: The Concepts behind Organizational Health Intervention Research, 327–350.

Nielsen, K., Yarker, J., Munir, F., & Bultmann, U. (2018). IGLOO: An integrated framework for sustainable return to work in workers with common mental disorders. Work and Stress, 32(4), 400–417.

*Ochentel, O., Humphrey, C., & Pfeifer, K. (2018). Efficacy of exercise therapy in persons with burnout. A systematic review and meta-analysis. Journal of Sports Science & Medicine, 17(3), 475.

Oliveira, S., Roberto, M. S., Veiga-Simão, A. M., & Marques-Pinto, A. (2021). A meta-analysis of the impact of social and emotional learning interventions on teachers' burnout symptoms. Educational Psychology Review, 33(4), 1779–1808.

*Panagioti, M., Panagopoulou, E., Bower, P., Lewith, G., Kontopantelis, E., Chew-Graham, C., Dawson, S., Marwijk, H., Geraghty, K., & Esmail, A. (2017). Controlled interventions to reduce burnout in physicians: A systematic review and meta-analysis. Journal of the American Medical Association Internal Medicine, 177(2), 195–205.

Papazian, L., Hraiech, S., Loundou, A., Herridge, M. S., & Boyer, L. (2023). High-level burnout in physicians and nurses working in adult ICUs: A systematic review and meta-analysis. Intensive Care Medicine, 49(4), 387–400.

*Perski, O., Grossi, G., Perski, A., & Niemi, M. (2017). A systematic review and meta-analysis of tertiary interventions in clinical burnout. Scandinavian Journal of Psychology, 58(6), 551–561.

Peterson, U., Bergström, G., Samuelsson, M., Åsberg, M., & Nygren, Å. (2008). Reflecting peer-support groups in the prevention of stress and burnout: Randomized controlled trial. Journal of Advanced Nursing, 63(5), 506–516.

Regina, J., & Allen, T. D. (2023). Masculinity contest culture: Harmful for whom? An examination of emotional exhaustion. Journal of Occupational Health Psychology, 28(2), 117.

Reid, R. J., Coleman, K., Johnson, E. A., et al. (2010). The group health medical home at year two: Cost savings, higher patient satisfaction, and less burnout for providers. Health Affairs, 29(5), 835–843.

Saboonchi, F., Perski, A., & Grossi, G. (2013). Validation of Karolinska Exhaustion Scale: Psychometric properties of a measure of exhaustion syndrome. Scandinavian Journal of Caring Sciences, 27(4), 1010–1017.

Salmela-Aro, K., Rantanen, J., Hyvönen, K., Tilleman, K., & Feldt, T. (2011). Bergen Burnout Inventory: Reliability and validity among Finnish and Estonian managers. International Archives of Occupational and Environmental Health, 84, 635–645.

*Salvado, M., Marques, D. L., Pires, I. M., & Silva, N. M. (2021, October). Mindfulness-based interventions to reduce burnout in primary healthcare professionals: A systematic review and meta-analysis. Healthcare, 9(10), 1342.

Salvagioni, D. A. J., Melanda, F. N., Mesas, A. E., González, A. D., Gabani, F. L., & Andrade, S. M. D. (2017). Physical, psychological and occupational consequences of job burnout: A systematic review of prospective studies. PloS One, 12(10), e0185781.

Salyers, M. P., Bonfils, K. A., Luther, L., Firmin, R. L., White, D. A., Adams, E. L., & Rollins, A. L. (2017). The relationship between professional burnout and quality and safety in healthcare: A meta-analysis. Journal of General Internal Medicine, 32, 475–482.

Sauter, S. L., Murphy, L. R., & Hurrell, J. J., Jr. (1990). Prevention of work-related psychological disorders: A national strategy proposed by the National Institute for Occupational Safety and Health (NIOSH). American Psychologist, 45(10), 1146–1158

Schein, E. (1990). Organizational culture. American Psychologist, 45(2), 109–119.

Schoeps, K., Tamarit, A., de la Barrera, U., & Gonzalez Barron, R. (2019). Effects of emotional skills training to prevent burnout syndrome in schoolteachers. Ansiedad y Estres, 25(1), 7–13.

Shirom, A., & Melamed, S. (2006). A comparison of the construct validity of two burnout measures in two groups of professionals. International Journal of Stress Management, 13(2), 176–200.

Simionato, G. K., & Simpson, S. (2018). Personal risk factors associated with burnout among psychotherapists: A systematic review of the literature. Journal of Clinical Psychology, 74(9), 1431–1456.

*Soriano-Sánchez, J. G., & Jiménez-Vázquez, D. (2023). Effectiveness of interventions on burnout syndrome in nurses: A systematic and meta-analytic review. Revista Acciones Médicas, 2(1), 7–23.

Spector, P. & Nixon, A. (2023). Assessing and Managing Mistreatment and Work. In The Routledge Companion to Mental Health at Work. Routledge.

*Suleiman-Martos, N., Gomez-Urquiza, J. L., Aguayo-Estremera, R., Cañadas-De La Fuente, G. A., De La Fuente-Solana, E. I., & Albendín-García, L. (2020). The effect of mindfulness training on burnout syndrome in nursing: A systematic review and meta-analysis. Journal of Advanced Nursing, 76(5), 1124–1140.

Swider, B. W., & Zimmerman, R. D. (2010). Born to burnout: A meta-analytic path model of personality, job burnout, and work outcomes. Journal of Vocational Behavior, 76(3), 487–506.

Thomas Craig, K. J., Willis, V. C., Gruen, D., Rhee, K., & Jackson, G. P. (2021). The burden of the digital environment: A systematic review on organization-directed workplace interventions to mitigate physician burnout. Journal of the American Medical Informatics Association, 28(5), 985–997.

Thompson, M. J., Carlson, D. S., Kacmar, K. M., & Vogel, R. M. (2020). The cost of being ignored: Emotional exhaustion in the work and family domains. Journal of Applied Psychology, 105(2), 186.

Tims, M., & Bakker, A. B. (2010). Job crafting: Towards a new model of individual job redesign. SA Journal of Industrial Psychology, 36(2), 1–9.

Trépanier, S. G., Fernet, C., & Austin, S. (2013). Workplace bullying and psychological health at work: The mediating role of satisfaction of needs for autonomy, competence and relatedness. Work & Stress, 27(2), 123–140.

Tutty, M. A., Carlasare, L. E., Lloyd, S., et al. (2019). The complex case of EHRs: Examining the factors impacting the EHR user experience. Journal of the American Medical Informatics Association, 26(7): 673–677.

Valcour, M. (2016). Beating burnout. Harvard Business Review, 94(11), 98–101.

Van Bogaert, P., Van Heusden, D., Verspuy, M., et al. (2017). The Productive Ward Program™: A two-year implementation impact review using a longitudinal multilevel study. Canadian Journal of Nursing Research, 49(1), 28–38.

Van Weert, J. C., van Dulmen, A. M., Spreeuwenberg, P. M., Ribbe, M. W., and Bensing, J. M. 2005. Integrated in 24-hour dementia care, on nurse-patient communication during morning care. *Patient Education and Counseling.* 58(3):312–326.

Walker, J. 2025. Burnout: The Dirty Truth About How Employers Benefit From It. Forbes. https://www.forbes.com/sites/jasonwalker/2025/02/05/burnout-by-design-the-dirty-truth-about-how-employers-benifit-from-it/.

*Wang, Q., Wang, F., Zhang, S., Liu, C., Feng, Y., & Chen, J. (2023). Effects of a mindfulness-based interventions on stress, burnout in nurses: A systematic review and meta-analysis. Frontiers in Psychiatry, 14, 1218340.

*West, C. P., Dyrbye, L. N., Erwin, P. J., & Shanafelt, T. D. (2016). Interventions to prevent and reduce physician burnout: A systematic review and meta-analysis. The Lancet, 388(10057), 2272–2281.

Westman, M., Etzion, D., & Danon, E. (2001). Job insecurity and crossover of burnout in married couples. Journal of Organizational Behavior: The International Journal of Industrial, Occupational and Organizational Psychology and Behavior, 22(5), 467–481.

Woo, T., Ho, R., Tang, A., & Tam, W. (2020). Global prevalence of burnout symptoms among nurses: A systematic review and meta-analysis. Journal of Psychiatric Research, 123, 9–20.

World Health Organization. (2022). International Classification of Diseases, Eleventh Revision (ICD-11). Geneva: License: CC BY-ND 3.0 IGO.

Yang, F., Fei, Y., Guo, L., Bai, X., & Li, X. (2023). Job crafting intervention for job burnout and work engagement among young construction project management practitioners in China. Engineering, Construction and Architectural Management.

Ybema, J. F., Evers, M. S., & van Scheppingen, A. R. (2011). A longitudinal study on the effects of health policy in organizations on job satisfaction, burnout, and sickness absence. Journal of Occupational and Environmental Medicine, 53(11), 1251–1257.

Yildirim, N., Yesilbas, H., & Kantek, F. Interventions to reduce nurses' burnout: A systematic review and meta-analysis. 2023. 20(4), Japan Journal of Nursing Science.

Appendix E

Biographical Sketches of Planning Committee Members and Speakers

WORKSHOP PLANNING COMMITTEE

Reshma Jagsi (*Chair*) is chair of the Department of Radiation Oncology at Emory University and Winship Cancer Institute. A graduate of Harvard College, Harvard Medical School, and the University of Oxford, where she studied as a British Marshall Scholar, she completed her residency training and an ethics fellowship at Harvard before joining the faculty of the University of Michigan, where she served as the director of its Center for Bioethics and Social Sciences in Medicine. Gender equity in academic medicine has been a key area of her scholarly focus. She has authored more than 400 articles in peer-reviewed journals, including high-impact studies in the *New England Journal of Medicine*, the *Lancet*, and *JAMA*. Her research to promote gender equity has been funded by R01 grants from the National Institutes of Health (NIH) as well as large independent grants from the Doris Duke Foundation and several other philanthropic foundations. She has mentored dozens of others in research investigating women's underrepresentation in senior positions in academic medicine and the mechanisms that must be targeted to promote equity. She has served on the Steering Committee of the Association of American Medical Colleges' (AAMC) Group on Women in Medicine in Science and the *Lancet*'s advisory committee for its theme issue on women in science, medicine, and global health. She serves on the National Academies of Sciences, Engineering, and Medicine's Committee on Women in Science, Engineering, and Medicine and the Advisory Committee for Research on Women's Health for the NIH. An internationally recognized clinical trialist and health services researcher in breast cancer, her work is frequently featured in the popular media, including the *New York Times*, the *Wall Street Journal*, and NPR. She is a member of the American Society of Clinical Investigation and Association of American Physicians and has received the Leadership Award of the AAMC's Group on Women in Medicine and Science, LEAD Oncology's Woman of the Year Award, American Medical Women's Association's Woman in Science Award, and American Medical Student Association's Women Leaders Award. She is a fellow of the American Society of Clinical Oncology, American Society for Radiation Oncology, American Association for Women in Radiology, American Association for the Advancement of Science, and the Hastings Center.

Kelley Bonner leads Burn Bright Consulting, a consultancy specializing in developing customized plans to address burnout and enhance workplace safety and wellness. Prior to this, she was the Workplace Violence Prevention and Response program manager at the National Oceanic and Atmospheric Administration (NOAA) and a specialist for the Primary Prevention of Violence in the United States Air Force (2017–2018). Her expertise lies in developing actionable strategies for workplace safety, including burnout prevention, employee wellness, stress management, fatigue management, and sexual assault/sexual harassment prevention. She has successfully managed large-scale programs and created the first comprehensive sexual assault and sexual harassment (SASH) prevention platform at NOAA. She is certified in mindfulness, compassion fatigue, resiliency, workplace violence, and psychological safety. Her work has been recognized as "revolutionary" by Anita Hill and "a benchmark in her field" by the Pentagon. Bonner served on the Gender Policy Committee for the White House and the International Women's Economic Security Council, aiding the Biden administration in developing a national framework for workplace safety. She has been endorsed by the National Academy of Sciences (NAS) as a thought leader on SASH and has been a speaker at several national events and an active participant in their Action Collaborative (2018–2022), co-leading their evaluation working group. She is a licensed clinical trauma professional with additional certifications as a master resiliency trainer, Green Dot implementer, mindfulness trainer, and emotional intelligence practitioner, and she has trained in post-traumatic growth and acceptance and commitment therapy. She earned her Clinical Compassion Fatigue certification in 2018.

Elena Fuentes-Afflick is chief medical officer at the Association of American Medical Colleges. Prior to joining AAMC, she was professor of pediatrics and vice dean for the School of Medicine at Zuckerberg San Francisco General Hospital at the University of California, San Francisco (UCSF). Throughout her career, Fuentes-Afflick has personally managed and mentored faculty and staff on a range of caregiving issues in the context of academic medicine. In 2010, she was elected to membership in the National Academy of Medicine and has served on numerous consensus committees, the Membership Committee, and the Diversity Committee; was elected to the Governing Council and the Executive Committee of Council; and was elected Home Secretary. In 2020, she was elected to the American Academy of Arts and Sciences. Fuentes-Afflick obtained her undergraduate and medical degrees at the University of Michigan and a master's degree in public health (epidemiology) from UC Berkeley. She completed her pediatric residency and chief residency at UCSF, followed by a research fellowship at the Phillip R. Lee Institute for Health Policy Studies at UCSF.

Lonnie Golden is a professor of economics and labor and human resources at Penn State University, Abington College. His Ph.D. from the University of Illinois was in economics, focusing on labor economics. His research analyzes trends, patterns, determinants, and consequences of hours of work and nonstandard employment in labor markets, organizations, households, and individuals. Specifically, his research focuses on measuring employment/job quality, underemployment and overemployment mismatches, overtime work, part-time work, work schedules, labor and workplace flexibility, and outcomes such as overwork, health, earnings differentials/disparities, happiness, work-family time balance, and personal time-use; and relevant policies such as the Fair Labor Standards Act, Fair Workweek (predictive/secure scheduling), overtime regulations, paid leaves, independent contracting work, and work-sharing/short-time compensation. He has co-edited two books, *Working Time* and *Nonstandard Employment*, and numerous papers and scholarly articles in leading academic journals such as *Industrial Relations, Monthly Labor Review, Health Affairs, Cambridge Journal of Economics*, and the *Journal of Economic and Family Issues*. He has received grants or commissions from the Urban Institute (including WorkRise), the

International Labor Organization in Geneva, the Economic Policy Institute, and the Center for Law and Social Policy in Washington, D.C. He is affiliated with the Project for Middle-Class Renewal at the University of Illinois School of Labor and Employment Relations and with the Work-Family Research Network.

Alicia Kowalski is a full-time professor of anesthesiology at the University of Texas MD Anderson Cancer Center, where her academic passion is promoting and supporting professional engagement and career sustainability for individuals and organizations in healthcare and has multiple peer-reviewed publications in this realm. This fervor led her to obtain her Chief Wellness Officer certification from Stanford Medicine. At her organization, she served as the sole clinical faculty representative to the institutional council CREWS (Career Resiliency Engagement Wellness and Sustainability) during its entire existence, helped implement a robust infrastructure to support professional well-being across all communities, and served as the University of Texas MD Anderson liaison to the University of Texas System Task Force for Physician Well-being. She is the lead instructor of the Chief Wellness Officer Training and Certification Program through a collaboration with the Institute of Physician Wellness. Additionally, she founded and chairs a national symposium, Burnout to Brilliance, for physician well-being and career sustainability, which earned Congressional Recognition. She and her sister founded the Charles S. DeJohn, MD, PhD Scholarship fund for physician education for wellness and career sustainability. Kowalski participated in the Veterans' Health Administration Executive Management Fellowship through Congress as a mentor to establish chief well-being officers at numerous VA locations across the country.

José A. Pagán is chair and professor of the Department of Public Health Policy and Management at the School of Global Public Health, New York University. He is also chair of the Board of Directors of NYC Health + Hospitals, the largest public healthcare system in the United States. Pagán is a member of the National Academy of Medicine. He has led research, implementation, and evaluation projects on the redesign of healthcare delivery and payment systems. He is interested in population health management, healthcare payment and delivery system reform, and the social determinants of health. He also served as chair of the National Advisory Committee of the Robert Wood Johnson Foundation's Health Policy Research Scholars and was a member of the Board of Directors of the

Interdisciplinary Association for Population Health Science and the American Society of Health Economists. Pagán received his Ph.D. in economics from the University of New Mexico.

SPEAKERS

Bryant Adibe is the Jay S. Sugarman Practitioner in Residence in the School of Public and International Affairs at Princeton University. Previously, he served as system vice president and chief wellness officer at Rush University System for Health in Chicago, Illinois. He also held the distinction of off-site, full professor of organizational change and leadership at the University of Southern California. At Rush, he founded the Center for Clinical Wellness, an innovative facility designed to study and treat the effects of burnout and emotional exhaustion on healthcare workers. His work has been featured by the National Academy of Medicine, American Medical Association, American Psychiatric Association, and other leading outlets. Adibe is a graduate of Cambridge University. He earned his medical degree from the University of Florida College of Medicine. He completed clinical clerkships in emergency medicine at both Harvard Medical School and the Stanford School of Medicine. As a graduate student, he studied health policy and evidence-based healthcare at Oxford University.

Youngjoo Cha is an associate professor of sociology at Indiana University Bloomington and Yonsei University. Her research interests are in gender, work, and family. Her major line of research investigates how the trend toward long work hours reinforces gender inequality and what organizational and institutional conditions help to challenge this trend. Her other research focuses on the effect of marriage and parenthood on the gender pay gap, the role of Asian stereotypes on labor-market outcomes for Asian women and men in the United States, and conditions under which discrimination lawsuits undermine workplace inequality. Her recent work appears in *American Sociological Review*, *American Journal of Sociology*, *ILR Review*, *Gender and Society*, and *Sociological Science*.

Natalia Cineas is senior vice president, chief nursing executive, and co-chair of the Equity and Access Council for NYC Health + Hospitals, the largest municipal public healthcare system in the nation, serving 1.4 million New Yorkers annually in more than 70 patient care locations. She serves as clinical lead for the organization, directing more than

9,600 nurses: planning, overseeing, and evaluating all aspects of clinical operations, services, and nurse education to ensure the delivery of quality, safe, standardized, and cost-effective nursing care to patients and the community. As co-chair of NYC Health + Hospitals' Health and Equity Access Council, she is actively engaged in identifying and defining systemwide strategic diversity and inclusion priorities. Cineas previously held nursing leadership roles as senior director of nursing and deputy chief nursing officer at New York City's Mount Sinai St. Luke's Hospital and as patient care director of neurosurgery and the Neurosurgical Intensive Care Unit at Columbia University Medical Center New York Presbyterian Hospital. She holds a master of business administration in healthcare from Northern Arizona University's W.A. Franke College of Business, a doctorate of nursing practice from George Washington University, a master of science in management and a bachelor of science in nursing from New York University, and a bachelor of arts in psychology from Stony Brook University.

Arla Day is a professor in occupational health psychology at Saint Mary's University, director of the CN Centre for Occupational Health and Safety, a fellow of the Canadian Psychological Association, and a former Canada Research Chair. Her research focuses on leveraging the positive aspects of work to create healthy workplaces. In her role as project director for the EMPOWER Partnership (a collaborative group of researchers and organizations, workplace experts, and stakeholders), she develops and examines evidence-based solutions to foster psychologically healthy workplaces by supporting workers, strengthening work groups, and developing leaders.

Liselotte Dyrbye is senior associate dean of faculty and chief well-being officer for the University of Colorado School of Medicine, the first to hold this newly created position. Dyrbye began her work at the Mayo Clinic in 2001, where she has made many creative contributions to education programs, taught medical students and residents, and implemented several innovative programs in support of faculty development, diversity, and well-being. She is professor of medicine and medical education and co-director of the Mayo Clinic Department of Medicine Physician Well-Being Program. Dyrbye graduated from the University of Wisconsin Medical School in 1996 and completed an internship and residency in internal medicine at the University of Washington School of Medicine. After working in private practice for a few years, she accepted an appointment at Mayo Clinic in September 2001, where she rose through the ranks to become professor of medicine and medical education at the Mayo Clinic School of Medicine in 2014. She earned a master of health professions education from the University of Illinois at Chicago College of Medicine in 2009. She has also led significant initiatives to promote faculty development at Mayo Clinic, including serving as assistant dean of faculty development for the Mayo Clinic School of Graduate Medical Education and creating and implementing Mayo's Academy of Educational Excellence. Through these efforts, Dyrbye has helped create useful and popular programming, including short videos, that can fit into the busy schedules of faculty. The "Take5" videos are broadly available for use in Mayo Clinic faculty meetings and cover key topics of interest, such as how to deal with patients expressing bias toward learners. In 2018, the videos were viewed more than 33,000 times.

Eve Kerr is Kutsche Memorial Chair of Internal Medicine, professor of internal medicine, and section head of the Division of Gender Medicine at the University of Michigan Medical School. She has dedicated her research career to understanding how to more effectively translate advancements from clinical and translational research to routine practice in order to improve patients' health and healthcare. In particular, she is internationally recognized for developing innovative, clinically meaningful methods to assess and improve quality of care and decrease low-value care. She has led major studies that demonstrated a significant U.S. Department of Veterans Affairs quality advantage over community care, developed "clinical action measures" to improve the intensity of blood pressure treatment that were implemented VA-wide, and developed new measures that assess and promote appropriate care. In addition to her faculty appointment and role as division chief of general medicine in the Department of Internal Medicine, Kerr is a senior research scientist at the VA Ann Arbor Center for Clinical Management Research, and the founding director of the Michigan Program on Value Enhancement. She has been recognized for her scholarship, leadership, and mentorship through election to the National Academy of Medicine, Association of American Physicians, and American Society of Clinical Investigation; selection as a master of the American College of Physicians; and the VA Undersecretary for Health Award for Excellence in Health Services Research and the Society of General Internal Medicine John M. Eisenberg National Award for Career Achievement in Research.

Jean King is an active neuroscientist and Peterson Family Dean of Arts and Sciences at Worcester Polytechnic Institute (WPI). Previously, she was the vice provost of biomedical research and professor of psychiatry, radiology, and neurology (with tenure) at UMass Medical School, where she had been a faculty member since 1994. Together with other administrative leaders at WPI, King has launched new undergraduate and graduate programs in learning science, neuroscience, interactive media and game development, and artificial intelligence (AI) and has expanded undergraduate research opportunities. Her research is broadly focused on the adverse effects of stress on the brain, body, and behavior, with current projects on chronic pain and youth and young adult mental health. She has been the recipient of continuous extramural funding from the National Institutes of Health (NIH) for more than two decades. She has published more than 100 original scientific papers in highly respected international scientific journals and more than 10 book chapters and review articles in major neurophysiology journals and is an editor of the New York Academy of Sciences publication *Roots of Mental Illness in Children*. A major current research project is centered on the use of AI to predict the response to mindfulness for chronic pain, supported by a 5-year NIH grant through the HEAL (Helping to End Addition Long-term) initiative.

Alden Lai is an assistant professor of public health policy and management at New York University (NYU). He studies how the jobs and work environments of healthcare workers can be improved to increase employee outcomes (e.g., well-being, retention) as well as organizational performance (e.g., program implementation, patient safety). He uses theories and frameworks from psychology, organization science, and health services research in his work. Lai's research has appeared in both management and healthcare journals, including *Academy of Management Discoveries, Health Care Management Review, Medical Care Research and Review*, and *The Milbank Quarterly*. He has an affiliated faculty appointment in the Department of Management and Organizations at NYU Stern. He has advised federal and state governments, health systems, international and nonprofit organizations, corporations, and philanthropies internationally. His professional experiences include being a management consultant, social enterprise strategist, and education researcher. He currently serves as executive advisor to the Global Wellbeing Initiative, a collaboration between the Wellbeing for Planet Earth Foundation and Gallup Inc. to foster a more globally inclusive understanding of well-being for research, practice, and policy. Lai also serves as chair of the Health Care Research Stream for the Industry Studies Association. He is co-editor of an upcoming book by Springer on professional development for early-career researchers. Previously, he served as chair of the European Health Psychology Society's early-career researcher division and was an executive committee member in the Academy of Management's Division of Health Care Management.

Christina Maslach is a professor of psychology (emerita) and a core researcher at the Healthy Workplaces Center at the University of California, Berkeley. She received her A.B., magna cum laude, from Harvard-Radcliffe College (1967), and her Ph.D. from Stanford University (1971), and has been on the Berkeley faculty since then. Maslach is the pioneer of research on the definition, predictors, and measurement of job burnout. This work is the basis for the 2019 decision by the World Health Organization (WHO) to include burnout as an occupational phenomenon, with health consequences, in the International Classification of Diseases 11th Revision. She created the Maslach Burnout Inventory, the most widely used instrument for measuring job burnout, and has written numerous articles and books, including *The Truth About Burnout*. Several of her articles have received awards for their significance and high impact, including her longitudinal research on early burnout predictors, which was honored in 2012 as one of the 50 most outstanding articles published by the top 300 management journals in the world. Recently, she received the 2017 Application of Personality and Social Psychology Award, as well as several lifetime career achievement awards. In 2020, she received the award for Scientific Reviewing, for her work on burnout, from the National Academy of Sciences. In 2021, she was named by Business Insider as one of the top 100 people transforming business. Her latest book, *The Burnout Challenge*, was named by *Publisher's Weekly* as one of the top 10 books in business/economics for fall 2022.

Rene Pana-Cryan is chief economist and director of the Economic Research and Support Office in the Office of the Director of the National Institute for Occupational safety and Health (NIOSH). She also comanages the NIOSH Healthy Work Design and Worker Well-being Cross-Sector Program. Her interests include understanding how to improve the design of work, management practices, and the physical and psychosocial work environment in order to enable workers to thrive and contribute productively at work, at home, and in society. She is particularly interested in understanding the economic factors that affect work arrangements and the effects of work arrangements on the well-being of workers and their families. Pana-Cryan joined NIOSH in 1996 as a postdoctoral Prevention Effectiveness fellow.

Carolyn Porta is the associate vice president for clinical affairs for the University of Minnesota. She is a professor in the School of Nursing, and an adjunct professor in the School of Public Health and the Center for Spirituality and Healing. Porta is a forensic clinician and scientist committed to promoting the health and well-being of individuals, families, and communities. Her current scholarship focuses on the science of trauma-informed practice, leadership, and organizations, and system-level strategies to strengthen the healthcare workforce and mitigate threats to their well-being. She has extensive experience in clinical service, team science, mixed methods clinical trials, interprofessional clinical training, and strategic and operational leadership of large-scale research and workforce development initiatives (more than $100 million in funding and more than 115 publications).

Joan Y. Reede is dean for diversity and community partnership at Harvard Medical School. Appointed in January 2002 as the first dean for diversity and community partnership, she is responsible for the development and management of a comprehensive program that provides leadership, guidance, and support to promote the increased recruitment, retention, and advancement of underrepresented minority faculty at Harvard Medical School (HMS). In 1990, Reede founded the HMS Minority Faculty Development Program and currently serves as faculty director of the Community Outreach programs. In 2008, she became the director of the Harvard Catalyst Program for Faculty Development and Diversity. In addition, she holds appointments of professor of medicine at HMS, professor of society, human development, and health at the Harvard T. H. Chan School of Public Health, and assistant in health policy at Massachusetts General Hospital. The impact of Reede's work is reflected in the numerous programs she has created to benefit minority students, residents, scientists, and physicians. She created and developed more than 20 programs at HMS that aim to address pipeline and leadership issues for minorities and women who are interested in careers in medicine, academic and scientific research, and the healthcare professions. She has developed mentoring programs for underrepresented minority students from the middle school through the graduate and medical school levels. She has also designed a training program for middle and high school teachers, developed science curricula for public schools, implemented research and exchange clerkship programs at HMS, and designed and implemented innovative fellowships in minority health policy for physicians, dentists, and doctoral-level mental health professionals.

José E. Rodríguez is associate vice president for health equity, diversity, and inclusion (HEDI) at University of Utah (U of U) Health. He served as interim associate vice president beginning in August 2018. Rodríguez is a professor in the Department of Family and Preventive Medicine and has extensive background in diversity work in the healthcare arena. In addition to his HEDI position, he is a family physician and associate medical director at U of U Health's Redwood Health Center. Prior to joining the University of Utah, Rodríguez co-chaired the Council on Diversity and Inclusion and co-directed the Center for Underrepresented Minorities in Academic Medicine at Florida State University College of Medicine. He is an accomplished academic, publishing numerous articles on the importance of underrepresented minorities in academic medicine. Rodríguez received his M.D. degree at Weill Cornell Medicine in New York City and his B.A. at Brigham Young University.

Tait Shanafelt is the Jeanie and Stew Ritchie Professor of Medicine, associate dean and chief wellness officer at Stanford Medicine. A hematologist-oncologist by training, Shanafelt is a leading researcher on clinician burnout and its impact on quality of care, access to care, and the healthcare workforce. Prior to his position at Stanford, he was a professor of medicine and hematology at the Mayo Clinic and served a 3-year term as president of the Mayo Clinic voting staff from 2013 to 2016. He was the founding director of the Mayo Clinic Department of Medicine Program on Physician Well-Being and led a number of initiatives at Mayo to mitigate burnout and improve physicians' sense of fulfillment and well-being. He has published more than 325 peer-reviewed manuscripts and research studies, including more than 125 on the topic of healthcare professional well-being. His research in this area has involved physicians at all stages of their career, from medical school to practice, and has included many multicenter and national studies. In 2018, he was named by *Time* magazine as one of the 50 most influential people in healthcare.

Julie K. Silver is the senior associate dean for faculty experience and success. Her research and clinical work has focused on improving gaps in the delivery of healthcare services. She has published many scientific reports focused on surgical prehabilitation and cancer rehabilitation. Her ground-breaking work on "impairment-driven cancer rehabilitation" was initially published in the journal *CA: A Cancer Journal for Clinicians*—a high-impact factor oncology journal that is published by the American Cancer Society. Impairment-driven cancer rehabilitation was subsequently incorporated into the American Cancer Society's *Cancer Facts & Figures*. Silver co-founded the Cancer Rehabilitation Group for the American Congress of Rehabilitation Medicine—a research-focused interdisciplinary professional society.